THEY MAKE
CHEESE
IN
NIMBIN
...don't they?

They Make Cheese in Nimbin Don't They? © 2024 Sheldon Baverstock

All Rights Reserved. No part of this book may be reproduced in any form or by any electronic or mechanical means including information storage and retrieval systems, without permission in writing from the author. The only exception is by a reviewer, who may quote short excerpts in a review.

This book is a work of fiction. Names, characters, places, and incidents either are products of the author's imagination or are used fictitiously. Any resemblance to actual persons, living or dead, events, or locales is entirely coincidental.

Publisher NextSearch
Second Edition October 9, 2024

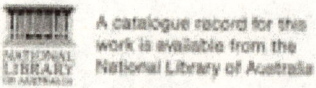
A catalogue record for this work is available from the National Library of Australia

We acknowledge the Bundjalung people
and pay respects to the Elders, past, present and future.

THEY MAKE CHEESE IN NIMBIN

...don't they?

Sheldon Baverstock

About the author

Born and raised in South Africa, Sheldon began writing towards the end of a long and successful career in IT. After many years in South Africa, tenures with various global IT companies saw the family set up new homes in England, New Zealand and Sydney, Australia where they currently reside. He has two daughters and two sons.

Other novels by Sheldon Baverstock

One Black Ear
The First Canary

Acknowledgments

Once again a huge thank you to my wife, Dagmar, for her considerable guidance with the storyline and proof reading of several drafts of this book. Her tireless, razor like focus never fails to astound me; nor her intolerance for "over writing". She never misses a thing.

PROLOGUE

Black Water

THE YOUNG WOMAN WATCHED her father staggering up the steep incline towards their home. The southerly wind, howling across the freezing waters of the Cook Strait into the North Island, threw him against the wooden handrail time and time again. Despite her deepest wish for him to be blown over the rail and down the steep bank, he managed to hold on until each gust subsided and he could start his ascent again.

'Blow the bastard down the steps then, won't you?' she muttered to herself, desperate to avoid the pain that was coming. She wondered how much she hated him. The drinking, the abuse of her mother and herself.

From the window, she could see the cable car track rising like a roller coaster from Lambton Quay towards her, to their suburb. It was transportation he had chosen not to pay for, climbing the steps alongside the track instead. *Spent his remaining few dollars on a last beer no doubt*, she thought to herself.

The pubs closed early in New Zealand, even though the war was over, so he would have been hell bent on an emphatic end to the "six o'clock swill" before they were all thrown out and told to go home. Taking a last look across the grey swells of the distant harbour, South Island, lost in the haze above them, she let go of the curtain and called to her mother to hurry.

'Dotty, where'd the bitch hide my booze?'

She hated the way he used her name like that, like she was a little girl; would feel affection, notwithstanding how he had just referred to her mother. They were normally his first words as their front door crashed open, and mostly to no one, as she had already taken her mother across to their neighbour's where they could shelter until he passed out. Sometimes she got her timing wrong or had to work late and when that happened, it invariably meant when she got home, she would find her mother sporting another big ugly bruise and her father snoring, passed out across their bed. The bed her mother refused to leave.

For what seemed the hundredth time, as they waved to her father far below on the quayside, her mother turned to her with the same anxious expression on her face. Most of her recent bruising had subsided, she was pleased to see.

'Do you think he will be alright, Dorothy. It's a long time for us to be away. How will he cope?'

'Mrs James is going to look in on him, Mum. And as you know, I have stocked enough groceries for months, they will last him until we get back,' she said. 'You need a break and we need to visit your sister. You know that, Mum. She's lost both her husband and her son to the war in the last few years. She needs our support.'

In reality, she had *bought* her mother's freedom, not just groceries, probably saved her life. She had bribed her father, offering him money, *enough to drink himself to death,* she hoped, so he would agree to them going on a "holiday cruise", including a visit to her aunt, who lived in a small town not far from Byron Bay.

Her plan was to *not* "get back". Once she became accustomed to feeling safe and secure, her mother would, she had decided, eventually trade losing him with not being in a constant state of fear. She was sure of it. Now the war was over and sea cruisers were safe, the opportunity to get her mother away had presented itself. Where she herself would end up in the future, she had no idea.

It was as if he was stationary and the burning city below him was turning. The rear gunner watched Hamburg rotate like a slowly extinguishing Catherine Wheel as the Lancaster banked away for home after dropping its load, turning steeply through the search lights and anti-aircraft flak. The full extent of the damage the bombers had wreaked on Hamburg, once again, was revealed through the now downward facing side of the glass dome he sat in. They were bombing and burning what they had not already reduced to rubble two days before.

Watching the burning city below him, made him think of the bush fires in Australia. As a teenage fire fighter volunteer in New South Wales, he had felt the heat of an out-of-control fire as flammable gas from the heated-up oil in the eucalyptus trees turned them into fire balls. He had chased down new fires starting three kilometres ahead of the main inferno, lit by embers carried by the relentless wind. Seen the countless dead, burning kangaroos and koalas. Down below, the burning bodies would be human.

He tried not to imagine what his hometown, Sydney, would look like if it had had the same twelve visits from the bomber he sat in the rear of, and others that thundered nearby in the dark sky. *The wreckage of the harbour bridge, twisted steel spikes painted in their special grey, pointing skyward, the shipyard nearby, obliterated. His beloved Newtown, rubble.* Britain's Bomber Command, intent on neutralising the output of Hitler's Ruhr industrial area had made *this* city, Hamburg, bear the brunt of their campaign.

It was over for him though, his last mission. Four more sky scanning hours on the way back to base as a *rear* gunner in his glass "thimble" and it would be over. He had defied the odds, the huge mortality rate for rear gunners. He was on his way back to "Oz" and the first thing he had planned was a visit to his parents on their farm, where peace and quiet would repair his damaged soul.

Half an hour into their return trip to base, the rear gunner could barely make out the burning city they had left behind. It was just a glow on the horizon, a setting sun. Much like its inhabitants might describe their future lives after the last few weeks.

He peered into the space either side of the glow as he scanned the starlit sky for the shadowy threat of a German fighter plane. There seemed to be nothing, not even the vague outline of another Lancaster. Just blackness. *We must be one of the last in the formation.*

Then he saw it. Flashes from a Messerschmitt cannon coming up from below, their preferred point of approach, intent on firing into the belly and fuel tanks of the Lancaster, causing a fire or even an explosion. Either one meant the end. He picked where the flashes started up in his sights but, before he could pull the trigger, a 20mm round from the guns below him tore through his fragile bubble, smashing through his gloved hand. All that was left of his thumb was a bloody hole in the body of the leather glove the thumb section had been part of.

Other rounds hit the belly of their aircraft and, within a few seconds, he heard his captain yelling, 'Fire...fire in fuselage...abandon aircraft,' over the static coming through his headphones and the scream of the wind through his smashed glass turret.

Quickly winding a cloth over what remained of his thumb and holding it in place with his four fingers, he slid open the flap doors at the rear of his turret behind his seat and felt for his parachute inside the fuselage. For the rest of his life, he would try, without success, to remember what transpired over the next few minutes. His only recollection was finding himself pulling the flap doors closed behind him and rotating his turret to the side. Then, opening the flaps behind him a second time, to the freezing night air this time, he leant his now parachute-carrying back out into the howling wind and was ripped into blackness.

From where the *seemann* stood at the ship's rail, the sea's surface far below felt remote, distant and ominous; icy black swells, pushing at the grey bulkhead, seemed to demand rite of passage. He imagined the heaving dark water was reaching for him each time the ship breasted a swell, the surface rising up to him, beckoning, *come to me, come down to me*, before falling away into the trough without him.

Shuddering involuntarily, he lifted his eyes to the horizon, trying to think of something more pleasant. He pictured his smiling wife the night he left home. Next to her, his young daughter, cheeks rosy from the *gasthaus* stove, eyes lost under the sailor's cap he had placed over her blond locks, *I can't see Papi, it's too big*.

He and his wife had spoken about trying for another baby. Everyone thought it was a good idea, except his father-in-law. The morning he left to join the destroyer docked in nearby Hamburg, his father-in-law, a man disliked by one and all in the village, had sniggered over his cup of coffee, 'What if it is not a boy? You don't need another *"grasmieger"*. What about your family name?'

That first night on board, they exchanged anecdotes about recent departures from loved ones. He had shared these comments with his new friends, all amused, he had missed what his father-in-law was saying.

'You see, a boy *stands* when he has a pee on the grass,' one said and they all laughed loudly.

Staring across the swells, he sighed deeply, *dark water as far as one could see*. Behind him, when the wind eased momentarily, he could hear snatches of his friends' conversation, their laughter, teasing each other. Once he thought he heard *his* name mentioned. Moving his eyes from the distant horizon he was about to turn and join them, when he caught sight of the two parallel lines closing in on the ship. Getting closer every second, the bubbles from the churn of the torpedo's propellors just below the sea's surface, picked up the last light of the setting sun.

The five of them had become good friends over the last few weeks. They would joke that it was fortunate they were *all* strong swimmers. *If we are sunk, we can swim together from the ship like rats would.* There was no time to reflect on their cynical joke in the pandemonium after the torpedoes struck. The explosion ripped the heart out of the destroyer and within 20 minutes, she was bow up, stern beginning to slide backwards, downwards through the oily surface.

Like the other oil and blood-spattered mariners crowding the decks the five friends clung to whatever they could, boots slipping now on the oily wet, inclining deck, waiting for orders. When none came, with the black surface rising up to meet them, in desperation they threw themselves over the rails into the icy water, hoping to reach one of the hastily lowered lifeboats.

The *seemann* sat in the second lifeboat, tightly holding the tow rope wound round a cleat bolted onto its wooden bow. The icy wind did nothing to dispel the stench of oil nor the taste of it. He felt it would choke him. Their boat was being towed as its motor had ceased to function, flooded during its hurried launch from their sinking ship. It had no power to steer it *bow first* into the swells, avoid being side on and rolled over.

He wondered where his friends were. He had last seen them a short distance from the lifeboat he was hauled into. It seemed like all four of them had clambered onto one of the tiny dinghies thrown from the ship. The tethered lifeboats rose and fell erratically in the darkness. As the lead boat crested each swell, its tiny light was lost to him until they too reached the top and it came back into view below.

The sudden lack of tension had the *seemann* in the rear boat instinctively pulling at the tow rope. It slid around the cleat in front of him.

'Sir, sir,' he yelled into the wind, 'there is something wrong.'

His officer did not respond. He had already observed that the small light they followed had been out of sight for too long. The front boat was on the other side of a swell, their boat was still at the bottom, wallowing.

It was a miracle, he thought. Struggling to stay above the surface with his sodden uniform and boots almost pulling him from his *schwimmweste,* he shouted out to what he guessed must be his friends. He had spotted the small group floating nearby in the moonlight, appearing between passing clouds as the storm subsided. *It must be them, only four on a tiny dinghy.*

'Hilfe! Hilfe!' he screamed in desperation, before choking on water that slopped into his mouth.

He saw one of them at last turn and look out towards him and then turn back to the others. He tried to get closer, but it was impossible in his exhausted state. Another mouthful of water had him coughing and choking. He knew he was done for. His aching arms just would not move fast enough to keep his shivering body afloat, his mouth above water. He closed his burning eyes, *rest a little,* he told himself. He did not even feel the icy water anymore, he was numb.

He opened his eyes to the sting of a cold hand slapping his cheek. He lay in the dinghy, his legs between those of his four friends staring down at him.

'Sit up. Sit up. Others have seen us haul you in and are nearly here already. We can't let them get in. It will be the end of us,' one panted.

Heaving himself up into a sitting position, he watched as one of his friends used the one and only paddle they had, to beat off the hands of a drowning survivor trying to pull himself up over the side of the dinghy. He watched in horror as the white, anguished face slipped away. The paddle was passed to another of the now five on the four-man dinghy, who beat off a desperate survivor on his side. He was aghast as the desperate, exhausted swimmer, hands outstretched, was swallowed by the black water. There were more and more around them. He knew if they were to survive, he would soon have to take his turn with the paddle, or his fists, which the others were now already employing. Forcing his frozen fingers to move, he undid the buckle of his sodden leather belt and pulled it from his trouser waist.

PART ONE

CHAPTER 1

Gasthaus Tricks

GLANCING OUT OF HER bedroom window from time to time, as she dressed for her night's work in the *gasthaus wirtschaft* downstairs, Eva marvelled at the vastness of the snow stretching across the surrounding fields and slopes. Glistening in the evening twilight, the whiteness rolled endlessly upward until, suddenly swallowed by the dark forest line halfway up the hill, overlooking their *gasthaus* and dance hall.

Her spirits fell a little as she recalled another snowy image that had stuck with her since she was very young. One she had created in her mind in the freezing cellar, helping her mother with pickling one morning. She had listened to her recount how her grandfather Franz had died. Why he had suffered a heart attack; before Eva was even born. Now shivering in the memory, Eva flung a shawl over her shoulders before heading down the stairs, to join her mother in the bar - in time for her father's trick.

There was actually no *snow*, as Eva imagined, in the account Magda gave her five-year old daughter that morning. The geese were scattered across the *green lawn* in front of the *gasthaus*. The sight of his beloved birds lying beheaded in the dull morning light, was too much for Magda's father. Too much for his heart.

As she listened to her mother's story in the icy cellar that morning, helping fill jars, the image a shivering Eva created in *her* mind was of bloodied snow, not lawn. There lay nearly 50 white geese, almost invisible against the snow, but for the trails of blood from their throats. Alongside each, a severed head with the outline of a gaping yellow beak, frozen open in their death throes. Eva had felt tears welling up in her eyes.

'It was the neighbour,' her mother was saying. 'He did it to spite your father because Kurt ordered him to leave our *gasthaus* the night before, for being drunk and swearing at him.'

Had Eva not been just five years old at the time, her mother might well have enlarged on the story. Mentioning perhaps, that the reason Eva's father was being sworn at by his neighbour was because he had just been told by the neighbour's equally drunk partner at their card table that his wife and Kurt had been spotted together recently in Kurt's car, the only one in the village and for miles around. Despite the misted-up windows, it appeared the two were enthusiastically engaged.

Had Eva been old enough to hear such an unabridged version, she might well have asked her mother *what she thought of such a situation?* and would have been told by Magda that she was long used to such behaviour from her husband. *It was part of her life.*

It was his *pfennige* trick that always got them, unable to believe what they had just seen happen before their very eyes. Old enough now to serve in the bar, Eva knew her father never let an evening in the *gasthaus wirtschaft* go too long without his entertainment. He made sure he was around to help Eva and Magda behind the bar at the start of the evening, keeping a watchful eye on who was bustling through the door, stamping snow covered boots at his threshold, emerging from overcoats. Whether they were new live-in guests at the *gasthaus* or just there for an evening to drink in the bar, once he decided there was a good number of new faces, he would dramatically slam down a glass tumbler on the counter.

With this loud thump, there would be an immediate reaction as the rowdy chatter died down.

'*Ja*, Kurt, now we see if your lungs are as strong as yesterday,' one of the regulars in the know would call loudly across the crowded room, ensuring Kurt was getting the attention he demanded.

Eva and her mother would continue serving and drawing pints of beer, Magda taking little notice. She had seen it all before. Eva was as captivated as she was every night she saw her father do his trick, glancing down the bar as she served, monitoring the trick's progress. Fascinated by the expressions on everyone's faces.

Wishing she could one day attract so much attention, Eva wondered if Kurt did the trick so he could have 5 or 10 minutes in his day when everyone around him at the time would respect him unreservedly. Stunned by the outcome and full of admiration, his distracted audience would forget they actually disliked the owner, resented him for the way he took the *gasthaus* from a distraught widow and for his infamous womanising.

Eva was just 15 when she began serving in the bar. Against her mother's wishes, but not her father's, who she could sometimes twist around her little finger. His *grey eyed beauty*, he called her no matter how many times she pleaded loudly, *'Nein, blau Papi, blau.'*

Kurt never allowed his sons to work behind the bar. Didn't trust them with the beer, he always told them. In any event, they were often sporting bruises or a black eye, from being beaten by him, so it was better they weren't seen.

He preferred his wife and daughter to be there. Kurt believed they were the reason they had so many regular patrons. He saw how they eyed Eva and tried to engage Magda in conversation, but he didn't care, so long as they kept spending their money. They never flirted with his Eva though. The story of what happened to the patron who had, was as well known, as was the court case that followed it. One of the many Kurt lost for beating other men senseless, along with the money in settlements the court ordered each time.

Now that his audience was engaged, Kurt carefully placed several pennies around the tumbler and stood back, immobile, staring intently at the empty glass for dramatic effect. Not shifting his gaze, he drew a deep breath, bending his small, wiry frame down slowly towards the counter. His first puff across the coins was half-hearted, to build up curiosity. The coins did not move at all. Those who were visiting the bar for the first time would smile and shake their heads. *This guy must be drunk,* one mumbled once, receiving a glare from Kurt with a quick turn of his head over his almost childlike shoulder, making the onlooker shrink back into the circle of bodies gathered around the bar counter. Eva glanced from face to face. Disbelieving. Curious. Expectant. Cynical. She marvelled at how her father could get a whole bar full of drinking, talking individuals to become still and give him their undivided attention. *If you disliked someone, why pander to them, why not ignore them?* She smiled at the scene before her, not sure what *she* felt for him.

Taking her eyes off the throng around Kurt for a moment, to push a jug of deep brown ale across the counter to an expectant hand, Eva smiled at the image of herself, *a naïve five-year-old holding his hand, walking through the forest, not having a clue what she would learn about him after this time.* Glancing back towards the trick in progress, she sighed, *I learnt a lot more about those doors you slipped through, Papi.*

Eyes fixed on the pennies, Kurt drew in a deep breath before bending slowly forward, bringing his lips close to the nearest one. There was silence around him as the onlookers waited. Suddenly, he began. The air left the depths of Kurt's lungs with a roar like an angry bear confronting a rival. One of the coins lifted slightly and then fell back as he continued to blow. Suddenly, it flicked up, bounced upwards off the side of the glass and, still spinning, caught the rim, knocking itself inside with a rattle. Open mouthed, his audience stared and before they had recovered from their initial astonishment, another coin clinked into the glass and then another, as the bear roared.

There was laughter and applause from his audience. One young man approached the now upright Kurt, slapping him on his wiry shoulder to congratulate him. With no response from Kurt, he withdrew, embarrassed, to rejoin his friends and smiling at Eva, who was taking the glass and pennies off the counter. She smiled back, holding his gaze until he blushed and looked away. Turning from the bar counter, Eva was confronted by a disapproving stare from her mother. She smiled back and winked, drawing a wagging finger from her mother.

'I have told you about flirting with these men Eva. They will think it's an invitation to help themselves to something and then all they will get is your father's fists,' Magda whispered. Eva giggled and squeezed past her as she was summoned to the end of the bar by two thirsty patrons.

'Don't worry *Mutti*, I won't forget what you have told me. Like you, I can see what is going on.'

CHAPTER 2

From Noble Beginnings

Kurt Borbounet liked to claim "blue blood" ran through his veins as a result of having a father who was a French nobleman. When asked, his version was that in the late 1800s there had been a family feud resulting in his mother, pregnant with Kurt, having to leave France in haste to take refuge in Germany. His mother and his father had never reunited, he said.

Magda's version, the one she recounted to Eva as a teenager, went more along the lines of there being 'some randy Lord who left his sperm in countless places,' getting one of the maids of the royal household pregnant. That maid, it turned out, was Kurt's mother. Being a feisty, young woman, she kicked up quite a fuss when she found she had conceived and before Kurt was even born, demanded a title for what she was sure would be a son, but the lord would not agree to this. Instead, she was offered a considerable sum of money on condition she was to remove herself to Germany with a promise to never return.

This maid's son turned out to be a small, wiry, young boy who, she was convinced, had huge lungs because of how loud he cried as a baby and, in later years, yelled. She always said her son was small because the rest of his body had had to yield to the demands of his lungs as he grew. Kurt was a strong boy, nonetheless, and very fast on his feet.

He became a miller and, as small as he was, he could lift and carry heavy sacks of flour with ease. People marvelled at his ability to swing them from the stone floor of the mill storeroom to his shoulders in one smooth movement, all the time singing the only French song his mother had taught him, *La Madelon,* which told of young soldiers flirting with a girl in a tavern.

As a young boy, Kurt spent a great deal of time in the forest around the village and when he wanted to, could disappear for days on end. It was this ability to disappear when he wanted to, and perhaps the fact that he made the community's much needed bread, that enabled him to escape the first world war when all other young men were sent to the *front*. He was not an agreeable individual and was disliked by most local men, exacerbated perhaps by the fact that, unlike them, he had avoided doing his time in the army and was attractive to women, including *their* wives, while they only had the rats in muddy trenches.

It was his experience as a miller that gave Kurt the chance to work his way into one of the prominent families of the village. When her sister died at a young age, it left the family's younger daughter, Magda, sole heir to the family fortune, which included money, a mill and bakery, and a popular *gasthaus* with a large pub and dance hall, surrounded by farmland with orchards. Already employed by Magda's parents in their mill and ever observant of the family, the implications of this bereavement did not go unnoticed by the young Kurt.

He found women enormously desirable and, although small and wiry, Kurt was a vicious fighter who won all his encounters and there were many, due to cuckolded husbands in the district seeking, what they thought would be easily taken, revenge on a smaller man. He was shrewd though and, in the case of Magda, he never approached her directly. Instead, he ingratiated himself with her parents by working harder that any of the young men they employed, without complaint or demand for more pay, like most of their other workers. Kurt had his eyes on a far bigger prize. His opportunity came one day when Magda's father grew weary of dealing directly with workers and Kurt was promoted to overseer. He never smoked or drank alcohol, so he was also a trusted asset to have watching over the *wirtschaft,* where Magda's father was convinced they were losing profits, due to thirsty staff sneaking drinks. He knew of Kurt's aggressive reputation, so he was confident his employees would soon be pulled into line.

With its pub and attached *saal,* where dances were held regularly, the *gasthaus* was widely known and an attraction for people from many surrounding villages. Having to spend time in the *gasthaus* gave Kurt the chance to be near Magda, without seeming obvious. They were often in close proximity as the family also made it their *home.*

Whenever Magda came near, tending to her duties, he began flirting with her if her parents were out of ear shot. That's as far as he allowed it to go though. He had a much bigger role for Magda to play in his future than he had ever had for his other *distractions* in the village. He was able to put his plan into action when one morning, Magda's father died of a heart attack. He had a notoriously weak heart and many said, the final straw must have been seeing all his geese with their heads chopped off by a spiteful neighbour, ordered out of the bar the night before by Kurt.

The "spiteful neighbour" countered that he had seen, as he walked to work that morning, with his *very own eyes*, as bleary as they were from a heavy night of drinking and card playing, the geese dispatched by Kurt as they gathered on the lawn at their feeding place in the early dawn light.

The funeral was a large one with family and extended family arriving from far and wide. The village church was small and cramped so many bypassed this part of the ceremony and headed for the *gasthaus* where free beer and food were bound to be plentiful.

As the drink flowed, the conversation level soon increased to keep up, with anecdotes about the deceased and other funerals attended. A story about some *dearly departed soul* farting loudly in his coffin while the preacher droned on from the pulpit had just brought roars of laughter from those gathered at the bar when the door burst open.

'*Sie kommen,*' a large young women said, panting from her walk up from the church.

The family, hastily gathered at the windows and fuelled with several pints of Pilsner, were soon openly grumbling about the scene before them. The loudest complaints initially came from the family of Magda's deceased father, but soon everyone was voicing disapproval. Coming up the road, Magda's mother clung to the unpopular Kurt and, in return, he supported her like her *dutiful son*. His expression, as he walked alongside Magda, that of a grief-stricken sibling.

As the evening proceeded, the funeral guests became drunker and drunker. Kurt, for once, urging the bar staff to dispense drink freely. The funeral attendees paid less and less attention to the poor widow as the beer flowed. This was when the sober Kurt seized his opportunity, taking Magda's forlorn mother aside to propose a solution to what she had kept repeating to everyone was a hopeless situation - *a woman left alone to look after a family and a business without a husband.*

Drawing close to her ear, Kurt said as quietly as he could over the raucous conversation around him, that he was prepared to marry Magda and take over as *man of the house*. He would manage her business affairs, provided he was the sole decision maker. Thinking her wealth would be safe if *a son-in-law,* someone part of her family, was looking after it and seeing a chance to shirk her future responsibilities, Magda's mother jumped at the offer and immediately began announcing the engagement of her daughter and Kurt to everyone in the room, including her incredulous daughter.

Both family and friends were appalled that the much maligned, and clearly manipulative, Kurt was not only to become "family" but would also have his hands on the wealth of the man who had created most of it as a result of so many years of hard work. As one side of the family pointed a finger at the other, the drunken words exchanged soon became abusive. It wasn't long before punches were being thrown. The feud that followed the funeral saw Magda and her mother ostracised by everyone as the root cause of the anger. They had gained a son and husband but lost their family. It was the perfect outcome for the victor of the evening's punch up, satisfied that his plan had been perfectly executed.

Magda confided in Eva before her daughter was barely a teenager, that not long after her *arranged* marriage to Kurt, her mother began to gain weight and fell ill, her body covered in festering sores. She was instructed to stay in her room by her new son-in-law and finally, to Magda's dismay, was *locked* in there by him lest the guests saw her.

Kurt forbade everyone, including his new wife, from going near the room other than to take food and drink to her. He allowed a doctor to see her once, but when he suggested hospitalisation, Kurt ordered him out the house, threatening to sue.

'Besides the poor doctor, your father was always suing someone or being sued. It was where all our money went. To your father's lawyers and the victims of his wrath,' Magda told Eva.

'Losing all our money was one thing, but what he did to my mother I can never forgive. I hope you and your brothers never do anything so cruel to me, Eva.'

So, in her room is where Magda's mother stayed, neglected until she died in a terrible state, leaving Kurt in total control of the family fortune. As her slowly dying mother faded away, Magda had begun to feel a transfer of her husband's aggression from her mother to herself. She could see it in Kurt's eyes. There had been little romance in their marriage, of course, but now it seemed her new husband had begun to *despise* her.

Even at her young age, Eva sensed that her mother was trying to forewarn her about what to expect from certain men, *perhaps all men?* Be on your guard, was what she heard as she watched her mother catch the tears trying to escape. Eva tried to suppress the horror she felt for the scene her mother had described. Tried to imagine what *she* would feel like, what she would have done, if it was her mother who was dying, uncared for on the other side of a locked door in her own home.

CHAPTER 3

Young Eva

EVA WOULD NEVER FORGET the trips her father took her on to the forest when she was a young girl, before she reached her teens and felt self-conscious being seen with him. They had plenty of money then and Kurt was the proud owner of a car. A three-wheeler Goliath - Eva loved the name - in which they would race through the forest, down the bumpy tracks, Eva screaming and laughing as she bounced up and down on the seat, nearly banging her head on the car's metal ceiling.

When they were deep in the forest and had come to a stop, Kurt would give her one of the little buckets he always brought along on these rides. They would race to see who could fill theirs with blueberries first, stopping only if a deer went crashing through the undergrowth, disturbed by their laughing and Eva's screams of excitement.

Sometimes her father would curl his berry-stained fingers and hold them up at her like a wild thing, growling at her as he peered over a bush.

'I'm the monster of the forest and I need a little girl to eat. EAT. EAT. EAT.'

She would scream and run to the car as fast as she could, pulling the door open, pressing on the hooter, holding it down.

'There monster, that will scare you away, won't it?' she yelled over the raucous beeping sound.

Kurt would put his stained hands over his ears and spin around and around.

'Oh no, oh no, I can't take that noise. You are free little girl, please stop that noise,' which brought a wagging finger from Eva.

'Naughty, naughty monster.'

The game was always the same each time, signalling the end of their berry picking. *Time to go home my little Eva.*

Sometimes if there were no berries, her father would stop the car and they would stroll through the forest, hand in hand. He would teach her about the various plants or wildlife they saw. It was the only time she felt close to him. Unafraid of what he might do or say next. Those times always reminded her how some of the girls in her class occasionally said they *loved* their father or mother. Eva remembered how, in the car on the way home, he was always quiet. She assumed he must be thinking of all the jobs he had to do when he got back to the *gasthaus*. All the guests he had to please.

She knew he worried about the lady guests if they were alone. Without their husbands they were sad and lonely, he told her once. He said it was his job as owner of the *gasthaus* to comfort them, to try and cheer them up. She had seen him open the door to one of these ladies' rooms without knocking one morning and enter quietly, which surprised her, as she had been told over and over never to enter a room like that. Her mother always said how rude it was to just walk in on someone. That day, her mother must have also seen him forgetting to knock, because she was really angry with him that evening at dinner.

Eva rocked her doll in her arms as she knelt in front of the hearth. She felt the warmth from the already hot coals on the doll's porcelain face as she kissed its cheek gently, whispering quietly in the stillness of the deserted bar room, still a bit smoky from the newly lit fire.

'Hush now, my darling, *schlaf gut,*' she said, wrinkling her nose at the smell of smoke in the doll's hair.

During winter, when the weather was at its worst, the only warm place in the *gasthaus* was in the bar area where there was a large coal stove. Each morning, Magda would leave the kitchen for a few minutes, hoping her pots would not boil over, to make the fire early so the large room would be warm in time for the opening of the bar. Clumping up the cellar stairs with a bucket of coal, she prayed the pots would be alright without anyone to watch them. Kurt had decided the other cooks should leave, as they were an unnecessary expense when he had a wife who was an excellent cook and could provide for both her family and the patrons of the *gasthaus*.

The cellar below the *gasthaus*, where the coal was kept, was huge and when she was not in the kitchen or laundry, Magda had to be down there. She worked tirelessly, preparing jars of preserved fruit and pickles, making cheese and also sausages from pigs they slaughtered themselves. Throughout her life, some nights in her sleep, Eva would hear the screams of those pigs being slaughtered in the yard.

She was just deciding whether she should try and brush the smell of smoke out of her doll's hair, when her mother came staggering into the room with a huge bucket of coal. Eva noticed the dark rings under her mother's eyes were even darker after shovelling dusty coal in the cellar. Magda slammed the bucket onto the wide brick hearth and sank into a chair beside the stove's open door. Instead of shovelling the coal into it, she leant back in the chair.

'Let me rest for just a few minutes,' she yawned. She had been up since dawn as usual.

Eva smiled up at her already dozing mother. There was something special between them, a relationship born during their time in the cold cellar together, listening to her stories as she helped fill jars. Sadly, the stories were seldom happy ones, not for her mother, anyway. Eva was in the midst of telling her doll a much happier story about a mother goose who had found her baby in the forest, when she became aware of a burning smell. She examined her doll's hair carefully, wondering if it was the same smell of smoke she had noticed earlier. As Eva's eyes lifted above her doll's golden curls, towards the stove, the source of the smell came into focus. Magda's long skirt had grown so hot the hem was beginning to smoulder.

'*Mutti. Mutti. Du brennst,*' Eva screamed in panic. She jumped up, shaking Magda's arm as hard as she could. '*Mutti!*'

Magda finally came out of a deep sleep as Kurt ran into the bar room from the main *gasthaus* hallway. Eva was initially relieved to see her father arriving to save the day as Magda slapped at her smouldering skirt. Relief turned to fear though, as she watched him pull her mother out of her chair and hit her across the face. Eva screamed, as she saw her mother fall heavily to the ground before being dragged to her knees by her father, all the time yelling,

'Stupid bitch! Stupid bitch!'

Eva heard herself screaming, 'Stop it! Stop it!' before hurling her doll at her father's back and running from the room in terror.

Eva was the youngest of three siblings and the only girl. She had very few memories of happy childhood times. Her brothers received regular beatings from their father and, being so young, Eva at first thought the beatings were just because they were *boys*. Kurt never laid a finger on her, well, not until she was a teenager. As she got older, Eva began to surmise she had just *not* been told what they had got up to. Perhaps things *not fit* for a girl's ears, like those she had heard whispered by one of the really naughty girls in her class.

The one thing she *could* remember them being punished for, was making her fall down the *gasthaus* steps. The boys had hidden under them in the dark alcove of the staircase. They gave her a fright with dog-like growls as she passed on the steps above them, making her tumble down the remaining few steps with a scream, just as her father was passing in the hall.

A sobbing Eva had looked behind her mother, as she was helped up and comforted in Magda's arms. Through her tears, she saw her father dragging the boys out of the front door. They never appeared at dinner that night and in the morning, Eva was shocked to see they both had eyes that were swollen and closed.

There were times when the three of them did have fun. Both boys had old bicycles they rode everywhere, leaving their little sister distraught she could not join them. She asked her father for a bicycle, but Kurt just laughed saying, 'Ah, my grey eyed beauty, you are so small, how could you ride a bicycle?'

Eva turned her attention to the boys, begging them to take her on the cross bar of their bikes. Notwithstanding the dire outcome for them if she got injured, they finally agreed. One day, out of view of the *gasthaus* and their father, one of them heaved her onto his cross bar in a side-saddle fashion and off they went. Eva's little hands gripped the cold metal of the handlebars so tightly her knuckles were white. She did not feel the discomfort of the metal crossbar pushing into her legs, alternately screaming and giggling with excitement at each bounce over a bump or splash through a puddle in the road.

Eva felt quite secure with the warm arms of her brother on either side of her little shoulders, preventing her from falling. She could feel his warm breath on the top of her head as he panted up a hill. Then they were flying down the other side, her hair blowing behind and laughing as her other brother overtook them, unencumbered by a screaming little sister on his crossbar and long blond hair blowing into his eyes and mouth.

After a few outings with her brothers, Eva, giggling, could not resist announcing one night to everyone at the dinner table, how much fun she had been having. The blood drained from the boys' faces and her mother's mouth opened in shock. It was understood by all that Kurt demanded dinner was to be in silence. If breaking *that* rule was not bad enough, announcing the bike riding was likely to bring down his full wrath on the boys.

Kurt glared at Eva and she dropped her head. There was a long silence before she lifted her face to him with big, wide open blue eyes.

'Sorry, *Papi*,' she whispered.

'If you hurt yourself, your brothers will pay. Now quiet,' was all Kurt said, calmed by her sorrowful look.

The boys continued eating, their breathing returning to normal after the fearful shock of their sister's revelation. Their relief slowly changed to uncertainty after a few minutes. Had their father given conditional agreement for them to continue taking Eva on their bikes or not?

Eva was determined she would show everyone that she could ride a bike. She asked her brothers repeatedly to teach her and they merely laughed, pointing at her legs as they did so.

'Those little legs will never reach the pedals,' they said.

'Can't you make the saddle lower?' she asked, but they laughed even louder at her request, saying even if that helped, she would still fall over and they would be in trouble.

Their derision just made her more determined. *Throughout her life Eva would find the more she was ridiculed for what she wanted to do, the more determined she was to do it.*

The dance *saal* was attached to the side of the *gasthaus* and had windows all along its sides with wide ledges outside. One wall of the *saal* had a road built alongside it, following the slope of the hill the building was cut into. This meant that by the time the road passed the last window, the window ledge was only a metre above it.

A determined Eva saw the opportunity this presented. She learnt from her brothers that once a bike was rolling forward, balance was easier. She just needed a way of being on a bike after it gained momentum, to show them she could balance, then they would *have* to teach her how to ride.

She chose an afternoon the boys had been instructed by Kurt to sweep the mill floors and stack empty hessian flour bags. Taking one of the bikes from where it leant against a wall, arms high above her head, gripping the handlebars, she struggled up the hill alongside the *saal*.

Once she toppled over, landing in a tangle on top of the bike, knees and elbows grazed. She was not to be deterred though and, after several minutes, finally had the bike upright again. The side of the *saal* blocked the view from the *gasthaus* so her struggles went unobserved.

Eventually, she had the bike leaning against her chosen window. Eva had turned the front wheel into the wall of the *saal* so the bike would not move forward. She ran around into the empty *saal* and, with the help of a stool, after raising the window, scrambled onto the ledge from where she was able to dangle a leg over the bike's saddle. Lowering herself gently onto it, she pulled her other leg over the window ledge and slipped it down between the wall and the bicycle.

Eva had to suppress a whoop of excitement at her success. She was finally sitting on the saddle of a bicycle. She sat there for several minutes, stationary, leaning forward, hands gripping the handlebars, legs dangling on either side of the bike. Revelling in her accomplishment, enjoying the feeling of riding a bike. *Well sort of.*

Taking a deep breath before pushing her foot against the wall for balance, she eased the front wheel away from the side of the hall, into a straight position. Immediately, the bike began to move forward down the incline. Her legs flayed out, seeking stability like a tight rope walker used arms. She jerked the handlebars this way and that to keep her balance.

Several times, she thought she was going to fall and land with the bike on top of her, but as it picked up momentum, she was able to keep a wobbly upright position more easily. Gathering speed, Eva's elation began to turn to concern, then fear and finally panic. Even if she had remembered the brakes, her little fingers could not have reached them as she hurtled towards a bend in the road.

Magda had just turned from the washing line, where she was hanging up newly washed sheets from rooms vacated by guests that morning. She saw, coming down the road at breakneck speed on a bicycle far too big for a child, her daughter, legs spread, eyes like saucers, screaming like a banshee.

Magda's initial response was to rush out to the road and try and grab the bike and its passenger as it came around the bend and passed by her. To slow it, but then she realised it was going too fast to make the corner. It was now off the road, hurtling straight towards her, probably would go straight *through* her, so she leaped to the side as the unstoppable apparition plummeted into the newly hung washing. Encased by the first soggy sheet she collided with, Eva blinded, did not know how many others she ripped from the lines before being enveloped in a feather duvet that provided a softer landing than she expected. Leaving its rider behind, the bicycle carried on a few more metres before crashing down a bank into the stream that fed their nearby mill.

Magda managed to bribe one of the mill workers to collect and repair the bike, without Kurt finding out about the incident, saving her two boys from beatings. She knew the one who deserved to be reprimanded would not get it from her father, so she punished her with many hours of pickle jar preparation and laundry work.

For Eva, the *saal* also served as a point of introduction to the joys of being a teenager. From time to time, it was used for dances and young and old came from miles around. One event that she had anticipated attending since she was a child, was the fancy-dress dance, the *Maskenball*.

At the end of the upstairs hallway, was a tiny window in the wall between the *gasthaus* and the *saal*. It was down at floor level, just above the old floral carpet runner and looked down into the *saal*. From within the *saal* nobody noticed the window as it was high up near the apex of the *saal's* ceiling. A wide-eyed face, pressed against the glass of this window, would be invisible to the happy dancing guests below.

With everyone already having fun at the dance, Eva was able to sneak out of her room to observe proceedings down below, careful not to wake her brothers who, no doubt, would have wanted to be involved and probably done something stupid, causing them to be discovered at the window by those below. Eva loved the, mostly, handmade costumes to go with the masks. Her favourites were the king, the queen, the angel, the devil and the very big baby whom she quickly identified as her mother. Her father, serving behind the bar, was dressed as a waiter, avoiding a silly *costume,* Kurt believed.

She had never seen her mother look so happy. She danced and danced. It seemed so many men were keen to dance with the still beautiful Magda. They wondered at her energy, how well she danced, knowing she worked such long hours for an uncaring husband.

Although she ended up with a terrible cold the following day, after lying on her stomach for so long in the cold dark passage, Eva was enthralled with what she had seen. She could not wait until she was old enough to go to such a dance, such a joyful affair.

CHAPTER 4

Becoming a Woman

GROWING INTO A TEENAGER, Eva had developed an optimistic and excitable personality, despite her sometimes awful surroundings. Although she was still her father's *favourite*, it was a trait that occasionally got *her* into trouble and not her brothers, especially at the dinner table.

Each evening, after Magda had placed their plates of food before them and sat down herself, the family fell silent for the duration of the meal, as decreed by Kurt. Eva could contain herself mostly, but there were times when words just bubbled out as they had about being taken on the boys' bikes. One evening, as her mother took her place, Eva popped out a request like a cork from a bottle of champagne.

'*Papi*, can I go to university when school is finished?'

Both boys smirked. They knew their sister was smart, they had watched her play "Skat" with the adults and remembered how incredulous they were at Eva's ability when she was just 12 years of age. Most considered Skat more complex even than Bridge.

'Not for girls,' one of the brothers said.

'SHUT UP!' Kurt yelled.

He turned to Eva.

'We don't have money for university. Especially not for girls. Now, quiet at the table,' he said, looking down at his food.

Eva looked at her mother, who shook her head slightly. She knew she would be held responsible later for what took place at the meal. Eva looked back at her father.

'It's not fair,' she said quietly.

'Arm on table,' Kurt commanded.

Eva knew what was coming. Putting down her knife and fork, she placed her arm on the table, leaving the underside near her elbow exposed, off the edge. She waited in silence.

Leaning across the table, picking up her fork and holding it upright in his fist, Kurt positioned it under her arm against the skin. He watched her intently. Her brothers smiled expectantly. It was their right to enjoy this, given the beatings they took regularly, although there would be one for them later anyway, for speaking at the table.

Slowly, Kurt applied more and more pressure. Eva knew the only thing that would stop it, the five little daggers in her tender underarm, were tears. As usual, she refused to give in. The room was silent, just the ticking of their old clock. The pain intense. Eva stared at the wall opposite, willing herself not to weep, but finally a tear popped into the corner of each eye and rolled down her cheek. Her father removed the fork and replaced it in front of her.

'To bed. Go. No food tonight. Go,' he said. 'GO!'

Eva jumped at his yell, then stood up and ran out of the room and up the stairs. Behind her, she heard the scrape of their chairs as her brothers were also sent out.

As she grew older, Eva and her mother became much closer than just mother and daughter. Now, two women needing to support each other in an environment dominated by a man, who in an instant could cause far more pain than he ever caused joy.

As far back as her memories went, Eva could remember *only* herself seeming to be the recipient of any joy in the family. The few times she saw her mother smile and laugh, were at the occasional dances in the *saal*, few and far between now, especially with a war being talked about. One other time, the smile when her mother heard Kurt had been jailed for a year.

That was a happy year. He had burnt the mill down to get the insurance money and, although he was finally charged and found guilty on the grounds of neglecting to ensure the Mill's electrical wiring was maintained in a safe condition, the judge found him not guilty on the main charge of arson and ordered a portion of the insurance claim should be paid to ensure his family would survive during his incarceration.

The insurance settlement brought welcome relief and the departure of her father presented an opportunity for Eva to enjoy what she had longed for since the night she had lain at the tiny hallway window, hour after freezing hour, staring down through decorations strung from the rafters below her at the dancers.

Although she was treated so badly by her husband, Magda did not consider leaving, had stayed to look after him and their children. There was little money left, Kurt having spent it over the years on lawyers and settlements arising from lost court cases or frittered it away on various affairs. So, the insurance money was cause for unexpected happiness. Magda had to admit to herself, as she listened to her excited daughter's suggestion, that maybe she did deserve a few hours of fun and enjoy the windfall.

'So, my daughter, you think I deserve to be happy and dancing? I wonder, though, if it is not also because you think, with your father away, you will persuade me to let you enjoy the evening as well?'

Magda waited for her daughter's reaction, watching her face over the basket of grubby sheets they were carrying down the stairs to the laundry in the cellar. Puffing unnecessarily hard, Eva put on her most pleading expression.

'*Mutti*, I have worked so hard lately in the *gasthaus*, and I *am* nearly eighte -'

'Seventeen years and two months.' Magda cut her daughter off with a laugh.

'Yes, but we have been learning dance steps at school. I would love to try dancing for real, at a proper dance. My teacher would be very happy to hear I had been able to go to a dance because of her dance lessons.'

Letting her end of the laundry basket drop to the stone floor with a thump, Magda put her hands on her hips.

'And would your teacher be so happy for you that she would come to the *saal* and get down on her hands and knees and polish the dance floor for us? Or would you like to do that? Polish a dance floor that is the length of this whole *Gasthaus*?'

'I will. I will, *Mutti*. The boys will help me,' Eva said bouncing up and down.

'Ah, so your brothers must be invited too, Eva? To make sure they don't ever tell your father you went to this dance and do the polishing? You have thought of everything, haven't you.'

Eva blushed and smiled, but her mind was already racing ahead.

Knowing most of the young girls in the village would attend, it did not take Eva's brothers long to be persuaded to take on the task of shining the dance floor, in return for dance lessons. There was an old radiogram in the sitting room and a few records left over after one of Kurt's rages about *loud music all the time.* Eva began teaching her two, suddenly very meek and shy, brothers some dance steps. It was an agonising process for all three, but the thought of being able to dance with one of the young girls of the village, drove the boys on. The dance would, of course, be a *maskenball,* similar to the one Eva had witnessed that night as a very young girl and it was soon the talk of the village and surrounds. Helping Eva with her Cinderella costume, Magda prayed word of the dance would not get back to Kurt.

From the start, the band was pestered by the younger of the dancers to play the more modern tunes. Older people sought more nostalgic melodies, probably because they knew a war was creeping up on them.

Eva, an *Aschenputtel* without a prince, danced to everything the band played. She had inherited her good looks from Magda and, like her, had blond hair and blue eyes, even if her father still insisted they were grey. Boys, some were more like young *men*, lined up to ask her to dance and Magda kept a wary eye on them from behind her feathered masquerade mask.

Her sons sat hunched over their table, heads resting on a newly starched tablecloth, exhausted from a whole day on their knees polishing the dance floor. Exhaustion, exacerbated by glasses of beer they had stolen off unattended tables in the early part of the evening.

Thank God their father isn't here, thought Magda as she swirled by her sons' table on the arm of a handsome villager, Magda knew Kurt considered one of his longstanding nemeses. He called Kurt *geese slayer* behind his back in the village.

Over the shoulder of her husband's enemy, she saw that Eva was dancing yet again with the same young man she had already danced with several times, to the annoyance of would-be suitors hanging around awaiting an opportunity to dance with her. He was tall and, with his thick slicked down fair hair and deep green eyes, Magda had to admit he was a very good-looking young man. *When the cat's away*, Magda smiled to herself.

Peter Baurst, enjoying his third dance in a row with Eva, decided the long trip on the train to attend the dance was totally worthwhile. Having been reminded by Eva of the fairy story, Peter was just saying he wished he could find a *shoe left behind* by her, when he felt a tap on his shoulder. It was a smiling Magda.

'I think you should let some of the other boys have a dance with Cinderella, don't you think?'

Peter smiled back at Magda and, with an awkward half bow, thanked Eva and began moving away, but Eva pulled him back with a quick grab of his hand.

'Its fine *Mutti*. There are many other girls,' she said.

'Oh, this is your mother, Eva? How do you do Frau Borbounet. I am Peter Baurst. May I dance with *you,* then?'

Eva glared at her dancing mother as she smiled back over Peter's shoulder, until her view was blocked by a smiling young suitor arriving for his long-awaited dance.

The band no longer had the dilemma of deciding what type of music to play to keep the dancers happy, as they were all so drunk they played whatever they wished. Sometimes replaying the tune, they had played only minutes before. Occasionally, one of their members would jump up and join the dancers on the floor, but no one noticed any change in the music. Generally, the drunker they got, the better they played.

The dance was over by about two in the morning and the band came staggering out of the *saal* to make their way up the Kirsch Allee where Eva and Peter had earlier picked cherries off the trees that ran either side of the narrow lane, each popping a cherry into the other's mouth as a farewell gesture.

Over their giggling, they had heard Eva's mother yelling for her to *come in out of the cold, immediately.* Eva slipped out of Peter's heavy coat and handed it back to the shivering young man. He gratefully climbed into it, basking in the aroma and warmth of the girl whom he decided he was going to marry one day. Looking back from the dark, as Eva entered through the door held open by Magda and seeing her backlit by the light inside the *gasthaus*, Peter waved, not knowing if she could see him. Turning, he stomped up the lane not caring if he made the last train or not.

By the time the band began following in Peter's footsteps, there would be no trains. The musicians swayed from side to side, up the snow-covered lane, cursing their heavy instruments and the bitter cold. Advancing a few steps and then retreating as many, they hauled their trumpet player up from the snow again and again, cursing him for being so drunk as they themselves swayed perilously over him.

The final time he went down, three of them were way ahead up the lane, leaving the trumpeter with just one supporter. He had slipped on a patch of ice and gone down heavily, crushing his instrument case. His friend struggled vainly to raise him on his own, his body was too slack, he was already asleep. Reeling dangerously, he shouted to the other three, but they kept going without acknowledging his call. He looked down at his fellow musician and shrugged. Then he struggled out of his heavy coat and laid it over him.

'When you wake up, you will be sober and able to...to get up,' he slurred, before staggering, and shivering without his heavy coat, through the snow to catch up to the others.

The following morning early Eva decided to go for a walk up *Kirsch Allee* to see if she could recapture some of the magic she had felt the night before. There was nobody around, most adults sleeping in with hangovers, leaving younger people to sleep as well instead of doing their Sunday chores and homework.

Eva felt no weariness, just excitement at the way her first dance had turned out. *What a wonderful evening.* As she reached the end of the lane, she noticed what looked like a frost covered overcoat lying in the road.

'Who could drop their coat, even take it off in this cold?' she asked herself. Then she giggled, *Peter had for her.*

It hadn't snowed again last night, but there had been a heavy frost. As she got closer, she realised it was not just a coat, but something much bigger. She crossed over to the other side of the lane to get a closer look and suddenly froze in mid step. A blue face stared up at her from the snow, frozen vomit everywhere, the mouth gaping open.

Eva did not hear herself scream, but her mother, lying in her bed did and was at the front gate opening onto the avenue in her dressing gown, barefoot in the snow, by the time a stricken faced Eva came running up to the *gasthaus*.

CHAPTER 5

Eva and Peter

MAGDA HAD NO REST and little sleep, yet she still found time to teach her daughter how to bake and make fine cheese. *Quark* and *Kochkaese* were Eva's favourites. She kept these recipes and all her others in a hard covered notebook, in handwriting that was unreadable to all but herself. On the cover, she had glued a grainy photograph of the cellar and its cheese making equipment, including the curd table over which she had heard so many anecdotes as they worked together.

Here in the cellar, Magda had told Eva so much about her past life experiences, some from the time when she was married to Kurt, some from when she was a young girl. It was during one of these cheese-making mornings, not long after the dance, that Eva steered their conversation towards the subject she wanted to raise.

'*Mutti*, do you remember your first boyfriend?'

Magda's head jerked up in surprise.

'That's a surprise question,' she laughed, knowing it was not one she could answer or recall joyful memories about. She had grown up in the shadow of her older sister who, as a teenager, seemed to have most boys in the village and surrounds totally enchanted. They never saw any attraction in the younger sister, regarding her as an enforced chaperone, forever hanging around when they wanted to flirt with her sister.

Magda's parents took advantage of this situation, always insisting her older sister take Magda with her wherever she went. Magda had hardly any opportunity to socialise on her own, until she was old enough to put her foot down and demand her time alone. Unfortunately, by this time, her sister had become seriously ill and she was expected to help with her bedridden sibling. So, there was still no time for teenage romances for Magda; Kurt had been her first and only man, she told Eva.

'Why do you ask such a question, my dear,' Magda asked her daughter with an expression she hoped was neutral.

'Oh, just wondered,' Eva said, avoiding her mother's enquiring look, concentrating on folding the curd they had just cut.

They worked in silence together for a few minutes and then Magda spoke, 'Has this got anything to do with the boy you met at the dance?'

'Which one?' Eva murmured.

'Which one?' Magda laughed. 'Perhaps the one you stood outside with in the freezing cold, in your thin dress.'

'I had his coat on,' Eva said in defence, unsure if she should have made that disclosure.

'Oh, I see. How gallant of him. I must say he is a good dancer,' Magda smiled, winking at her daughter.

Emboldened by her mother's light-hearted comments, Eva began to get excited and words started to bubble out.

'Yes, he is and he is such a good letter writer, as well. You know, he is an apprentice brick layer and will soon achieve his *Maurermeister* certification. Also, he wants to come and visit us – may he?'

Eva had just turned 18 when she and Peter were married in the small church in the village. By this time Peter had got his certification and was earning a good wage, so with the shortage of money in the family, Kurt was more than happy to have him in the household. He, nonetheless, always referred to Peter, with a cynical chuckle, as *Graf Habenichts*, due to his lack of wealth.

When Magda heard her sons also referring to Peter in the same way, she reprimanded them and told them, in no uncertain terms, just how little wealth their father had had until she came on the scene. They, of course, reported her comment to Kurt, hoping to infuriate him, but he snarled at them for not immediately telling her they disbelieved her. Magda, of course, also received angry words later.

The boys were also working now too, one as a baker and one as a policeman, so for the moment there was some extra money coming in, but for how long, no one knew. The looming war would soon start swallowing up Germany's young men so it was likely, Kurt feared, that this new source of income would dry up.

Soon after Peter and Eva married and she fell pregnant with their first child, one after the other, her older brothers also married and moved their pregnant wives into the *gasthaus* as well. Young families in small rooms, crying babies, Kurt providing late night entertainment with his mistresses through thin walls and the constant talk of war, put a strain on all. There were endless arguments and, now that they were strong young men, sometimes awful fist fights between father and sons.

Against this background Eva and Peter watched their daughter, Anna, grow into a little girl who, like her mother, was *the apple of Kurt's eye*. She was exceptionally curious, determined to try everything, including *Eierlikör*, licked off fingers dipped into the glasses, left in the bar after a previous night's gathering for Skat.

Some mornings, Eva would appear in the bar looking for her, but Kurt would have already hidden her under the bar counter, hearing Eva's calls as she came down the stairs. Once, when Eva caught them out, Kurt laughed and said they were just playing a hide and seek game.

'How could the little one answer your call, Eva? Then *Opa* would have known where she was hiding,' he said, winking at Anna under the counter and laughing out loud as she tried to wink back.

Anna was also one of the few people that lifted Magda's heart in her world of constant work and domestic unrest. It was because of this, Anna would find herself standing alone in front of the ice cream van clutching a coin in her tiny hand. The kids of the village would hear its bell when it was still a long way off, but it meant nothing to them. With the impact of the war across Europe there was very little money to spare, but Magda somehow always managed to find a coin.

She was dismayed when Eva announced she and Anna were moving out, as she had volunteered to be a nurse at a hospital in Hamburg. Half of Eva felt it was her duty, but she conceded to herself it would be a relief to be away from the domestic war in the *gasthaus*. Nurses were desperately needed when the allied bombing began its focus on Germany's industrial area, so the hospital even went to the trouble of finding Eva a room in a house near their building. The owner, they said, could babysit Anna in the evenings when Eva did night shifts, and a neighbour would care for her during the day.

Against Magda's wishes, Eva had decided Anna should stay with her in Hamburg. The *gasthaus* was not a place she wanted to leave her daughter, with Peter away all day working. Magda begged her to let Anna stay with them, where it was safe from the bombs, but Eva refused, promising they would return to the *gasthaus* whenever she had a few days off.

The night, Peter left to join his ship, a destroyer in Hamburg, he appeared to Eva almost relieved, not fearful in anyway. *Relieved to be leaving the chaos here, like I was,* Eva thought. It was that same night Anna was told she might be getting a sister or brother one day. Eva was still not convinced it was a good idea, given the war going on around them, both in the *gasthaus* and outside it.

Peter, nonetheless, decided Anna should be prepared for a sibling by employing what he thought was a very clever parable so Anna would know what the future held for her; he stood in front of her holding up a small slab of chocolate.

Anna jumped up and down, squealing excitedly, 'Thank you *Papi*, thank you *Papi*.'

'That is your present from me before I go,' Peter said as she took it from his hand.

'Soon, when you have a baby brother or sister, you will have to share gifts like this with them,' he said as he snatched the slab of chocolate back from her tiny hand. Tearing open the wrapper he snapped the dark square in half. 'You will be the oldest and it will be your duty to give half of everything to your young baby sister or brother,' he said handing her one half.

Anna shook her head and declined the gift. She said little more to Peter before he departed. Even though he tried to distract her, putting his sailor's cap on her head, but she pulled it off in anger because it was too big and fell down over her eyes, making him laugh.

Eva's instinct told her she had just witnessed an incident that would influence her daughter's attitude towards her siblings for a long time and one she herself would regret. She would refer to it often in future years, when arguing with Peter after Anna had been punished for something or the other, *your stupid parable started all this.*

CHAPTER 6

Eva's Ashes

EVA HEARD ONLY THE sound of her own footsteps as she strode through the ward towards the small room at the end, where the nurses stored their coats and bags, along with the cupboards full of medicines and dressings. It was quiet at this time, the *midnight shift,* unless ambulances arrived or there was an air raid. Even the smell of ether seemed less confronting. Arriving at the door, she reached for the latch, but the door swung open before her and the *Oberin* pushed past her on the way out.

Recovering from her surprise at seeing the senior nurse in the hospital at such a late hour, Eva took in the fact there was now a bed in the small room and in it a patient, his head and the hand that lay on the blanket beside him, swathed in bandages.

'He must be kept separate, keep the door locked, even when you are in there,' the matron said sternly.

'He is a prisoner of war. Well, while he is alive, he is. Which I don't think he will be for long. An airman. One that has been bombing us for weeks. He's been hanging above the snow in a tree all night after he parachuted from his aircraft. One of our boys must have shot them down. Now *we* must nurse him,' she snarled ironically as she turned and walked off. '*Schweinehund!*' she threw back at Eva.

Slipping out of her coat, Eva moved to the bed, to her patient. He had become *her* patient the second the *Oberin* made it clear she did not care whether he lived or died. Only that he must be kept separate and locked up, as she had been instructed by her superiors.

Eva took his unbandaged hand in hers. It was as cold as ice. Putting her hands under the covers, she felt other parts of his body. He was freezing. Eva wasted no time finding several hot water bottles, filling them and placing them against his body. He seemed to murmur something, but she was not sure. His whole face was covered in bandages; his nose, cheeks and ears ravaged by frostbite.

The airman was not able to free himself from his parachute harness, swaying all night above the snow, his parachute snagged in the tree he had crashed through. Saved from freezing to death by the heavy shearling leather jacket and pants, rear gunners wore against the cold in their glass turrets.

He was fortunate the doctor attending him had a great interest in the treatment of frostbite. He had studied before the war with a Russian friend, and they had managed to maintain some contact during the war. The Russians had advanced knowledge of frostbite classification and remedy as a result of their war with Finland and some of this information and technique the airman's doctor had learnt from his friend. Whilst others cared very little about the patient who had been bombing them for months, the airman became a *project* for the doctor, much like he was to Eva. He was determined to save the man's ravaged skin with the knowledge he had acquired and apply what he would learn, trying various treatments on this airman, to future frostbite cases.

Eva was not surprised when it happened. She had nursed him for months, during which time she had even taught him to speak some German while her English improved dramatically. They would talk for ages some evenings when the wards were much quieter. He told her all about his past life and his family and their farm. This was when he was happiest, when she was near him, he told her. He could handle the physical pain, but the memories of the last few years, that came when he was alone, left him distraught.

She had celebrated quietly, alongside his doctor, as his health improved and the final removal of his bandages revealed his recovery from frostbite. Held his hand when his mental wounds overwhelmed him some nights, when he shed tears for his family and his home he missed so much. It was on one of these evenings, *the midnight shift,* when he looked so sad, Eva had been moved to lean over and take him in her arms. Whispering in his ear like a loving friend, she felt his arms move around her. Felt the warmth of his lips on her neck.

Later, she would remember the last clear thought she had had was, *thank God they insist on the door being locked at all times.*

It had been a restful weekend in Lauenburg for Eva. Less so for Anna because, much to her irritation, her Nanna's friend and her granddaughters were continually wanting to *feel if the baby already moved*, giggling and guessing whether it was a baby girl or a baby boy.

'It's a boy, I know,' Anna insisted irritably. 'We don't want another girl. Opa said so.'

'Can we play now?' she continued, tugging at the hand of the girl nearest to her.

During the weekend, Magda's friend did not mention Peter, whom Eva had not heard from since he sailed from Hamburg. She seemed more concerned with the fatigue she saw in Eva. Having these Lauenburg friends to play with meant Anna was fully occupied, and their grandmother convinced Eva try and catch up on her sleep after months of double shifts at the hospital. Insisting Eva retire to her room, she sent the children out to play.

'*Spielt draussen. Spielt draussen*,' she whispered to them, waving her hands in the direction of the back door, like she was flicking a fly away from her baking bowl.

Even from Lauenburg, they had seen the sky lighting up over Hamburg, heard the non-stop thunder of the bombs. Eva knew this Monday morning would be frantic in the hospital. The bus driver got them as close as he could to the tiny house the hospital had found her. They stumbled the rest of the way over smouldering rubble and splashed through puddles of water left by fire engines trying to save burning buildings and the people inside them.

She had barely prepared Anna a bowl of porridge and thrown on her uniform, when there was a loud knock at the door. The neighbour, who babysat Anna, stood before her.

'You won't need that anymore,' she said pointing at Eva's stained uniform. 'Or *me*, to look after Anna, I mean. It's gone. The hospital. Gone.'

Without another word, the woman, exhausted from being awake all-night sheltering in an underground station, turned and walked away. Eva pulled coats off hooks from the door she had just closed and, slipping into her own, called her daughter.

'Arms up, arms up darling. We're going to the hospital.'

Mouth still full of porridge Anna could barely mumble her protest at going back out onto the cold, scary streets.

Motionless, in front of the huge smoking mound of crushed timber and bricks, Eva imagined she could still hear the sounds of a normal day in the hospital. Voices over the echoing footsteps in the long passageways. Nurses calling out to colleagues, commands from doctors standing in doorways. Groans from beds in dark recesses.

But all Eva was hearing were the calls of rescuers as they dug at the rubble, trying to find survivors, respond to any faint cry they might hear or be directed to by their Alsatians. Too much time had passed by now. They were mainly finding bodies, or parts of them. Eva moved away quickly when there was sudden shouting and frantic digging, lest Anna be exposed to something horrifying.

They were both rocked by a sudden gust of wind laden with ash and dust from the surrounding rubble. What fell on the street had been shovelled to either side, leaving enough space for a fire engine, or an ambulance should there be a *discovery* of someone clinging to life under the rubble. Another gust tore at the hem of her uniform and, as she pushed it down against her leg, she *noticed* a lorry moving off slowly. One of the doors crashed open as its wheels bounced through a hole in the road and she gasped when she saw rows of bulky, black plastic bags, one on top of the other.

Through her tears, she tried to summon into view the building she had entered every day, but nothing appeared. The image before her remained the same one that had stunned her when she came around the corner into the street dragging her daughter with her. A few broken, sagging brick walls and the remains of a chimney stack at a crazy angle, poking out of a mountain of smouldering bricks and ash where her hospital used to be.

'Are you crying, *Mutti*?' Putting her arm around Anna, Eva breathed deeply, trying to make the hospital smells come back, antiseptic in the corridors, in some rooms the odour of blood and wounds, but there was only acrid smoke. She shuddered and began to sob. Tears, cool on a face, warmed by the mountain of hot rubble before her. This was all that remained of the building, her workplace, she had hurried away from on Friday in her grubby nurse's uniform to start her weekend break.

The hospital had become a kind of bubble for Eva, a place where she was shielded from her life in the *gasthaus*, where there was no acrimony between people. She felt empathy for the nurses she worked with and those they cared for, felt a happiness in her heart she had last enjoyed when she first met Peter.

Although there had been anxiety and suffering around her,

the opportunity to nurse those in such an environment, brought immeasurable rewards. Seeing a patient return to health, begin smiling once again, brought joy to all those who worked there, especially after caring for someone for many months as she had for her 'Aussie' – as he sometimes referred to himself.

Robert had emerged from his cocoon of bandages like a butterfly and it was not long before the young airman's charming grin won him many nurse friends. Even the *Oberin* had felt it and Eva would smile to herself, watching her speak to him in broken English, her *senior nurse* full of concern for his need to rest. She imagined tapping her superior on the shoulder and enquiring innocently, 'Isn't he the *Schweinehund?*'

And now her bubble had been shattered. She had lost all her hospital friends, colleagues and patients that she cared so much about, in an instant. All her precious emotional attachments, that made her feel happy each day, ripped from her heart. Her feeling of loss was palpable.

Anna was also feeling the heat from the shattered remains, her little hand sweaty in her mother's tight grip. Instinctively, she tried to stop her mother crying by distracting her with a request.

'*Mutti*, can you take my coat off? I'm warm.'

Anna's sister was also warm. Inside her mother's womb, she enjoyed a different warmth. Eva moved her free hand, still clutching her sodden handkerchief to her abdomen.

'Gone,' she murmured between sobs.

'*Mutti*,' Anna said pulling at her mother's hand.

With the hospital demolished and Peter's return possible, Eva decided, rather than volunteer for another hospital, it would be best for her to return to the *gasthaus* where it would be safer for Anna and herself. She had lost so much that weekend. With the intense bombing that had taken place, it was a wonder *they* had survived. Anna and her babysitter had sometimes spent hours in the local bomb shelter.

Magda had begged Eva to send Anna back to *her* when the bombing of Hamburg became almost a daily occurrence, but she had refused knowing her brother's sons, whom Anna hated, would bully her constantly with Peter gone.

Magda was far too busy to keep an eye on the boys and any reprimand from Kurt, brought on yet another fight between him and their mothers, who struggled to cope alone, their husbands away at the *front*. Anna was delighted with her mother's decision to return *home*, where she would be spoilt by her grandparents again.

As it turned out, with Magda and Kurt so busy trying to keep the *gasthaus* going, they had little time for Anna. It was the Estonian refugees who spoilt her, offering her bread with sugar sprinkled on it. Eva tried to stop it, but Anna always found one willing to give her what she wanted. The refugees had taken over the entire *saal* and some were even moved upstairs by the authorities, on the floor where Magda, Kurt and their extended family had their rooms. Magda and Kurt had to both accommodate the refugees and feed them.

CHAPTER 7

Baby Sister

CHRISTA WAS THE ONE highlight for the extended family in the *gasthaus* trying to survive the environment they were forced into by the war and what was yet to come. There would be many dark revelations for German people to confront when it came to an end.

Her sister's birth wasn't a highlight for Anna. She was still smarting from being told she was going to have to share everything with this unwelcome addition to her family. At school one day, her teacher called the class to attention to make an announcement.

'Girls and boys, we have a very lucky girl in class today. I have just been given a message that Anna and her parents have been given a wonderful present, just this morning. While she has been here at school, a cute little baby sister has arrived.'

Anna could still hear the class clapping as she ran down the hall in tears to the entrance door of the school. Walking home from the village, she vowed to herself she would not return to the school, to hear silly questions about the baby. She was determined to change things back to the way they were, although how, she did not know.

Eva was just as determined to change things for her daughter. To find a way to alter Anna's perception, that her baby sister, Christa, was a threat and would usurp her standing with her mother and father. It was the first thing she said to her returning husband when she introduced him to his beautiful second daughter, whom he seemed less than enthusiastic about.

'Any chance we get, we must let Anna see that we think so much of her, we are comfortable with trusting this new baby to be in her care, without us being around. For her to look after Christa on her own,' she said to him.

With a shrug and a faraway look in his eyes, he said, 'We get used to anything after a while, learn to love it, even.' Then seeming to come out of a dream, he said, 'If we had had a son, she would have been happier, I think.'

Eva noticed Peter had done a lot of shrugging since he had come home. A few months before she returned to the *gasthaus* from Hamburg, she was notified that Peter's ship had been sunk and although there were some survivors, nobody knew yet who they were. Once postal services were reinstated, to Eva's relief, she received a letter from him, saying he was in Ireland, having been picked up by an Irish trawler.

'Lucky for him the *Kriegsmarine* hadn't blown the trawler up,' Kurt laughed, '*Graf Habenichts* saved by our Irish friends; now he will soon be back to see he has yet *another* daughter.'

Eva's brothers had also added a few snide remarks about how they would soon have another person to support in the *gasthaus*, but Eva knew they both just longed to start an argument, so she ignored them. They had also recently returned from the *front*, the one more or less unscathed, the other very traumatised after years in a Russian prisoner of war camp in Siberia.

Knowing her war-stressed brothers could explode at the slightest provocation, Eva tried to avoid any conflict. She worked hard to keep the peace between her brother's sons and Anna, because if Kurt reprimanded them for bullying his beloved granddaughter, the fathers would immediately react, keen to show him, he could not treat *their* sons like he had treated them, willing to use their fists, as they already had. Revenge for their own painful upbringing. The time under constant bombing in Hamburg had not hardened Eva; she still dreaded these violent confrontations.

Peter arrived back from the war seemingly unscathed, but as the weeks went by after his return, she would come to believe he preferred to be back there, interred in Ireland, not home with his family. It was the only time he seemed happy, when he was speaking of his time in Ireland.

She once asked Magda if she had noticed how distracted Peter was since returning and her mother sighed and said she should not be surprised.

'It is no wonder he is like he is Eva. What a place to come home to. Your husband came back from the war to the war. Families at war in this house, his home,' she said bitterly.

Mutti's right, no wonder he hardly notices his daughters, Eva thought.

Distracted he might have been, but Peter did support his family, Eva had to concede. Builders were in short supply in Germany and there was much to rebuild, so he was able to find work easily. He worked long hours for little money, in good weather and bad. He left early and arrived home in the dark, exhausted. Eva worried though, that as tired as he was, he did not fall asleep easily, seemed to be restless when he slept, waking up often.

As spring began to wrest the countryside back from the clutches of a cold dark winter, Eva suggested to Anna one fine morning, that she take baby Christa for a walk in the pram. The clear night had coated the pine tree foliage around the *gasthaus* with frosty crystals. *Show her the Tannenbaeume,* although Christmas was a long way off. She watched her daughter's face, waiting for a response, but Anna's expression was impassive. Eva never stopped being hopeful she would eventually accept and grow to enjoy her young sister.

Standing beside the old pram handed down through several generations, with its big wheels, her head was barely above its sides, Anna watched as Eva wrapped the baby in a thick, pink blanket and drew a knitted pink baby bonnet over Christa's blond curls. Picking up the matching woollen mittens, that had fallen under the pram and handing them to her mother, Anna asked where she should walk to.

'Why don't you walk up the hill behind the *gasthaus*? That is the sunniest place to be in the morning,' Eva smiled, 'But hold on tightly to the pram, it's steep in some places.'

There were two narrow gravel roads running either side of the *gasthaus*. They met at the top of the hill behind it, so Anna could have taken either and ended up in the same place. Unfortunately for her, instead of choosing the one that ran close to the *saal*, the one her mother had used for her first abortive attempt at bicycle riding, she chose the one that ran a little distance away from the side of the *gasthaus*. Through the kitchen window, it was in full view of the bench Eva worked at.

Anna was surprised at how heavy the pram felt once she started up the hill. She panted quietly as she pushed on the pram's bar, which, because of her size, she had to look under not over, slipping occasionally on the loose gravel. All the while, Christa gurgled happily in the bouncing pram, but Anna already had enough experience to know this would soon be followed by some increasingly noisy fussing, the prelude to a good cry.

'Which I will probably be blamed for,' she said to herself as she fought the resistance of the incline.

They were near the crest of the hill when Anna slipped, both knees crashing into the gravel. It was the last straw. She yanked the pram around irritably, pointing it down the hill.

'Alright pram, you want to be going back down the hill, let's go then,' she said out loud.

Anna ran as fast as her little legs could take her, but because the pram was soon beginning to get away from her, she let it go crying, 'Go then, stupid thing,' before slowing to a panting stop as it careered down the hill.

After a short distance, the pram's wheels hit a patch of rough gravel knocking it from side to side, swerving like a car driven by a drunk driver, before flying off the edge of the road. Its front wheels rammed into a ditch toppling the pram forward, flinging blanket wrapped Christa through the air into a roadside thicket, dense enough with leafy bushes to give her a soft landing. Anna began to grasp the enormity of what had transpired as she ran up to the scene of the accident and saw, the foliage that had saved Christa, appeared to be stinging nettles.

Eva had watched the whole episode, frozen at the window, pot in one hand, spoon in the other. It all took place, it seemed to her, in slow motion. By the time she reached the scene, Anna was trying to hold Christa and rub her own nettle stings at the same time, whilst the baby cried uncontrollably from the burning skin on *her* face.

Taking the screaming Christa in her arms, Eva cast around in the thicket for the antidote she always used as a young girl when stung. Then feeling the back of her skirt yanked, she swung around and Anna thrust a handful of Dock leaves at her before turning back to the bush for herself.

That evening, the red marks from her father's belt matched the colour of the marks the nettles had left, but Anna had not let the tears fall while Peter hit her. Later, she cried in bed when no one could see her. She wondered why her mother did not punish her at the time. Instead, leaving it to her father to arrive home and deliver a much more painful punishment. Eventually, the tears stopped, replaced with a slight smile at the image of her baby sister flying through the air like an escaped pink balloon. Downstairs in the kitchen, as she swayed gently, soothing the blotch-faced baby in her arms, Eva remonstrated with her husband.

'You and your stupid chocolate story. You should be the one getting the belt.'

Her builder husband merely raised his shoulders, before shovelling another spoon of dinner into his mouth, *much like he shovels cement, I suppose,* Eva observed to herself. Looking at the nettle marks on Christa's face, she thought, *I probably didn't need to tell him, probably wouldn't even have noticed his baby's face. Poor Anna.*

Noises that normally found their way through the walls of a full *gasthaus* in the quiet of the night, generally signalling another of Kurt's affairs, had lessened as he got older and the number of guests diminished. They were replaced now though, with even more disconcerting sounds. Peter's restlessness in bed had been exacerbated by vivid dreams. Agonised groans as he replayed his time on the lifeboat in tortured nightmares. Waking up moments when a wet hand reached from black water, or an open mouth retreated below the oily surface. Sometimes the hand or teeth would suddenly leap back out of the water, try to grab him by the throat or bite his belt-wielding fist.

When they first started, it was often only an image of an old woman, a mother, or a young woman, a wife. They would just watch him while they sobbed, him standing before them with his belt hanging loosely from his hand, but as time wore on the dreams became terrifying. Sometimes, Eva and her daughter would be woken by grunts and moans, sometimes by a sudden howl that would have them sitting bolt upright in bed and Christa standing up holding the sides of her cot, beginning to cry.

The nights Peter had these dreams, left Eva drained. She would spend an age calming him after making him a warm drink, but when asked, he refused to tell her about them. Once Eva asked him if it was something that had happened to him in the war, but he looked away and said it was best not to talk about it.

Eva would lie awake after he had finally gone back to sleep, thinking what a mess her life had become, but for her two beautiful daughters.

She worried that the future for all of them looked so bleak and the more that was published about what had transpired in Europe during World War Two, the worse she felt.

Peter would always be his normal self in the morning, grumbling at his daughters as they argued over their dolls. Eva, making his breakfast and food for his lunch box, staring out the kitchen window at the distant weeds and wildflowers, hiding the ashes and rubble of the mill Kurt had burnt down. The demise of the mill seemed to have initiated a happy time in her life. Her father away, her first dance, meeting Peter, a kiss under the cherry trees, being in love, pregnant with Anna. Where had all the happiness gone?

Now, all there seemed to be was the anxiety born of bickering amongst families in the *gasthaus*, the arguments, the hardship her mother had to endure. At least, Magda's now grown-up sons had put a stop to their mother's physical abuse by Kurt. Happy memories were clouded by early images of the beatings her father handed out to her mother and her brothers, his affairs, her mother's loud angry words through the thin walls, 'No I don't want to Kurt, I'm so tired.' Then her moans.

CHAPTER 8

Abandoning Ship

'ALL ALONE, GRÜBCHENGESICHT? THOSE beautiful dimples make *me* want to smile too.' Eva heard from above her as she stacked bottles on the shelves under the bar counter her two-year-old Christa sat on, playing with her dolls. Rising from her kneeling position, Eva said, 'No, mother *and* barmaid are right here, *Guten Abend*.'

The woman laughed in surprise and putting an apologetic hand on Eva's arm, returned her greeting, '*Guten Abend*. You have a beautiful daughter. My husband and I would like a room for the night. Is that possible?'

'Thank you. Of course, come with me,' Eva said as she took Christa in her arms and lead the way to the *gasthaus* reception.

The woman's husband was standing in the hall with their suitcases and, as they came through the *wirtschaft* doorway, he smiled a greeting to Eva who called up the stairs for Anna to come down and fetch Christa. Slipping behind the reception counter, Eva opened the large leatherbound register and turned it around. While her husband began filling in details, the woman greeted Anna halfway down the stairs, beckoning Christa to come up to her.

'Goodness, another beautiful girl, you are lucky,' she said to Eva.

Smiling a *thank you*, Eva was just handing over keys to their room when Kurt came in through the front door, having stamped his feet free of snow on the door mat outside.

'*Guten Abend*,' he said, smiling at them both, but leaving his eyes on the woman who, it seemed to Eva, was not at all offended by the uninvited attention.

'Ah, Eva has done the paperwork I see, so let me take you up to your room,' Kurt said, picking up both their heavy cases. 'May I lead the way?' he inquired with his most charming smile as he started up the steps, carrying their luggage like it weighed very little. Eva shook her head and with a wry smile of her own, headed back to the *wirtschaft* to finish stacking her bottles.

It was Friday night and Peter made sure he got home earlier than usual, in order to enjoy the beers and fun evening in the bar he forsook during the week, having to leave so early in the morning. Still carrying his heavy bag of tools, he detoured past the main *gasthaus* door in the direction of the *wirtschaft's* outside entrance and, light-hearted at the thought of the work week being over, he clomped up the few steps to the large double doors.

The newly arrived couple, still marvelling at the *pfennige* trick Kurt had just executed, were seated at the bar counter on stools as Peter opened the door. His stamping in the doorway, accompanied by a waft of cold air, had them both momentarily looking over their shoulders towards the door. Still holding it open Peter examined his boots for remnants of snow while the man watched him open-mouthed.

'Peter!' he said in astonishment, 'Is that you!?'

Everyone in the bar jumped as Peter's heavy tool bag crashed to the wooden floor; he stood transfixed at the entrance. The face he now saw was one of the faces, the man's inquiring voice had brought instantly to mind, before he looked up. Of one of his four friends staring down at him as he lay exhausted, half drowned, squeezed between their legs in the tiny dinghy.

Motionless in the doorway, he could feel the dinghy rising and falling, taste the salt in his mouth, smell the oil. Behind the bar, Eva saw the blood had drained from Peter's face and without knowing why, she half expected him to turn and leave but he didn't. He seemed to gather himself, forced a grin as strode forward, his hand out.

'Hans, is that you, after all this time!? When they separated us in Dublin, I had no idea what became of you and Wolfgang and Axel,' Peter said, pumping his friend's hands with both of his.

After introducing his wife to Peter, the two ex-mariners became engaged in an animated conversation between swallows of beer, remembering all the good times on board the destroyer, avoiding any reference to their dinghy. When they did reminisce about the torpedoing, tacit agreement the incident was a *memory to be forgotten*, took them from how they reacted at the moment of impact, directly to their rescue by the Irish trawler and their time in Ireland.

Out of the corner of his eye, Peter saw Kurt was captivating Hans' wife with his anecdotes, touching her arm occasionally. Glancing between both, it seemed Hans appeared just as unconcerned about what was going on as Magda, who had joined Eva behind the bar after preparing the evening's meal.

'And where is Wolfgang nowadays?' Peter asked.

'Oh, he emigrated to Australia, not too long after the end of the war. Similar to here, there is a building boom going on and being a builder, he found work easily. He has set up his own business and looking for workers himself. He keeps writing to me and saying he needs a good electrician; that I should join him there.'

Hans seemed very knowledgeable about Australia, from having been in regular contact with Wolfgang who clearly did his research before applying to his new country for residence. It seemed, from what Hans said, that following the war Australia had become very sensitive to its relatively *small* population, compared to other nations in the Pacific region.

The country's vulnerability during the Pacific war, bombed by the Japanese and attacked by its submarines in Sydney Harbour, led to new government policies focused on building population; its often-used slogan of the time, *populate or perish*. So, an intense drive for immigrants took place in the late 1940s and, although Australia took many displaced people fleeing persecution in Soviet Bloc countries, the Department of Immigration initially preferred Dutch, West German and Danish applicants when it came to immigrants from Europe. In order to house the expanding population, new suburbs were being built but the war years had taken their toll, resulting in a shortage of skills and materials.

'Being both German *and* a builder, they welcomed him with open arms, our Wolfgang,' Hans laughed.

Peter laughed as well, clinking glasses with Hans as he went on, 'Wolfgang has made quite a name for himself as a quality builder. Because of the demand and shortage of materials, brick veneer instead of solid walls has become the standard. Faster and cheaper.' Hans took a mouthful of beer and, wiping either side of his moustache with the inside of a finger, he glanced at his wife and Kurt before continuing, 'But not for Wolfgang, only solid brick walls for him. High quality work, this is where he has found his niche. He has started his own business and his affluent customers love what he delivers.'

They laughed together at memories of Wolfgang on board their ship. He was always pointing out bad workmanship. *That could sink us, boys,* he would say, indicating what he believed was a design flaw.

'Ah, Wolfgang, always knows better,' Hans said shaking his head with grin. 'I got a letter from him a few weeks ago and he asked me, yet again, to join him. He says the shortage of skilled workers in Australia is getting worse.'

Lying in bed that night, Peter wondered if the chance meeting with Hans would bring on a bad nightmare or had he had enough alcohol to keep him asleep? He thought about Wolfgang as he lay next to a gently snoring Eva and, for once, pictured him not waving an oar above his head, instead, on a sandy white beach in faraway Australia, his big body dripping from swimming in the waves.

As they had readied for bed earlier, he laughed at Eva's excitement over the snippets of conversation she overheard between he and Hans.

'Just imagine living in a lovely warm country like that. Making a fresh start. Getting away. Taking the children on holidays to the beach. You could get a job with Wolfgang easily,' Eva prattled on as she did when she got excited.

'Don't be silly,' Peter said, joining her in bed. 'It would be so far away from our families.'

'Oh yes, of course. Wouldn't that be bad?' Eva laughed facetiously. 'We would miss all this terribly,' she said sweeping her arm above her head simultaneously, looking from left to right with a smile. 'Our lovely *gasthaus* family.'

When he awoke, having slept peacefully right through the night, Peter jumped out of bed and began dressing.

'What are you doing? There is no work today. It's Saturday. You know, our *special* morning,' Eva said, looking across at Anna in her bed and Christa in her cot, both asleep. 'Look, they're asleep,' she whispered in dismay at his departure, but Peter was already on his way through their door.

'I must speak to Hans,' he said closing the door.

He ran through the *gasthaus* front door as Hans was reversing his car for his early departure. He stumbled down the snowy pathway yelling for him to stop.

'Hans. Hans. One minute please.'

Panting, he told Hans he had thought about their conversation and would he mind asking Wolfgang the next time he wrote to him if he might consider him as one of his workers?

'You would go to Australia?' Hans asked, sounding incredulous, looking up through his half rolled down window.

'Maybe. Maybe. I don't know. Maybe,' Peter said, bending over to make himself heard over the car's loud engine. As he did, he noticed

Hans' wife had a swollen lip. She ignored his greeting, staring straight ahead through the windscreen.

'Okay, I will then. *Auf Wiedersehen*,' he waved and the car thundered down the driveway between the cherry trees Eva so loved.

Back in their bed, shivering after peering out of the window to see what Peter was up to, Eva heard her husband stomping back up the stairs and, stretching luxuriously in their small bed, she smiled to herself.

Peter had already been gone three months when his letter arrived with the news that the Australian authorities had granted Eva and the girls visas to travel to and live in Australia, so she could make arrangements to join him. He suggested they travel by sea, as his expensive plane trip had taken three days and was unpleasant and extremely tiring. With all their possessions and two children, one a two-year-old, Eva would find it very difficult.

What Peter did not know, was that most ships available to migrant travellers to Australia, were converted troop carriers with few facilities. There were vast open areas where men and women were accommodated separately, sleeping on bunk beds either side of communal dining tables.

He said once again, as he had in his previous letters, he was enjoying being there, working in the warm climate was a lot easier than in Germany and he was being paid very well. What he did not tell her was that his nightmares had got more frequent and more intense since being in Wolfgang's proximity. In fact, Wolfgang had already commented on his frequent drinking. It had been more of a joke than a criticism, but nonetheless it was made.

'You need Eva here to get you under control, hey Peter?' he had laughed.

Anna was very curious the day several men came with a big wooden box and, as directed by her mother, put it in a room, normally used for storage, off the main bar area. When she went to investigate after the men had followed Eva back out of the bar, she found the room was locked. Looking through the keyhole, she saw the box standing in the middle of the room. It seemed huge to her, almost filled the room. *Could it be a doll's house for us to play in?*

Her mother told her not to be so nosy, when she asked about it and, under no circumstances to mention it to her Nanna, which was not very likely since Magda had not left her room for days. She had become increasingly frail even after the refugees left. She had no respite, as now guests began to return and were even more demanding. Caring for her own family, the refugees forced on them and now, the returning *gasthaus* clientele, had finally got the better of her. Eva could see in her mother's face she had given up, did not care about *anything* anymore. She hardly showed interest in her grandchildren.

When her father insisted Magda move into a small room of her own, Eva feared she could see history repeating itself. She insisted he call a doctor to see her mother, which he finally did, but scoffed at the diagnosis of exhaustion and need for rest. When the doctor said, if she did not have the care she needed, he feared the worst for her, Kurt threw him out of the *gasthaus*, threatening legal action.

Eva could feel a growing distance between her and her mother. Perhaps it was fear of seeing her mother in the same situation as her grandmother, not wanting to be part of it, exposed to the trauma. Another side of her thought, more likely, she was distancing herself from her mother because of her anxiety over revealing she and the girls were moving away *to the other side of the world*. The inevitable heartbreak she would see in her mother at the news.

There were times in the dead of night, as she tossed and turned alongside Anna, that an ugly thought edged its way into her mind. She pushed it away before it had a chance to reveal itself, trying to think instead about how she could fulfil her duty as a daughter to a sick, vulnerable mother, if she was not living with her. There it is, *that* thought again, clinging to her mind. She tried not to imagine what it might do to her mother, being told her daughter and granddaughters were leaving forever, maybe returning only for occasional visits. *Would it be the final straw? Be careful of that thought, lest it manifest itself as a wish.*

Then it was there. Yes, it would be best if her mother died, before they departed. Tormented, Eva lifted and slammed the back of her head against the pillow. *Oh my God*, she rebuked herself, knowing she was a coward. Unable to be honest with her own mother. She couldn't bear it; she didn't have the courage. *You're a coward, you're a coward.*

Anna had been growing much closer to her little sister, even though she was forced to drag her along with her wherever she went. Christa loved being with Anna and any move her older sister made towards a door drew loud plaintive cries to go with her.

'Chrissie *mit*, Anna. Chrissie *mit*.' Always followed by a parent calling from somewhere, 'Take Christa with you, Anna.'

The box that had been brought, had Anna fascinated. She had noticed her mother going into the room regularly, always with a bag. So, one day, she peeped through the keyhole and saw her busy putting things into the box. Behind her, Christa was tugging at her dress.

'Chrissie *mit*.'

She lifted Christa up so she could look through the keyhole, but Christa had no idea what she was supposed to do, so turning her little sister's head to face her with her hand, Anna closed one eye and pointed at the door. Christa, screwing up her entire face, trying to close one eye had Anna giggling uncontrollably, which in turn Christa thought was funny and she burst out laughing. Eva yanked open the door before Anna could escape.

'What are you doing here at the door? Go, go and play.'

Nobody had asked Eva how she felt about Peter being so far away. Recently, she had begun to believe they assumed she would eventually join him, as no one inquired about his return from his contract in Australia anymore; *or maybe they have just forgotten Graf Habenichts,* she thought wryly.

She resolved to tell no one until the day of their departure, not even her daughters. Eva surprised herself with her ability to alone organise every aspect of the clandestine move and the intense focus had kept her mind off the inevitable. Could she bear the anguish on her mother's face?

When the men came back a week before their departure, this time with a trolley, to collect the now full wooden crate from where it sat under lock and key in the storeroom, Eva responded to inquiring looks from her brothers with a simple response, 'That storeroom needed to be cleared out. Full of old stuff that could be sold. We need money.'

It brought nods of approval from them and a compliment from Kurt on her initiative, saying *if he couldn't remember what was in there, then it was not worth keeping.*

On the day of their departure Eva and the girls came downstairs carrying a suitcase each. A tiny one for Christa. It had been Anna's lunch box when she first went to school, a smaller one and a backpack for Anna and Eva heaving a much larger one, which the taxi driver hurried across to take from her after being reprimanded by Kurt.

'That's a big case for just a few days with Margaretha and Dieter, Eva,' Kurt had laughed when she announced they would be away for a few days, visiting her old school friend, maybe for a week.

'Yes, I know,' she laughed, 'but as you know, they are having a baby and I have lots of things I don't need anymore. In these times, they will be a big help to them.'

Her brothers wanted to know who would do the cooking while she was away. Eva laughed, 'You both have wives. Did their mothers not teach them to cook? Is that why they have never helped Mutti and I in the kitchen? Now we will find out.'

Eva told Christa and Anna about their forthcoming trip on the train to Rotterdam, where they were to board their ship to Australia. Eva's choice of a Rotterdam departure was a serendipitous one. Like Peter, Eva was unaware of how bad sailing on an ex-troop ship was or that this was what most migrants to Australia had to travel on. Departing from Rotterdam, not Hamburg, meant they would sail on the *Johan Van Oldenbarnevelt*. Referred to as the *JVO*, it was a large Dutch ship which, after working as a British troop ship, had been refurbished with cabins and entertainment areas before joining the Australian migrant trade route.

'When will we see *Papi*?' Christa had responded.

'Christa will fall in the sea,' was all Anna said, knowing that it would be her task to make sure that did not happen.

Eva did not hear their responses; she was thinking of the envelope she had left on the bar counter in the *wirtschaft* for her mother and father. With an overwhelming sense of guilt and heavy heart, she wondered if it had been discovered yet.

CHAPTER 9

The Flamenco Dancer

It was the huge red fan that caught Anna's eye as she strolled along the deck holding Christa's hand tightly. The woman had her back to them, gazing out to sea, waving the fan near her face. But as they walked by, it was as if she sensed they were there, because she swung around to look at them. The fan snapped shut with a flick of her wrist. Now it was a red *conductor's baton* held in slender white fingers tipped with long crimson fingernails.

Anna's eyes flicked from the fan to the woman's red lipstick, to the matching red flower pinned into the pitch-black hair piled on top of her head, to her eyes as she smiled down at them.

'Two beautiful young girls taking in the view. Can you even see over the rail, Dimples?' she asked Christa.

'Say *Guten Morgen*,' Anna said to Christa in German, and the woman immediately switched to German to return their greeting. Her eyes were big dark pools and gazing up into them, Anna half expected to see herself and Christa reflected in there.

Christa pulled at her hand, wanting to keep going, but Anna, intrigued by the person before her, held her back. Since they had boarded the day before, Anna had barely been aware of where she was, totally focused on her task of ensuring Christa did not get lost or, worse still, fall overboard. Now, for once, Anna was near something that was not a potential threat to her little sister, a person who was fascinating; although she was what her mother called a "stranger", she supposed.

'You speak funny,' she said to the woman, 'and you have a very big fan and a summer flower in your hair. It's still winter.'

'That is because I am from sunny Spain and am a flamenco dancer,' she said, suddenly tilting her head back, flicking the now raised fan open and giving it a flutter. She thrust a thin leg forward awkwardly from where it had been hidden by her long dress. Holding her pose she added, 'And anyway, we're sailing towards summer.'

'You're so funny,' Anna giggled.

'And you're so cheeky,' the woman laughed.

Reaching down and picking up, what looked to Anna like, a small black suitcase that stood beside her, she said, 'Come, let's sit over there at the tables and chairs near the shop. I'll buy you and your sister - she is your sister? - an ice cream.'

Christa no longer wanted to move on. Happy to be still for a while if ice cream was involved. When they reached the tables near the ice cream vendor, Anna lifted her sister onto one of the chairs next to her and they both looked at the flamenco dancer expectantly.

'Right, I will get your ice cream. The show can't begin until the audience has got ice cream, can it?' she laughed gaily as she made for the ice cream counter.

Glancing excitedly between their new friend now at the serving counter and the mysterious case she had put on their table, Anna did not even think of her promise to their mother to not *speak to strangers*, never mind sit at a table with one.

'What is that?' Anna asked, pointing at the black box with a finger covered in ice cream scraped from Christa's nose, *use your spoon, Christa, what a mess.*

'This is my *tocaores*, my guitar player who travels with me,' Rosa said.

'Would you like to hear him play, girls?'

'Yes. Yes please,' Anna responded excitedly, clapping her hands.

Christa's face broke into a grin, dimples smeared with ice cream. She tried to emulate her big sister's clapping, small sticky hands nearly knocking her ice cream cup off the table, but for Anna's speedy retrieval. As Rosa unclipped the catches of the case, Anna could hardly believe they were going to see a tiny man with a guitar slung over his shoulder hop out onto the table, but before Rosa could lift the top, they heard a loud exasperated voice from behind them, 'THERE YOU ARE!'

Eva weaved between the other tables and chairs as she headed for her missing daughters.

'I told you not to stop anywhere on your walk, until you got back to me. What are you up to?' she asked, lowering her voice as she got closer. Rosa stood smiling in greeting.

Beautiful face, but tall and gangly, went through Eva's mind.

'I am sorry, it is my fault. I stole your girls for company. They are so beautiful! Like their mother,' Rosa added, making Eva blush slightly. 'And one of them is so cheeky,' she laughed, pinching Anna's cheek gently.

'Yes, and also doesn't do what her mother tells her to do sometimes,' Eva responded.

'Anna, look at Christa's face, ask the ice cream man for some napkins so you can wipe it please,' Eva said as she sat down on the chair Rosa had invited her to take.

It wasn't long before Eva and Rosa were chatting like old friends. Eva felt herself warming to the somewhat eccentric character who sat opposite her as she revealed that she too was sailing to join her husband who had found a job in a *far-off land*. She was to disembark when they berthed at Cape Town, about halfway to Australia. She would then travel to Stellenbosch where her husband, a wine maker in Spain, had found a job on one of the wine estates.

'Jorge says there are beautiful mountains all around where we will live and the most beautiful countryside, but I have also heard that there are plenty of snakes and spiders,' Rosa said with an involuntary shudder.

'I had a spider in my suitcase today, luckily only a small one,' Eva said.

'Rosa has a small man who plays a guitar in *her* suitcase, *right here*,' Anna exclaimed wiping at Christa's face as she jerked from side to side in protest.

Eva turned to chide Anna for interrupting, but Rosa laughed out loud and hugged her. Anna could smell Rosa's perfume and feel the slightly oily softness of her hair on her cheek.

'Darling, I meant my guitarist's music is in here. His *music* on his records travels with me,' Rosa said as she opened the top of the case revealing a turn table with a record sitting on it. She unclipped a small silver crank handle from under the lid.

The crank reminded Eva of a much bigger one her father used, to get his car's engine started when she was just a young girl. As Rosa inserted it into the side of the record player, Eva recalled how he would push it into the hole in the front of his Goliath, just below the bumper, and then stand back and smile at her, doing a winding motion with his hand, *go on then my girl, crank as hard as you can, get the beast going.*

She felt a tear as she remembered the warmth of his hands over hers, helping her turn the crank, *what had he thought when he found and read my letter.* Rosa, in the meantime, was busy winding, *almost lovingly*, Eva thought. Anna was bouncing up and down on her chair, excited to learn what was going to happen next. Christa, bored, was eyeing the deck rail nearby, keen to look down at the sea.

After completing her winding and moving a small lever next to the rubber covered metal disk the record sat on, making it spin slowly, to Anna's delight and even Christa's fascination, Rosa eased down an arm from where it too nestled in the lid. It looked a bit like a bugle with a needle on the end of it. She gently placed it on the edge of the record.

After a few scratchy sounds, loud chords played on a classical guitar, floated from the hollow in the lid filling the space around them. A flamenco dancer had to appear next, surely. Heads turned expectantly at the adjoining tables and passengers standing at the nearby deck rail, collars turned up against the breeze, swung around to look.

Rosa stood, scarlet fan flicked wide open across her breast and peeking demurely above it made her announcement:

'Tonight, my fellow passengers, during dinner, I will dance for you.'

Eva felt excited as she dressed for dinner. She had been ill the first night and disappointed that a chance to "dress up" and go to dinner with people she did not know, meet new friends after many years, had to be postponed because of her sea sickness. It had been years and years since she last went out and now, she was out of the *gasthaus*, sailing to a new adventure. She felt like she was on holiday.

Her good spirits were suddenly dampened when her clandestine *gasthaus* departure drifted into her mind, so she was glad to be distracted when the cabin door opened and Anna dragged a protesting Christa through it.

'Why didn't you come to dinner with us like the other mothers?' Anna demanded over Christa's pleading, 'Want to go up, on the deck, Anna please.'

'She wouldn't eat her vegetables. Only a little of her meat. And dessert. Then she cried and everyone stared.'

'Too much ice cream with your Spanish lady, I think,' Eva said without taking her eyes off her reflection in the mirror. Her hair was too fine, she hated it, but she thought her blue eyes made up for it, *blau Papi, blau*.

'Can I come and watch Rosa dance, please *Mutti* please?' Anna said delivering a request of her own.

'Don't be silly darling, it is dinner for *grownups* and who would look after your baby sister? Should I ask the captain to babysit?' Eva laughed. 'Anyway, I am sure Rosa was just joking. They won't allow some passenger to just jump up and dance.'

Eva felt a little overwhelmed when she was met at the entrance to the ship's restaurant by the maître d' who informed her she had been invited to dine at the captain's table. Being led past the others, she was convinced everyone must be staring at her, noticing her every blemish. She wondered if Anna had been correct about the seams of her stockings being straight. With relief, she found that Rosa was also at the table and, as the maître d' pulled out the chair opposite the Spanish woman, she looked up from an animated conversation with a distinguished looking young man.

'Oh no, I am now no longer the one to catch our handsome captain's eye. The beautiful Eva has arrived to usurp me,' she cried out with a dramatic downturn of her mouth.

Eva felt her cheeks warm as she sat down, not even hearing the maître d' introducing her to the captain and the others at the table. The passengers near where she sat seemed friendly and being used to working in the *gasthaus* bar, meeting new people with the English she had learnt at school and from her Australian patient, she had the confidence to begin talking to these complete strangers. The conversations seemed a mixture of German and Dutch with English the common thread. Rosa, in addition to her home language, was fluent in both German and English.

A sip from the glass of champagne placed in front of her, with the captain's compliments, also helped Eva to relax. With a smile, she looked in his direction and catching his eye, she raised her glass, mouthing a *thank you*. He, in return, raised his glass and smiling, nodded his head slowly saying, 'As Rosa has already said, we welcome a charming young lady to our table. I hope we will enjoy other times together. Welcome on board.'

Before Eva could respond, there was a sudden clatter of castanets as Rosa - no one had even noticed her leave the table - struck a classic flamenco dancer's pose in a small open space encircled by the dining tables. One of the waiters stood back, with a flourish, from Rosa's portable gramophone as the first chords of a classical guitar joined the rhythm of her castanets.

The captain gave his purser opposite him a perplexed look, then he just shrugged his shoulders and turned to politely watch Rosa's unexpected cabaret. Enough wine had been consumed for everyone to ignore the scratchy recording and Rosa's unorthodox dance technique, although there were a few sniggers from a man and his wife, which many at her table clearly resented.

As she too glared at the couple, Eva thought she noticed in the distance, over the woman's shoulder, a movement in the small round window of the waiter's door which led into the children's dining room. She was about to turn her eyes back to the dance, when a forehead, topped with blond hair, rose slowly into view. Eva knew, when the eyes appeared, they would belong to Anna.

She had a sudden image of herself, about the same age, lying on her stomach on a cold *gasthaus* floor, she could smell that dusty carpet even now, looking down through a small window at dancers in the *saal*, enjoying her mother gliding around the newly polished dance floor. The mother she had deserted, without so much as a goodbye, a few days ago.

Entering the children's dining room through its main entrance door, Eva saw one of the kitchen helpers with her back to her. She was holding Christa, her head on the woman's shoulder fast asleep and, alongside her, on a dining room chair, Anna clapping as Rosa came to the end of her dance.

Sneaking quietly up behind them she asked, 'And what do you think you are up to?'

The helper jumped, waking Christa momentarily and Anna was saved from falling off the chair by a quick grabbing hand from both the helper and Eva.

* * *

As the weeks went by, passengers got to enjoy the dance duo made up of Rosa and Anna, who had been a quick learner. They would appear suddenly in different places on the ship, each morning or afternoon, Rosa carrying the little black case and Anna tugging Christa behind her.

Once the music was playing, Rosa's body would burst into movement, castanets clicking, high heeled shoes stamping. Next to her, Anna would be pirouetting, skinny arms raised, waving her Japanese *sensu* with its one bamboo piece missing. Not quite a *pericón* that Rosa waved, given to her by a lady who always laughed and clapped at their performances.

'You need a fan, too,' she smiled, bowing slightly, offering it to Anna who resisted at first, until she saw the slight nod from her mother alongside the woman.

During their dance, Christa would rock from side to side, raising one shoe off the ground after the other, or jump around jerkily in front of them trying to clap at the same time, dimples as usual, a source of additional pleasure for the audience enjoying the trio. Sometimes Eva would go with them, changing the records and winding up the gramophone or just keep Christa amused when she got tired of dancing.

Eva and Rosa had become friends. Rosa had shown her how to paint her nails - always bright red - and to do her eye makeup the way she did hers, which Eva loved. They shared many stories about past times, how hard the previous few years had been, recovering from the war and how hopeful they were for a bright future in their chosen *new* countries. Rosa insisted they speak English so Eva would be prepared for the adjustment she would need to make in Australia.

Sometimes they spoke of their husbands. Superficially at first, but as they realised how many common issues they had with their men, they became more open. Laughing often at the inadequacies they had to put up with in their respective partners. Talking to Rosa made Eva see that it was not her that had to assume responsibility for Peter's happiness, help him with his depression, his nightmares, his frustration that he did not have a son. He needed to work those things out for himself.

Absorbed as she was, Eva was not aware how close they were to their halfway stopping point, where she would lose her new friend, so when one afternoon, an excited Anna and Christa came running up to where she and Rosa sat in the sun on the upper deck, their announcement was a shock.

'*Mutti, Mutti.* We can see the mountain. It's flat like a *table* just as they said, come and look on our side,' Anna cried.

As the ship eased ever closer to Cape Town, they could see the city nestling below what the tannoy informed them was the famous Table Mountain and nearby, Lions Head. The announcement was in English first and Eva surprised herself when she realised, she understood it and didn't need to wait for it to be repeated in German. It reminded her that she needed to start speaking more English to her daughters now.

Arms wrapped around Christa, holding her so she could see above the ships rail, the new bright red nails of her left hand caught her eye and she smiled contentedly.

'*Papi* is going to be surprised when he sees your nails,' Anna had observed when she saw them for the first time.

'Look, that mountain looks just like a lion's head. Like the picture of the world's cities on the wall at our school,' Anna cried excitedly.

'And that's *exactly* what it's called, my clever girl. Oh no, I am going to miss my little dancer,' Rosa said and then promptly burst into tears. Handing Christa to Anna and taking her soon to be lost new friend into her arms, Eva felt tears on her cheeks as well.

A few weeks later, they were once again gliding across calm blue waters of a harbour entrance. This time, the towering cliff face of North Head greeted them as they sailed into Sydney Harbour and before long, the famous Sydney Harbour Bridge came into view in the distance. Eva overheard someone at the ship's rail say it was referred to as "the coat hanger". That it had claimed 16 lives during its construction.

Just like in Cape Town Harbour, the grey sides of the *Johan Van Oldenbarnevelt* were eased gently towards the wharf by tugboats that reminded Eva of German shepherds on the farm near their *gasthaus*. She had seen them once manoeuvring a large bull through a gate, back into its paddock.

Even before mooring lines were thrown down to workers far below, to ease over bollards on the edge of the quayside, Anna, a few metres along from Eva, had made an exciting discovery. Pulling herself up to the top of the ship's rail, jamming the toe of one shoe onto a protruding bolt to take her weight, she was able to hold herself up and see down to the quay side.

'Look *Mutti*, that man sitting down there has white stripes painted on his tummy. He's blowing into a long pipe; I can hear the sound. Can you?' she said pointing excitedly, 'It sounds like a growl, a swarm of bees.'

Eva was not really listening to her daughter as she scanned the faces of the people looking up from down below. Christa was squirming in her arms, trying to see what Anna was so excited about, wanting to be put down so she could go to her. Finally, Eva saw her husband. He was not looking upwards like everyone else, scanning passengers for one they would recognise. He wasn't looking for the faces of his loved ones he had not seen for many months. Peter stood near the edge of the quay, gazing down into the water between the ship and the concrete wall of the quay. He seemed transfixed, unable to turn away from the image below him, an oily rising and falling green surface darkened by the giant ship's shadow.

As they descended the gangway, Eva put Christa down, believing she did not need to worry about her falling overboard. But when they reached the wharf and began making their way through the crowd to where they had seen Peter, another danger arose.

Anna had spotted Peter, who was still at the edge of the quay looking downward and took off towards him with Christa trying to keep up.

'*Papi, Papi wir sind da,*' she yelled as she ran towards him.

Her voice made him look up and he turned towards her, with a smile.

'Yes, *you are here*. Time to try some English, my girl,' he laughed as he hugged Anna.

'Mind Christa, Peter, the edge,' Eva called, trying to catch up, but Peter had already snatched Christa into his arms as she ran towards him.

Eva raised her own arms as she joined them, preparing to embrace her husband, but he did not respond. Glancing between her shiny red nails, extended towards him, and her blue eye shadow, he remained still and kept his arms around his daughters, then looking away from Eva he said, 'What is all that colour for?'

PART TWO

CHAPTER 10

Settling in Sydney

WOLFGANG HAD BASED HIS business in nearby Chatswood, because it was close to a railway station and the Pacific Highway, convenient for the delivery of materials. Within a year, his business was thriving. His *"German attention to detail"* already well known and sought after.

When Peter joined him, he was able to take on even more projects. The demand kept growing and Peter had never worked so hard. On his arrival in Sydney, accommodation was scarce but, after being introduced to the owner by her niece who worked in the office, he was able to rent an outside room in the garden of a large house. The woman's aunt, Mrs Craymillian, was an eccentric 85-year-old who collected buddhas.

'My aunt is very rich,' the woman in his office had said, 'but never spends a penny on anything but buddhas. That's why the house is such a wreck. But at least it's a start for you, Peter.'

From a few inches high, to some bigger than her, the buddhas and other bric-a-bac were everywhere, filling her lounge room so you had to turn side-on to get from one end of the room to the other, without knocking her precious icons over. Buddhas stood throughout the garden, some in shrines the old lady had constructed out of bits and pieces of junk she found left on the street verges by neighbours, some overgrown by weeds, weathered faces and bodies barely visible.

Peter spent a great deal of his spare time fixing things around the house, much to the old lady's delight. When he told her Eva and the girls were joining him in Australia, she insisted they all stay with her until they found a house to rent. Peter was grateful but concerned that moving into the main house meant she would be exposed to the sounds of his nightmares.

Dragging her crying sister in from the garden a few days after moving into their new home, Anna announced, 'There are a 153 of them and Christa has been bitten.'

'And which one of the 153 bit her?' laughed Peter.

'This country has *lots* of things that bite,' Eva observed, reaching down for a weeping Christa.

'No *Papi*, an *insect* bit her; I meant 153 buddhas. Granny told me what they're called. That's how many there are outside in her garden.'

After he had moved in, Peter had called the old lady Mrs C, but when Eva introduced her to the girls and she said they should call her "granny", it immediately became what Eva and Peter called her as well. She seemed to love being called granny and acted like one, taking the girls by their hands and leading them around the garden, teaching them the names of plants and insects, of which there were many in her jungle-like back yard. As the weeks went by, Eva suspected this was when clandestine lollies were handed out too.

Eva sometimes heard them, out of sight in the overgrown vegetation, chattering to her in German, already including an occasional English word granny had taught them. Christa finished all her questions with, 'Hey Granny?' in English, which made the old lady smile. *Soon they will be translating for granny,* she thought to herself. *They never even said goodbye to their real granny,* she felt the remorse. *Left her on the other side of the world.*

Concerned about Peter's nightmares, Eva knew she would have to find them a house to rent as quickly as possible. Not an easy task with the post war increase in immigrants to the country. It was for this reason, after weeks of unsuccessfully searching for a house to rent, Eva convinced Peter he should ask Wolfgang if she could have a job in their office, which he kept telling her was a shambles.

'I am good with numbers, you know that and if we have more money, we might be able to find a house that is available, because most others cannot afford the rent being asked.'

Once she had started working in the office, Eva had seen, very quickly, that Wolfgang had done his research on Sydney's post World War Two housing expansion well, when he decided the suburb of Forestville offered many opportunities for builders. Land from the original Soldier's Settlement scheme had been subdivided and was being sold as residential land just before he arrived in Australia. It was in demand by affluent Sydney city dwellers who were looking for a move to the fresh air and the leafy surrounds of the North Shore. It was also of interest to new arrivals, immigrants who had come to the country with money, unlike herself and Peter.

Eva approached her work in the office in the same way she played Skat. Steely focus on the numbers, be it dollars, weight of sand or length of timber. Within a month, she was the default office manager. Wolfgang was delighted, the burden of administration and organisation was lifted from his shoulders.

During that same month, Eva had also gained an understanding of how property development worked. Whenever one of the developers came to the office to make a payment or with a query about his project, he would find himself still there after an hour and several cups of Eva's excellent coffee.

Captivated by Eva, they could not stop talking, impressing her with their expert knowledge of the ins and outs of the property business, the tricks to making big profits by buying a plot of land and building a house on it, knowing where to find savings during construction and then selling it on at a profit.

Wolfgang's suppliers also loved Eva. She drove a hard bargain, but she was fair, and they were always paid on time. Instinctively, they all knew, there would come a time when they would be returning the favours she did for them.

Eva watched Peter as his breathing slowly returned to normal. His sudden loud groan as she woke him from his nightmare *must* have disturbed granny, she assumed, but there was no sound from her room. She had helped him change his sweat-soaked pyjamas and he now sat on the edge of the bed in silence, head hanging. She knew not to ask him anything about the dream, his answer was always the same.

'Are you able to sleep or would you like to talk a while? I have an idea for us.'

'I can't sleep, but we must go to the outside room if you want to talk or we will wake granny. Once again,' he added with a sigh.

Speaking quietly in the darkness of the outside room, slapping at the mosquitos which thrived in the lush back yard, Eva outlined her plan for setting up their own building business.

'In this way we can find a place to live and create good income, instead of making your friend Wolfgang rich,' she concluded.

'*Zwei Fliegen mit einer Klappe schlagen*,' she chuckled.

Peter scratched at the stubble on his chin. 'What will Wolfgang say? He will be furious.'

'Who cares?' Eva said. 'He has so much work he will probably not mind having to turn some away.' We will be rich, I know,' she implored. 'You don't want to be struggling forever, do you?'

Eva knew they both thought of her father at that point, how he used to refer to Peter and she hoped he would take her seriously.

Eva gauged the elderly lady's expression hopefully, judging Mrs Craymillian's response to what she was saying to her. As much as granny loved the family staying in her home, Eva knew in the last few months she had grown tired of Peter's anguished cries as he awoke, the sounds of her trying to calm both him and the crying Christa in the middle of the night.

Granny didn't need the rent, *heaven knows*. What she needed was her house to herself again, so she and her many buddhas could enjoy quiet times together once more; and what Eva needed was space for her family. Granny loved the girls, even though Anna had already beheaded one of her treasured buddhas with a rake, chasing the bush turkeys which thrived in her overgrown garden. Living in such close proximity to them, their new "nanna" did not get much time to herself. There was always something they were asking her to do with them. A little hand would slip into hers and off she would be taken on a new adventure in the garden.

'I'm sure it's not very peaceful for you having such a big family right on top of you. We really are trying to find a place, but it's a struggle, Granny,' Eva said, bemoaning the fact that as a result of the government's post war obsession with getting more people into Australia, there were now no houses to rent and they could not afford to buy one.

'It's such a pity,' Eva sighed, 'Peter could build us a small house very quickly if only we had ground to build on. He's a fast builder and I can get materials cheaply from our suppliers I work with. They love me, not having to wait ages anymore for Wolfgang to get around to paying their bills.'

Giving Mrs Craymillian a mournful smile, patting her hand, she went on, 'I would love to be able to give you your home back. If only we could find the money to buy one of the new plots in Forestville, Peter could build us a little house during the weekends and in no time, we would be inviting *you* over to visit.'

Granny's eyes lit up.

'Why, I could lend you that money. Of course,' she laughed. Eva, hoping she was disguising her manipulative behaviour, allowed herself a look of surprise.

'Really, Granny? You would do that?'

'Yes, sure,' she said, smiling inwardly at Eva's shrewdness. 'All I have to do is phone my lawyer and tell him to arrange it with you.'

Rosa sighed, as she always did, gazing up at the Jonkershoek Mountains, overlooking the town of Stellenbosch in the heart of South Africa's wine country. Their house had a long veranda, or *stoep*, as the locals called it, with a perfect view of the mountains. She liked to come out and sit here when she was feeling down. It seemed to put things in perspective.

So what if Jorge couldn't keep his hands off their domestic workers? Being able to easily afford the low wages people were paid in South Africa, meant she did not have to cook or clean for him, did not have to wash his dirty clothes or iron them. The garden was always a picture, thanks to Bertus who came every weekend to tend it when he was not working in the gardens at the estate Jorge was employed at. Rosa often wondered when Bertus ever spent time with his family.

'Madam.'

Rosa jumped slightly, lost in thought she had not heard Miriam approach through the French door.

'Does the madam want coffee now?' she asked in the dialect of the black population of the Western Cape.

'Ah yes, Miriam, that would be lovely.'

She watched the departing maid swing, what Rosa believed was, an ample rear as she headed the length of the veranda towards the kitchen. Miriam was the latest of Jorge's conquests. Rosa often thought it was because he was so small in stature that he had to continually acquire new conquests. *Makes him feel bigger, maybe,* she smiled wryly to herself.

They only lasted six months or so, before he found a reason to sack them. Rosa was seldom told about it, but she knew a dismissal was coming because Jorge would suddenly start paying *her* attention in bed. Then they just disappeared and a new face appeared. The cook always seemed to avoid retribution from him, maybe because she was a good cook *as well as bedfellow,* Rosa mused.

Rosa looked back up at the *Jonkershoek* and suddenly Eva came into her mind. They had been looking up at a mountain the very last time they were together. Now if she thought she had a husband who made her unhappy, her friend might well be in a worse situation. They had exchanged letters regularly over the years, sharing happy and sad times like old friends, although they had only been together on a ship for a few weeks.

Eva had been most distressed when Rosa told her she no longer danced, that she just did not feel like it. *Oh no Anna will also be sad to hear that,* Eva had lamented in an answering letter. Rosa did not bother to say that she knew everybody was just being kind. *They just humour me, an ungainly dancer with skinny legs and big breasts.* She also did not tell Eva that since being in her new country, she had become less inclined to do many other things she had found rewarding before.

Ah my Eva on the other side of the world, fast asleep right now.

A teaspoon rattled falling from a saucer onto the metal tray behind her.

'I brought rusks for dipping in your coffee as well, madam.'

The small house Peter built, so they could move from Mrs Craymillian's house, turned into one of many he built over the years. The first few they lived in and sold on, after Eva established a garden to increase the value. Once they had accumulated enough cash, they were able to settle permanently in one, but Peter continued to build other houses which they sold on in a market that could not get enough.

Before Eva knew it, they were affluent. Anna was in her final year at high school and Christa was about to become a senior. They were fluent in English, although Eva insisted they spoke German in the home. Anna was already talking about her desire to go to university, a conversation that sometimes had Eva unconsciously rubbing the underside of her arm.

They had reconciled with Wolfgang, in fact shared projects sometimes, and Peter was the owner of a Mercedes Benz, something he had coveted for many years. At Chatswood Motors, to the salesman's surprise, they paid cash for it. Eva liked to keep as much of their profit as she could "under her pillow". *Why should the tax people know everything?* She would decide what was fair to pay them.

The one thing that still seemed to allude them, was peace at night. As hard as Peter worked, no matter how exhausted he became, his sleep was often disrupted. The nightmares were getting worse and the visits Eva organised to various psychologists came to nothing when he refused to share anything with them. It was as though he did not want the nightmares to stop. That he deserved them, deserved to be punished for what he had done. Or that he was too ashamed, felt too guilty to let anyone else know what happened that night.

Eva was slightly surprised when the letter came, although excited seeing the post mark. She had written to her father to ask after the family but did not expect to hear back given her sudden unannounced departure from the *gasthaus*. The reply, somewhat cold, was from her brother and his news confirmed, what Eva always knew in her heart would be, the sad outcome of what she initiated all those years ago.

She wiped at the wet mark from one of her tears, smudging a word. Dabbing her eyes so she could focus, she continued reading her brother's untidy handwriting.

After Eva and the girls left, her mother had never fully regained her health and had fallen ill with pneumonia during one very cold winter. The local doctor had been hesitant about a house call because of his previous run ins with Kurt and when he final got to the gasthaus, Magda was in a bad way.

Her brother said they were all together at her bedside when she passed, and he wished Eva had been there because their mother always blamed herself for her daughter's sudden departure and it would have been a relief for her, if Eva had been there at the end to reassure her. Eva's shoulders shook as she sobbed, placing her face in her hands, the letter slipping from between her fingers. It would only be later when she reread the letter that she would see the rest of it was about Kurt who had been diagnosed with terminal cancer.

CHAPTER 11

Mind the Gap

LIKE MOST AUSTRALIAN TEENAGERS, Anna did not give much thought to cold weather, especially when it involved *travel*. As she stepped down off the train and her white moccasins made contact with the icy concrete platform, her mother's words rang in her ears as she fussed over Anna's packing.

'You were old enough before we left Germany to remember the cold, surely? And this year the winter has been very bad, I hear. Fashionable summer shoes will not help you in the snow Anna.'

There had been no one to meet them at the station, of course. This would be a surprise visit to her grandfather on the way to see Peter's mother in East Berlin. Shivering in her light coat as they walked to the *gasthaus* she had last been in over a decade before, Anna looked around, trying to remember her childhood surroundings. She seemed to remember the cherry trees on either side of the lane they walked up, *or were they part of one of her Mutti's stories about herself as a young girl?* The trees were adorned with bright red cherries glistening against the snow, clinging to the dark branches they hung from. Had she had winter boots on, she would have waded into the snow between the lane and the trees to try one.

Her teeth chattered involuntarily and once again, in her mind, she rebuked her mother for coming up with the idea of such a visit. Anna was convinced her grandfather would not even remember her and if babysitting her father wasn't bad enough, Eva insisted he was so disorganised he needed *hand holding* when travelling, then delaying their arrival in Berlin was.

She could not wait to start enjoying exciting experiences in the famous city, the reason she agreed to accompany her father, even if at some point travelling to the east was a bit intimidating for her. But Eva was adamant they visit Kurt. Born out of guilt, she admitted to herself. Her brother's letter regarding their father's cancer had also mentioned that he lived alone in the *gasthaus*, seldom leaving it. There was no indication, though, of what they might expect should they visit. He did say that Kurt had not been the same since their mother had died.

In the year that followed Eva's unexpected departure, her brothers had also left the *gasthaus* with their families, leaving Kurt and Magda alone. To their surprise, he had taken over the task of looking after his ailing wife without complaint. In fact, they had lived together, until she died, more harmoniously than they ever had, her brother said.

Hearing a faint voice in response to his knock on the front door, Peter pushed it open and entered, Anna behind him. The stench that hit them took their breath away, but they continued on in, calling out Kurt's name as they went.

'Kurt. Kurt. *Bist du hier?*'

'*Ja, ich bin hier,*' they heard someone say faintly.

Peter and Anna followed the sound of the voice to one of the downstairs rooms that had been converted to a bedroom. They passed by the stairs Anna had hidden under so many times and below them, the internal door leading to the *Wirtschaft*. It hung open, the huge room deserted, all the furniture gone. Even the huge old bar counter Kurt did his trick on, had vanished.

Entering the room, they found Kurt, the outline of his body, almost childlike, under a filthy duvet. The smell was terrible. In the corner was a bucket and they guessed this was where it was coming from.

'*Graf Habenichts, wilkommen,*' Kurt said through a hacking cough.

It came back to Anna immediately. Eva had told her he always called her father that, *Count HaveNothing*.

'*Mache den Eimer leer,*' her grandfather croaked, pointing at the bucket. Peter hesitated, appalled, but realising he had little option but to empty it for Kurt.

He moved across the room holding his breath. As he picked it up, Kurt finally acknowledged Anna was in the room. It seemed to take him time to realise, the teenager standing alongside his bed was his *little Anna*. Smiling eventually, he said how much she looked like her mother.

'*Ah, meine liebe Grosstochter. Du siehst genauso aus wie meine Eva.*'

As she watched and waited for his next words, the faraway look in his eyes made him appear like he was recalling a distant memory. Continuing in German he said, 'I am sorry I am not well enough to take you to the forest, my darling granddaughter.' He tried unsuccessfully to waggle the fingers of his barely raised hands. 'To be your monster like I used to be for your mother,' he laughed, but this brought on a coughing fit which lasted over a minute; *forever* it seemed to Anna.

Eventually, the heaving and gasping subsided and he pointed to the chair beside his bed. He did not seem to hear her repeated greeting as she sat, or ignored it. He pushed a pencil and paper pad across his bedside table to her, before he spoke again.

Restarting his sentence several times, coughing and catching his breath each time, he instructed her to write down any two sets of three numbers; the first she was to multiply by the second, but to read them to him before she started doing the calculation on the paper. She did as he bid and after she had the answer written down, he gave her *his* answer with raised eyebrows. They did this several times and each time he was correct.

His subdued chuckle at her surprised expression was more a cackle punctuated with gasps. Anna thought he might die at any second and prayed her father would return. Suddenly, without sitting up, Kurt pulled open the drawer next to where he lay and rummaged around in it with a long skinny, white hand. He handed Anna a slab of chocolate from, what she could see was, quite a collection. Returning his hand to the drawer, he continued to fumble, searching for something. Finally, he withdrew his hand, which was holding a crumpled, dirty one page letter which he handed to Anna.

'All I was left with, when my Eva was gone,' he said hoarsely, almost a whisper. Anna thought there might have been tears in his eyes. She looked away from him to scan the letter Eva had left for her parents the day she departed with her and Christa.

When Peter re-entered the room and put the now empty and rinsed bucket down alongside the bed, Anna stood to allow him to take her chair and be near his father-in-law. Over the years, picking up certain remarks made between her father and mother during their arguments, Anna had guessed what probably had taken place that day, but to see this letter in her mother's messy handwriting, she felt overcome with the gravity of the unannounced departure, the effect it must have had on her grandparents. Re-reading the letter in the faint light of the grimy bedroom window, as Peter struggled to achieve a harmonious conversation with Kurt, she wished there was some way she could right the wrong for all of them.

On the train back to Berlin, Anna unwrapped the chocolate slab and, after dumping the stale chocolate in the trashcan, slipped the wrapper into her travel diary. In years to come, she was glad she had; it was the last time she saw her grandfather. He died before they arrived back in Australia.

Eva had just got up from watching TV to go to bed when the doorbell rang, startling her. *Who could that be*, she wondered, *not Peter he has his own key?* She had been a little worried about him not being home yet, but the lunch Wolfgang had put on for his property developer clients was at the Watson's Bay Hotel, hours away from Chatswood on the other side of the harbour. He had not been keen to accept the unexpected invitation, but Eva had insisted he go.

'Think of all the new clients you might be able to find. Just mingle and chat.'

'And Wolfgang? He will know what I am up to.'

'Well, obviously, he doesn't care if he invited you in the first place. Anyway, he has more clients than he can handle. He will probably be happy if you stole one or two,' she laughed.

'Or maybe he trusts me, Eva?'

Turning the safety latch, she opened the door to reveal a dishevelled-looking woman of about her age. She was windblown, her ripped blouse held closed with a safety pin.

'Was your husband at Watson's Bay today?' she asked.

The sea was dark blue, almost black in the early evening light at the Gap, a set of towering cliffs near the heads that had welcomed his family to Sydney Harbour. Swaying at the edge of the cliff, staring down into the dark water rising and falling far below, Peter was transported back to the evening he stood at his ship's rail, moments before it was hit by torpedoes. Once again, he felt drawn to the menacing movement of the sea below him.

Drunk and staggering against the wind gusts that buffeted him, he looked back at the old wooden fence he had climbed over, wondering if he should go back to where it was safer, lean against it for support, *but then that was the whole point in climbing over it in the first place, to get close to the cliff's edge, to prove he was not afraid.*

He looked down at the water. Swells driven by the high tide heaved upwards, before crashing against rocks at the bottom of the cliff face. The sea had also seemed to climb towards him that evening long ago, *come down to me.* Below him now, the thundering waves were creating spurts of foam, spray carried by the wind cold on his face. He lifted his eyes, stinging from the salt, to look out across the ocean, half expecting to see two churning lines in the water coming towards him, but instead, he saw a small metal dinghy, or was it two. He blinked his eyes against the spray – and alcohol - a *tinny, they call them here.*

There was one person sitting inside and he could make out another in the twilight swimming towards it. As the swimmer got closer, the person in the dinghy moved forward, leant over its metal side.

'NO! NO!' Peter cried into the wind, stepping forward. A gust stopped him, forced him to take a step back. He squinted against spray and wind. It was okay, the swimmer was climbing into the *dinghy*.

Over the wind, he thought he heard a motor trying to start. They had lost the motor on *their* boat, hadn't they? That's why they were toppled into the icy sea. That's why they killed their own comrades. This time he was blinking, because of tears finding their way down his cheeks before being blown away at an angle. And, like that night on the ship, when he thought he heard Wolfgang and the others talking on the deck, he heard a voice behind him now. *Was it the wind?* He sniffed, wiped the back of his hand under his nose. The wind dropped momentarily and as he was about to look behind him, he felt himself yanked back and heard a woman shout,

'GET THE FUCK BACK HERE BEFORE YOU GO OVER, ARSEHOLE!'

She had hold of his shirt and was dragging him backwards from the edge. In his drunken state, Peter offered little resistance, even with her heels slipping in the loose gravel as she dragged him towards the fence, climbing nimbly over the wooden rail. But it caught Peter behind his legs and he went over backwards, arms flailing, a hand tearing the woman's blouse wide open before thumping his head into the soft sand of the path.

'Well, hopefully that should knock some sense into you,' she said, sitting down beside him, holding her blouse closed. 'Now what's this all about? Don't tell me you're just drunk and got lost.'

Eva gaped as the woman pointed over her shoulder with her thumb.

'Your husband, Peter's safely delivered from Watsons Bay, at the bottom of your drive. Asleep on the back seat of his flash Mercedes. Drunk as a skunk. I didn't want to drive in until I knew this was his house. Wolfgang didn't know the number and, in his state, I did not trust my passenger.'

'Thank God, I thought you were going to say he assaulted you,' a pale faced Eva said, glancing at her blouse.

'Oh, the blouse. No, just an accident.'

'Or had been killed.'

'Well, you got your priorities right,' the woman laughed, 'Now, you will have to help me with him, too heavy for me. Some guy named Wolfgang helped me back at the hotel parking lot. Supposed to be his friend. Didn't seemed too concerned to me.'

'Ah, the daughters,' she said as Anna and Christa appeared, looking puzzled, behind Eva. 'I hope for your sake, this is a first time for you two,' she said to the girls. 'Unlike for me. It was always the same, sometimes worse, when my father got home late.' She turned to fetch the car and its slumbering passenger.

'I'll bring the car up.'

Peter had become very vocal as they pulled him from the back seat of the car. Dorothy was the centre of his attention as they struggled to keep him upright, both women sagging under the arms he had around their shoulders.

'DOTTEEE. DOTTEEE. YOU SAVED ME FROM THE SEA,' he sang loudly, sounding a bit like a rabbi reading the Torah.

'I hate being called Dotty,' she gasped as they heaved him forward.

'DOTTEEE, WHY WERE YOU NOT THERE IN THE WAR? TO SAVE US FROM THE SEA, THE SEA. THE COLD BLACK SEA, SEA, SEA,' he bellowed.

Dorothy laughed.

'You weren't so happy up on the cliff, Mr. Sinatra.'

'*Papi* hush, please,' begged Anna. 'The neighbours?'

Eva was busy pouring Dorothy a coffee when a loud snore erupted from the spare room and thundered down the hall.

'Oh God, Anna, close that door, please. We've heard enough from your father for one night.'

Christa giggled but Anna had a frown on her face as she got up.

'*Papi* drinks all the time now. What will the neighbours think after tonight?'

'Don't you worry, Anna. All families have their problems and many of them have to do with booze,' Dorothy said as she re pinned her blouse. 'Your neighbours won't be any different. If it's not a husband who drinks, it's an aunt who gambles her family's money away, or a teenager who is into drugs. Or a pet cat that pees on visitors' laps or a dog that humps visitors' legs.'

Both girls laughed. They liked Dorothy, she treated them like adults, spoke to them like adults. *She was funny, too.* Eva hadn't, but both girls recognised her Kiwi accent, and after they commented on it, she told them how she had come to move to Australia. Glancing at Eva, she stopped short of telling them the full story, just saying her mother needed to get away for health reasons.

'Mum died many years ago, but I am still here, in little Nimbin. I bet you've never even heard of it,' she said with a wink. When they all shook their heads, Dorothy went on, 'We used to be part of a thriving dairy producing region, but with the decline in the 60s, Norco moved everything to Lismore. Nowadays, we're probably more famous for being a quaint little town in the "Rainbow Region", the Bundjalung people's land, whose beautiful Nimbin valley and Nimbin Rocks ensure tourism just about keeps us going.'

Driving down the Pacific Highway into downtown Sydney where Dorothy was staying, she asked without turning to look at Eva, 'Has Peter ever told you what happened to him during the war? When his ship was sunk?' Eva shook her head. She sensed what was coming.

'He was trying to kill himself tonight, wasn't he?' she asked, glancing at her passenger, *why didn't I offer her one of my blouses?*

'Honestly? I am not sure. Probably. But he was so drunk it was likely going to happen even if he didn't intend it to. He won't remember what he told me tonight and I don't know if it's the truth. But it *is* what haunts him and you need to know, I'm sorry. Can I tell you?'

They had just arrived in front of the hotel Dorothy was staying in and, as she pulled into a parking spot, Eva turned to Dorothy and said, 'Will I need a drink after?'

'Probably. Probably during,' she answered with a smile, touching one of the hands still clutching the steering wheel.

The woman at reception gave Dorothy's smeared torn blouse a look before reaching behind her for the room key, at the same time, trying to conceal her furtive glance at the burly hotel security guard loitering nearby. Grinning, Dorothy said, 'It's okay darling, I'm not a drunk *hoon* fresh from a pub brawl at the Kings Cross, speaking of which, where is your bar?'

Looking up the stairs, towards where the receptionist was pointing, Dorothy said, 'Eva, go and grab us a comfortable place. I'll just pop up to my room and change my blouse before I get arrested for indecency.' Walking towards the elevators she added, 'Make mine a gin and tonic, they're on me, room 324.' As the doors clanked open, she said, 'Thank you, tiger,' to the security guard who had pressed the button for her.

She's a character that one, Eva said to herself, starting up the stairs to the mezzanine floor.

Waiting for Dorothy, Eva reflected on the evening. Dorothy's arrival at their house, with Peter in the back of his car, was traumatic and she didn't expect the night to improve with what Dorothy was about to tell her. Nonetheless, she was suddenly enjoying herself. Alone and independent, out with an interesting woman, enjoying the evening. Not having to worry about what next little thing was going to trigger Peter's anger.

She and Peter seldom went out, unless it was to visit friends, of which they had few, or one of the local steak houses. His favourite was the Angus Steak Cave. Peter refused to try the Greek, Italian or any other restaurants that had begun popping up, as a result of the many new cultures arriving in the country.

'Wow, I've been looking forward to this drink,' Dorothy said as she joined Eva, sinking back into the plush armchair.

Eva sat stony faced, looking in front of her as Dorothy relayed a more coherent version of Peter's slurred, rambling account of what had taken place the night their ship was sunk. She had always guessed his fragile mental state had something to do with the sinking of his ship. He had never told her any details of the night they were torpedoed, but she knew it must have been traumatic for him.

When Hans and his wife had stayed in the *gasthaus,* she thought she might learn more overhearing their animated reminiscing, but they said little more about it than she already knew. They both spoke fondly of Wolfgang though, a name she had not heard until that night. As Dorothy spoke, Eva thought it was probably the worst thing he could have done, re-unite with Wolfgang, *a mutual daily reminder of a dark event in their lives.*

'He needs help Eva. He is going to do himself an injury or, at the very least, end up having a nervous breakdown. Even if it is neither of those, I have no doubt he will probably drink himself to death and ruin you in the process.'

Eva told Dorothy about Peter's nightmares and the attempts she had made to get him to open up to a psychiatrist. Dorothy was silent for a while before laughing ironically.

'Like my father. They do that, men. Make their wives suffer for the pain they have inside.'

Driving back home later, Eva agonised over who to turn to for support. She needed help with this. Dorothy had given her telephone number to Eva, but she was too far away. It was considerate, but she was unlikely to be able to help Eva persuade Peter to seek medical help. Squinting into the lights of the oncoming cars on the bridge, she thought it would be rather nice to be living so far away, far away from all her problems. But she had run away once in her life already.

Rosa took one last look at Jonkershoek Mountain before she climbed into the taxi. She would miss this view, but the decision was made. She had taken enough abuse from Jorge. Even now, the maids watched her from the veranda, ostensibly sweeping the floor but sharing comments in isiXhosa, no doubt about why the madam should be leaving in a taxi with two big suitcases, without saying anything to them, while her husband was at work. *Not difficult to work out ladies,* Rosa thought to herself.

Jorge had found Eva's letters; Rosa had been going through them, trying to find if Eva had ever given her phone number in one of them. They were lying next to where she sat on their bed.

'What's all this, letters from a lover?' he had teased, picking one up to scan it.

Rosa was hardly able to breathe with Jorge standing in front of her, reading. When he discovered from some of Eva's comments, that Rosa had clearly shared information about his affairs with their workers, he lost his temper. After gathering up all the letters, he tore open every drawer until he found her address book.

'No more writing to her about me, you understand?' he shouted at her as he left the room with the letters and the book.

'The airport, please,' she said to the driver as they drove down the driveway from her house. Once again, as she had every day since it arrived a week ago, she took the plane ticket she had purchased out of her bag and opened it.

Seat: 12E   Flight: Economy   Destination: Sydney

She read it quickly and closing her eyes, she put her head back and tried to absorb what she was doing. She rocked with the movement of the car as the driver navigated around the potholes in their gravel driveway Jorge was yet to fix. She was emigrating to a new country where she only knew one person, a friend whose full address she no longer had access to and could obviously not ask Jorge for.

CHAPTER 12

The Belt

EVA JUMPED AT THE sudden loud rustling in the tree she sat under. A possum, invisible in the darkness, leapt from the roof of their house onto a branch above her, causing it to bend downwards, its foliage shaking in the windless night. Scurrying along the branch, its outline appeared momentarily. Eva could see it must be a female as a joey clung to her back, not yet ready to give up the security she offered. *Unlike Anna,* she mused, *who could not wait to experience what life beyond the family had to offer.*

Eva thought her daughter's confidence probably came from knowing she *had* her family to rescue her if she took a fall in the outside world. This baby possum would not be picked up if it fell off or climbed off. Mother possums didn't go back to pick up young.

Peter, on the other hand, could not even begin to imagine his daughter leaving. Boyfriends at her age? *He knew what they were after.* He gave her little *freedom.* Anna interpreted it as little *trust.* *Peter need not have worried,* thought Eva, Anna's romances at high school had been one sided; she had seldom been asked out. *Maybe it was because she was always falling in love with her teachers,* Eva sighed to herself as she watched another branch bend as the possum pushed down on it, launching herself and her young one into their neighbour's tree.

Through the windows, she could see Peter moving from room to room. Stumbling, more accurately; he was drunk. They had argued earlier, or rather she had sat, stoic, while he shouted at her. *Anna being out for the night with a boy was all her fault.*

'She is like her mother, always must flirt, always must dance. Always must be with boys,' he yelled. *Always must have fun*, Eva thought.

It was the first invitation her father had agreed to, the 'end of school year' dance. The boy was the son of one of his few friends, hence his agreement, albeit reluctantly, to her going on a date, *at least he's German.*

'You will be home by eleven,' Peter commanded, 'otherwise, no more going out.'

As the evening wore on, the more he drank, the more paranoid he became.

'This is all your doing, Eva,' he shouted repeatedly. 'Anna is like your father, no morals. Good that the old fool is dead.'

Christa's school tennis team was leaving early in the morning for a long trip on the school bus. Eva told herself she was going to create some quiet in the house so her daughter could sleep, instead of lying in her bed listening to her drunk father rambling on.

'I am going for a walk,' she said, taking her coat from behind the door.

'What? It's too late for that,' but Eva was already through the door and down the steps.

'Stupid bitch, you will get attacked,' he yelled at the closed door.

In her bed upstairs, Christa turned over, yet again.

'This night is going to end badly,' she whispered to the vague outlines of the faces in the posters on her wall, pop stars staring down at her with concern, in the darkness.

History of Art was the only one of Anna's classes in her final school year the boys arrived early for. It was all about getting one of the front row desks, whereas in any other class, the seats at the back, that facilitated cheating in tests and clandestine pre-lunch bites of sandwiches, were most sought after. There was much pushing and shoving between testosterone-filled boys to acquire one of these front row positions. The attraction was the view the art teacher, Miss Finemour, offered of her cleavage, whenever she leant over her desk to retrieve a picture or note she wanted to reference during her lesson.

The girls in the class were resigned to the fact that this was how boys behaved, but Anna found it particularly annoying, mainly because the woman getting all the attention from them, was also getting the attention of the man she was in love with: her music teacher, Mr White. Anna knew this, because Miss Finemour had once sent a note to him during class.

'James, take this note to Mr White in the music room, please.'

James had barely got through the door when Anna raced passed Miss Finemour with a, 'Toilet Miss, emergency.' She caught up with James before he had even got to the end of the first corridor.

'Let me take that note, James. Please?'

'Why? No way,' James said. Then with a smirk, 'What will you give me if I do?'

'We'll just have to see when I get back,' Anna said, mustering a provocative look.

Snatching the note from his immediately outstretched hand, Anna made for the music room, hoping there was no class in progress and that Mr White would be alone, preparing a lesson or something. As she walked, she furtively opened the envelope and half slipped the note out, so she could read it.

Hi angel. Can't wait until tonight to be near you. Can't bear it. Let's meet in the park at lunch time. Share my sandwich with you like I share other things. Wink, wink.

Anna was mortified. When James saw Anna returning down the corridor, he straightened up expectantly from his slouched position against the wall, with a smile.

'Put your hand out,' she said. His hand shot up towards her, ready for a titillating experience.

Taking his wrist, she turned his palm upwards and slapped the envelope into his hand.

'Deals off. You take the note.'

Shivering slightly in the cool night air, Eva sighed at the inevitability of the situation. It wasn't Christa's tennis that had brought her out here. She was hiding from what she knew was coming. She slapped at the high-pitched whine near her ear. Sounds and images from her past returned. She could see herself running from the *gasthaus* dining room. Behind her, *Papi* going for her brothers. Another time, running from the bedroom upstairs, her father's hand poised above her mother, thrown to the cold floor. Her terror at his response, when he found Magda with her skirt on fire in the *wirtschaft*. Eva could still smell the smouldering material, even now as she stared into the brightly lit rooms of the house they lived in.

Eva feared the worst for Anna when she arrived back late, as she inevitably would, to her drunk father busy working himself into a rage. Face a man who carried the nightmare of how he came to be a *survivor*, images sometimes dulled by alcohol but only for a few hours, returning to penetrate the greyness he awoke in. Then into the background of his mind, rescued by the long days of hard labour.

It made her remember the nightmare that haunted *her*. Unlike Peter's, it had faded over the years, but it came to her now. Her father standing above her mother, smirking as he told her that her daughter had gone. *For good.*

'*Ja, your Eva we think is so wonderful, no explanation, no goodbye, just a letter left for us,*' he always said in the dream, throwing the crumpled piece of paper at the stricken face of her mother lying under her grubby duvet in her tiny room.

Her sitting up, reaching behind her to find the thrown letter. Her skinny white wrist suddenly exposed, emerging from her dirty night gown sleeve. Eva wept quietly, her sobs joining the muffled sounds of insects and other small creatures in the darkness around her.

Of course, they were late. *You don't stop dancing until the band stops and the band doesn't stop until midnight. And then they play 'one last one'.* Eva heard car doors close and a muffled laugh. Against the streetlight at the end of the driveway, two silhouettes became one, momentarily. Eva pictured her and Peter kissing for the first time under a cherry tree. She wondered if Anna had also fallen in love at her first dance tonight. Then a laugh and footsteps running up the driveway as a car drove off. Climbing the stairs onto the front deck, Anna raised her hand to reach for the door handle but it was wrenched open and her father's contorted face appeared before her.

'*Papi*, I'm sorry we...'

'WHAT DID I TELL YOU?' Peter shouted, grabbing her wrist, pulling her into the hall.

'We were dancing and it was such fun, we forgot. Just dancing, you can ask anyone,' Anna gasped, beginning to cry now.

The last time Peter slipped his belt from his pants to beat someone, he was rocking in a half-submerged dinghy on an oily sea. This time, he was rocking because he was so drunk, he could barely stand. Leaning heavily against Anna, he lashed the heavy leather across the thin white chiffon stretched across her buttocks. The *slap* of the belt and her scream of pain were simultaneous.

Anna fell to her knees as she pushed at him desperate to get away. He stumbled back slightly before raising the belt above his head, stepping towards her. She raised her arms over her head, a useless shield. Two arms reaching up from a black sea. A begging face. Wolfgang's voice somewhere behind him, *hit Peter hit*. Before he could bring the belt down onto his target, one of the others in the dinghy hit him in the back, hard. With a drunken lurch, he turned to look behind him in surprise. Christa stood there, clutching the remains of the torch from the hall table, now bent without any glass. Behind her, a statue in the darkness, Eva sobbed. She was a young girl. '*Stop it! Stop it!*' she was screaming, hurling her doll at her father's back.

Peter seemed stunned. Finally, he looked down at a cowering, weeping Anna and then back to an angry, young Christa, holding the torch above her head, ready to strike again. Reaching down to retrieve his trousers, that had slowly slipped to his knees, he lurched from the hallway, trailing the belt behind him.

Eva was just about finished with the preparation of the evening meal when she heard the sound of an unfamiliar car engine in the driveway. Looking out the kitchen window, she saw Peter's truck being reversed into their garage by one of his young workers and in the driveway, Peter climbing out of a different car. It looked brand new and if Eva was not mistaken, was what was referred to as a Volkswagen "beetle". After thanking his young worker and saying goodbye, Peter entered through the back door with a grin.

'I have a surprise for Anna,' he said.

Eva smiled at herself in the reflection of the glass oven door she had just closed. For years now, Peter tried to put nasty drunken and abusive scenes behind them with a gift for her. She had received many expensive diamond rings and necklaces. This time *she* was not the recipient.

'Now she has finished school, she will need a car to go to work in. Do you think she will like the colour?' Peter asked.

'What do you think Christa?' he asked the departing back of his younger daughter, but she did not look back.

Peter shrugged and Eva said, 'You can ask her yourself Peter. She will be down for dinner in a minute, but I think you will find she is planning to go to university not "work".'

Eva watched Anna put on a happy face, as *she* had done so many times over the years, show delight at the surprise, give the impression the stain of the past abuse had miraculously been wiped from her memory. The incident had evaporated. She was amused at the look on her husband's face when Anna enquired about the papers. *Where did it show that she was the owner of the car?*

That night after Peter had gone to bed and Christa was in her room, tackling a school project, Anna and Eva sat outside together. Anna had suggested they go out on the deck for a change, instead of watching TV. Eva sensed what was coming, the questions she was going to have to respond to.

Their conversation was fairly casual to start with. Anna told her about the courses she planned to take at uni and how she hoped Peter would change his mind about not paying for her fees. Eva said she would talk to him again about how unfair he was being. But she had to wait until he was feeling better, *you know how he has been, Anna.* They fell silent. Just the sound of the crickets in the darkness and a distant barking.

'Why did you let him, *Mutti*?'

Her mother was quiet.

'Why did you not protect me? I am your daughter. Why?'

Eva adopted an offended tone.

'What must I do when he is like that? How could I stop him? He's so big, so strong. His temper....'

'*Mutti*, *Christa* stopped him. You saw. A little girl. She hit him with your damn torch. She saved me.'

They sat in silence for a few minutes. Anna waiting for a response. Trying to force her anger to subside. To not direct it at her mother, to direct it at her father, *no more abuse no more slaps. The belt was the final straw.*

'I'm leaving tomorrow. For good.'

'Oh no,' Eva cried out quietly.

'*Oh no*, you say but you can't even tell me why you have always let him hit me. Even when I didn't deserve it.'

'When I let Christa's pram crash outside the *gasthaus*, her just a baby, you waited all day until *Papi* got home so he could punish me. Why not you? You could have punished me and not told him. Did he need to know a jealous sister did something stupid?'

They sat, not speaking once again. Finally, Anna sighed, 'At least I have told you I am leaving. Saying goodbye. Not like the way you left your mother. Our Nanna, all those years ago.'

'How do you know about that?' Eva said, shocked.

Anna laughed. 'I am not blind, *Mutti*. I can see. I can hear. I worked it out once I was old enough to put the pieces together.'

In the morning, Anna and her new car, packed with only the things she wanted in her life from then on, were gone. Only Christa got a kiss, still warm in her bed, tears slipping from her eyes, small wet spots on her pillow.

Glancing from Anna's empty bed, to her thinned out cupboards, to her denuded makeup tray, Eva wondered if her daughter would have better luck with her lecturers than she'd had with her teachers. She sat down on the bed and let her hand slide across Anna's pillow.

'My darling girl, I'm so sorry. I hope one day we can be happy again. One day,' she whispered, as the tears ran down her cheeks.

CHAPTER 13

The Big E

PEERING ACROSS AT THE building he had been searching for since leaving Redfern train station down the road, Peter contemplated his next move. On the opposite side of Regent Street in Sydney's inner west, the three arches above the building entrance reminded him of the Russian "onion" domes, *the "Holy Trinity"* he seemed to remember.

These arches, however, simply topped a window and balcony either side. So, this was the Empress Hotel, *the Big E,* JoJo's son had called it. The swing doors at the entrance to the pub had not moved since Peter arrived, so he assumed it must be fairly quiet at this time, just after lunch. Crossing the road, he noticed two police cars parked nearby but did not see any police around.

The bar was dark and stuffy. A few tables were occupied in the corner, their occupants appeared the worse for wear. They looked up momentarily, when the stool, Peter pulled from the bar, made a "chalk on blackboard" noise. He sat down opposite the barman, whose ample stomach rested against the dark mahogany counter, glass in one hand, cloth he had been using to dry it, in the other.

'You one of them?' he said quietly, nodding at the door and the police cars beyond it, Peter supposed. *'Plain clothed,* are you?'

'So, you think that rubbish will give you a roof as strong as I build?' Wolfgang laughed as he slammed shut the door of his ute.

Peter and his workers were on ladders busy installing *prefabricated* roof trusses, a relatively new 60s innovation that allowed for much faster roof construction.

'None of mine have fallen down so far,' Peter called back, signalling one of his team to turn down the blaring, paint-smeared radio hanging from a rafter. 'And I finish a roof three days faster than you do.' He grinned as he reached the bottom of his ladder and turned to shake his ex-boss's hand.

'*Wie geht's*. How can I help you my friend, this is a surprise visit?'

'I have some sad news. JoJo did not turn up for work at all this week and yesterday his son arrived on site.'

As Peter prepared himself, for what sounded like bad news, he was conscious of the banter above him, the workers hearing him and Wolfgang speaking German.

'Just telling his ex-boss what a crap brick-layer he has working for him, is all mate,' one called to a worker below him busy tapping a newly laid brick into position.

'Fuck off,' the brick layer responded. The others laughed while one mumbled something about bad language from *brickies*.

JoJo was one of the first Aboriginal workers Wolfgang employed. He turned up on one of their building sites, not long after Peter himself had arrived in Sydney, to work for Wolfgang. He complained bitterly about being paid half what non-Indigenous people were paid in the *Eveleigh* yards and claimed he did not care about travelling all the way to the North Shore every day, if he could earn a fair wage.

An elder, Uncle Chook, he met in the Big E had told JoJo about when he, as a young man, had worked on the Roseville Bridge construction as a concrete pourer. How he had been paid a good wage, sometimes even overtime.

'Go be a north shore fella, be a builder,' Uncle Chook had laughed, pointing to his empty beer glass and winking.

Within a few years, JoJo was as good a builder as any of them, turning his hand to carpentry and plastering, after joining Wolfgang as a labourer. He let JoJo work alongside his best tradesmen as a kind of apprentice to start with but paid him a fair wage anyway. Union officials, who occasionally visited, moaned about Wolfgang employing Aboriginal workers without the correct paperwork, but he was evasive, *you have no interest in these workers until I employ them and train them?* he would say with a questioning smile.

'Talk to the office manager. She will sort it out,' he always offered in the early days when Eva still worked in his office. The union officials were more than happy to deal with his attractive office manager.

'There's an Aboriginal kid here wanting to see you Wolfie,' one of his guys yelled above the screaming bandsaw blade cutting a hard wood post to size.

'*Ja, ja*. I come,' Wolfgang yelled back.

His face was familiar. He was the spitting image of his father.

'My name is Jay. My dad was JoJo, he worked here, he told me.'

'Yes, he does,' Wolfgang responded leading the young boy who must have been about 12 or 13 to a quieter place. 'Is your dad not well?'

The boy looked lost for a moment and then a tear ran down his cheek and he wiped it away quickly.

'My dad broke curfew last Saturday. Got drunk in the Big E.' He was quiet for a few moments, seemed to cast around, looking for words, pulled a grubby handkerchief from his pocket and blew his nose before continuing.

'Police took him in the hurry-up wagon. Next day they came back. Told the elder, my dad died of a heart attack. The elders say that must be lies, my dad was strong. Only got sick when he drank too much. His funeral was yesterday. I'm all alone now, got no ma, no *rellies*.'

Peter shook his head as Wolfgang recounted what Jay had told him. He was shocked. JoJo was the quietest, most gentle person. Even if he was drunk, he would never have got aggressive. Wolfgang went on to say Jay asked if he could have JoJo's job. Told him how the *whitefella* was going to throw him out as there was now no one to pay the rent for their room. Jay said he would have to live on the streets if he couldn't work.

'He said he would like to squat at our work site. Said it would be better than being on the streets of Redfern, which were dangerous at night for a young boy. I said it wasn't allowed. Gave him bus fare home though, and some extra.'

'Wolfgang we will have to rescue this kid. We owe it to JoJo. He was more than just a worker,' Peter said, wondering, *had the word 'rescue' resonated with Wolfgang.*

'I am a builder not a charity, not an orphanage, Peter. The elders in Redfern must sort it out,' Wolfgang said, turning and pulling open his truck door.

When Peter shook his head at the questions, the barman asked, 'So if you're not a cop you'll want a drink then?'

'A beer please. A cold beer.'

'That's the only kind we serve here. Pint or middy?'

Peter indicated the smaller of the two sizes with his hand held above the dark sticky counter. As he pulled the silver lever, the barman smiled and said, 'No, not with that accent you wouldn't be one of our cops, would you. From Germany are you, mate?'

'Yes, but here many years already,' Peter said. 'Building business, Forestville.'

The drink, in its cold misty glass from the fridge below the counter, a hedge against the heat of a Sydney afternoon, landed in front of Peter with a *plonk* on the old bar counter spill cloth advertising a beer he had never heard of.

Taking a sip, Peter looked around the bar casually before saying any more. He thought it best not to dive straight into a question about JoJo or his son. After watching the barman unpacking a large dishwasher for a few minutes, he asked casually, 'Do you know any builders around here that may be interested in working on the North Shore?'

The barman straightened his large frame from the dishwasher.

'A replacement for poor JoJo, hey?' Peter felt awkward. He should have known better. The Empress was the hub of Redfern. *Everyone knew everyone here, and everything about everyone.*

'Okay, so JoJo worked for us for a long time. He became a good work friend. We are worried about his son. He came to see us. Want to see if we can help him out. We owe JoJo.'

The barman said nothing. Held a glass up to the light before putting it down and taking another from the dishwasher.

'Any idea where I might find Jay?'

'Look buddy, you better speak to one of the elders before you do *anything*. You sound like you want to do good but any non-Indigenous interest in our kids is a *fair dinkum* hornet's nest. Especially around here,' he said waving his pointing finger in a circular movement.

He told Peter a little about the history of forced removals in the past, *still going on in the 60s,* and he soon realised how, one saying he wanted to help an orphaned boy, could be misconstrued.

'Chookie will be in soon. I'll introduce you. He's an elder, knew JoJo, and Jay of course. And don't mention JoJo by name, too soon after the funeral, its custom, say "Jay's dad".'

Uncle Chook was a bit stooped, and his face looked battered, but he had a twinkle in his eye, Peter thought and liked him immediately. The old man remembered the day he had advised JoJo to seek out a job on the North Shore. He listened intently to what Peter had to say.

'Look fella, we only just buried his dad, so no one knows what's going to happen with Jay but if you want to help, we will consider it if it's true that his father asked that you look after his son. I know

They Make Cheese in Nimbin, Don't They?

that's what Jay says his pa wanted. Said, *if something happens talk to my boss.*'

'I can pay for him to go to school or give him a job, or both,' Peter said. 'He says he will have to squat on the street now?'

'Maybe,' said Uncle Chook, 'or maybe we can find a family to take him. It will be hard in Redfern, for sure. People are poor, struggling. We all are,' he laughed tapping his empty glass.

Peter signalled the barman for two more beers. After a long silence and several sips of his middy, Uncle Chook turned to Peter and put his hand over the large, gnarled builder's hand.

'My friend, whatever happens, Jay must be here in the community as much as possible. He has lots to learn still about his people and our customs. He mustn't lose the Koorie language.'

He looked Peter directly in the eyes for several moments before saying, 'I will talk to the elders about this.' He placed his empty glass on the counter before turning and waving at the others in the bar and departed through the swing doors.

By evening Peter had quite a gathering around, there was lots of laughing and joking. He was popular. He was buying.

'You good man, German fella, good man.'

'Of course,' Peter laughed, 'All Germans are good blokes, let's drink to that. Barman, if you would please, more beer for my friends.'

'But not for old Crime here, he's had enough,' one young guy called.

Peter looked at the man whose name was Crime. He was grinning and making a rude sign at the one who had spoken.

'Why do they call you that?' he asked.

'Because "*Crime never pays*",' came the chorus around him, followed by guffaws of laughter. Even Crime joined in.

As the laughter died down, Peter felt the gentlest of tapping in the small of his back. He looked over his shoulder but there was nobody, so he swung around on his barstool. He knew instantly it was Jay. He saw a young JoJo before him.

'Uncle Chook said I should talk to you, find out what you had to say,' Jay said looking up at Peter.

'Ah good. Let me just finish here and I will see you outside. Have you eaten? Would you like a coke?'

He handed Jay a few dollars which he took eagerly and turned and left.

'See you later,' he called happily.

The others laughed. One said, 'You will be lucky to see him again.'

'Hey, that's our friend's boy,' another admonished.

It was nearly seven when Peter felt Jay prodding the arm he had folded on the bar counter as a pillow. He lifted his head and smiled at the young lad.

'I think we should talk another time, uncle. You bit drunk, hey?'

'Ok, call me a taxi. I come back tomorrow,' Peter said, standing and swaying across to the toilet.

Peter paid the taxi a return fare, insisting that Jay come along for the ride so they could chat. The taxi driver laughed. It was a first for him.

'Tell you what, mate. He can sit in the front on the way back. If I pick up a fare, I'll give the boy back half what you paid.'

There was not much *chatting*. Peter was snoring before they even got to the end of Regent Street. Jay and the driver talked instead. He had emigrated from Serbia and Jay was fascinated by the stories he told about how he came to be in Australia as they drove over the bridge and headed up Eastern Valley Way, to Peter's house in Castle Cove.

'We also came a long way to Sydney, but not over the sea. From Mudgee.'

When Eva heard the car in the driveway and, looking through the window, saw it was a taxi, she knew what to expect.

'Thank God. At least it's not a police car again.'

Peter had been brought home drunk a few times by the police. She heard stamping on the deck stairs as she unlatched the front door and opened it. Deep blue eyes stared up at her through curly black locks that had fallen down over them.

'This Peter's house, auntie?' Jay enquired, pushing his hair back behind his ears. 'Couldn't tell us, he's fast asleep. Taxi driver wasn't sure about the number he gave him.'

'Yes, it is, and you need help getting him out of the car, do you?'

'How'd you know?'

'Don't worry, let's just get him in.'

Having got Peter settled, Eva returned to the hall to thank Jay and see if such a young boy was going to be safe going back to wherever he had found her drunk husband. But there was no one. Just the sound of a car, she assumed the taxi, going up their quiet street. She closed the door, disconcerted at what had just transpired.

'Oh well,' she whispered to herself as she turned the TV back on. 'Wonder what I missed?'

Later as she lay wide awake in Anna's old bedroom, wondering what more she could do to help her husband, she thought she heard a sound out on the deck, between his loud snores.

'There it is again,' she said to herself, hearing a second scraping sound. 'Possums at my herb pots.'

She got up and pulling on a robe, shuffled down the hall. Picking up the torch she always kept near the front door, she peered through the lounge room window. The same blue eyes squinted back at her, blinded by her torch beam. Eva opened the window, and the face broke into a grin.

'I am waiting to speak with the uncle in the morning.'

Jay would always remember the contrasts of that first evening. The suffocating smokiness and smell of stale alcohol in the bar where he found Peter, the farting and snoring during the taxi ride home. And then later, after being discovered on the deck by Eva, the smell of the soap in the shower she led him to, the taste of the food she gave him, sinking into a bed that threatened to swallow him and Peter's snores echoing down the hallway.

CHAPTER 14

Shake-a-leg

THE MORNING WALK DOWN to the classrooms from the huge old iron entrance gates at the main road was something of a ritual for the pupils of the Rudolf Steiner School. The stroll under the old jacaranda trees fighting bravely to survive alongside Sydney's ubiquitous gum trees lining the potholed school track, was when events of the weekend were recounted, or analyses of yesterday's classroom antics took place.

The never closed gates - not since a metre long blue-tongued lizard was accidently crushed in them - were where you met up with a special friend or group before school started. In more senior years, a boyfriend or girlfriend, maybe. It was where boys and girls hugged without embarrassment as a result of the school being co-educational, with juniors and seniors sharing the same campus. These boys and girls, the makeup of the class seldom changed through the years, had known each other from a very young age.

This, of course, was not the case for Jay on his first day. Fortunately for him, Christa, now in her senior years, was there to walk with him, introduce him to her friends and several of his, soon to be, new classmates they met on the way. To his astonishment, each opened their arms to him with affection. His shyness and *first day* apprehension faded with each passing step - and hug - towards his new classroom.

With all the laughter and animated chatter, the group he walked with were oblivious to any vehicles behind them, so they jumped at the sudden *beep* from the large thudding Harley Davidson that had stopped near them. Giggling followed screams from some of the girls as its equally large rider grinned at them.

'Morning girls, just passing through if I may,' called the school's woodwork teacher.

'Morning Mr Sharpe,' they called back, shuffling to one side.

There was a flash of recognition between Jay and Mr Sharpe. His huge hand closed around the bike's brake and he smiled at Jay.

'You a new fella? Starting today?' he asked. 'Who's your mob?'

Jay grinned back. 'Wiradjuri. Dubbo.'

'That's Jay, my new brother,' Christa interjected over the engine noise.

'My mob too, Jay. Maybe we make a didgeridoo in my woodwork class, hey? That would be a good *year 8* project, one day,' he called over his leather clad shoulder as he and the large motorbike moved slowly past them. Jay's grin got even broader at his woodwork teacher's departing words.

'See you all in class,' Mr Sharpe called without looking back, waving his hand in the air.

The foster care authorities Eva applied to after they had cared for Jay informally for a few months, said his elders had to give their approval too, so it was fortuitous that Christa had not followed Anna to the private high school she had gone to, opting instead for what felt to her and Eva to be a more caring Steiner education. The school's focus on spiritual development, moral growth and social consciousness, not just academia, was bound to impress the elders more than a stuffy North Shore private school with its intense focus on academic results and sporting achievements.

Jay would have caring teachers in his new, unfamiliar environment and Christa nearby, to turn to if needed. Eva arranged for the elders to visit the school and they were impressed with its holistic approach, *if these people are aware of the whole fella, the soul and the heart, Jay's culture and ancestry will be embraced here.*

Even before they applied formerly to foster Jay, it was likely, the diligence Eva showed in the first few months he was with them, had won over the elders. She made sure he returned to his community in Redfern as often as possible to be involved in activities taking place or just to visit his friends. The kids soon got to know her, waving and calling out to her as she pulled up in her Mercedes Benz.

'Look, Jay's auntie in her deadly car. Hullo Auntie.'

Jay's new journey at school started and proceeded smoothly until his introduction to *Eurythmy,* an expressive movement art originated by Rudolf Steiner in the early 20th century. Jay would not be the first boy to feel paralysed with self-consciousness when asked to don a colourful flowing robe and sway and prance around, arms akimbo, to the sound of music and words.

And freeze he did. He simply went silent, refused to cooperate in any way, no matter how much gentle persuasion was tried by his teacher. Each lesson, Jay dutifully followed his classmates to the hall and, with a jump, took his seat on an old "wooden horse" left behind by the previous school that had occupied the buildings and out of use, as gymnastics was not in the Steiner curriculum. Each eurythmy lesson, he watched them silently from there, legs swinging as the others awkwardly tried to emulate their teacher's movements.

One day, on arrival at the hall, the class was surprised to see Mr Sharpe sitting alongside their eurythmy teacher. She stood as they gathered in their normal places - Jay on his horse - and spoke with a smile.

'Eurythmy art can take more than one form and we know art exists in all cultures. Today, we are going to try to create expressive movement art from our own country's culture and I've asked for Mr Sharpe's help.'

The big frame of the woodwork teacher rose from the chair, and he grinned broadly.

'Dance is an important part of Aboriginal culture, my culture. As important as painting or music and, like Eurythmy, tells stories. Thank you for allowing us to show you a little,' he said with a quick glance and smile at Jay.

With that he lowered his big frame into a semi crouch and the class heard rhythmic sounds from deep in his throat. Using the two small planks of wood, that looked a bit like boomerangs, Mr Sharpe started a rapid beat, punctuated with his grunts.

'SHAKE-A-LEG,' he called out as he shuffled forward, legs bent at the knee, one foot moving in front of the other at a time.

The class's smiles of astonishment at their woodwork teacher's antics were cut short when Jay sprung from his horse, clapping to the beat, legs bent, knees whipping outwards and back, body moving forward. After a short time, one of his classmates moved closer, caught up in the infectious rhythm, trying, not very successfully, to emulate Jay's movements. Soon the whole class had joined in, their woodwork teacher yelling out words of encouragement.

The Eurythmy teacher smiled to herself, *got him. Yes, but will this class ever be the same again?*

Jay and Mr Sharpe were intrigued, standing in the forest below the school buildings, watching the two elders patiently move from tree to tree, knocking on certain branches.

'It is best if the termites have eaten out the whole inside of the branch,' one informed them, knocking and listening.

'Also, not too thick,' Uncle Chook said. The other gave him a *what do you know about choosing didgeridoo wood?* look.

Jay and his teacher followed them from tree to tree, at the same time keeping an eye open for any snakes that might be around. Especially the legendry and deadly brown snake that came up from near the stream in the valley below - and about which there were many graphic stories amongst the pupils, but few actual sightings.

Across the valley through the trees, Jay could see the houses of the suburb, Castle Cove, he had moved to when he was taken in by Eva and Peter. It seemed like just the other day. Amongst those houses was the one he lived in with Christa, who was now in her final years at the school.

'Ah, looks like we found one,' said Uncle Chook when the other elder gave a thumbs up gesture to the sound he got from his knocking.

The didgeridoo project Mr Sharpe suggested on Jay's first day, had not come about until Jay was in year eight, the year when all Steiner pupils embarked on a project of their choice, normally under the guidance of a parent. As Eva and Peter knew nothing about the didgeridoo, or anything else Aboriginal, other than what Jay had taught them, he was going to have to rely on Mr Sharpe and the Redfern community for guidance.

His project had an added complication in that what he was making had to be *played* on the day the projects were exhibited to parents, pupils and visitors.

Exhibition day brought a visitor they had not seen at home for a few months. Anna decided she could not miss, what she felt was, a coming of age for Jay in the family. When she left, she had found a place to stay in Eveleigh, located midway between Sydney uni and Redfern, where most of Jay's community lived. The run-down old house she shared with four other students was near the railway workshops many Indigenous people had gravitated to from the country, hoping to find work and a better life. Unfortunately, the outcome was often not what they expected. Most ended up underpaid like Jay's father, living in squalid conditions in Redfern.

Jay sometimes stayed over with Anna – they made up a bed on the couch in the lounge - when Eva took him to visit his friends. He loved it. Listening to the students' animated conversations about their involvement in activities to improve people's lives, support for other activists trying to get things changed for people in Redfern. They sometimes asked him a question about Indigenous culture, listening intently to his answers. He felt so grown up, loving Anna's approving looks as he spoke.

One day, when he told her that for his year eight project, he had chosen to make a didgeridoo, she could hardly contain herself.

'Oh, what a wonderful idea,' she exclaimed, hugging him, making him blush in front of the others. 'The first thing I laid eyes on in Australia when we drew up alongside the quay was a man playing the didgeridoo way down below us. I had no idea what he was about then. White painted stripes on his body, big puffy cheeks and an amazing sound,' she laughed. 'I was only about nine, it was like something out of a nursery story. I have loved the sound ever since. Are you going to play it as well?'

'Uncle Chook says he will teach me. But I don't know, he is very busy nowadays. Maybe.'

'It's Anna,' Christa called, waving the receiver at the family around the breakfast table.

'She's at the station, can you pick her up, *Mutti*?'

'Can I go with you please,' Jay chimed in.

'Of course,' Eva called back to Christa, nodding yes to Jay and looking at Peter to judge his expression.

He had drunk far less since the night of the incident with Anna, but although she had visited occasionally, he had never apologised, believing his gift of a car was enough. Their conversation was superficial. He never asked her about university.

'You and Anna need to communicate with each other. You *have* to tell her you are sorry,' Eva kept saying to him, whenever the subject came up, but he just gave one of his shrugs.

'She took the car, didn't she?'

'And sold it at a loss to pay her university fees you refused to pay,' countered Eva.

Eva found she did not miss Anna as much as she had at first. They seldom spoke on the phone, had quick exchanges when Jay stayed over with her in Redfern. She wondered if it was because of him, he occupied much of her time, guiding him in his new life was quite demanding. She was enjoying having a son though, she had to admit to herself. *Funny,* she thought, *we all assumed without saying anything that he was going to be Peter's son, the one he always wanted, help him get over his war trauma. But no, he seemed to lose interest in Jay after a few months.* Once she asked Jay if he missed his dad, but he shook his head.

'Nah, *Mutti.*' He had started calling her that. 'Always remember my pa, but you and Peter are my ma and pa now.'

Staying over that evening for the first time since Anna had left the house for good, meant they ate together like a happy family again, toasted Jay's successful project, laughed about Uncle Chook arriving at the school unexpectedly to play the didgeridoo.

'He kept saying he was too busy to teach me. Maybe tomorrow? Maybe next week?' Jay laughed. 'But all the time he was planning to surprise me by coming himself.'

'Oh, but what about you and Mr Sharpe doing the shake-a-leg?' Anna laughed.

'We all do it now, in Eurythmy sometimes. Even in my year,' Christa said. 'Some say it was started by my brother here.'

Jay blushed and tried to change the subject.

'Mr Sharpe took Uncle Chook home on his Harley. Dropped him at the Big E. He said Uncle Chook asked him for beer money *'cause he was so thirsty, playing the didgeridoo all day.'*

They laughed at Jay mimicking Uncle Chook, but the mood changed when Peter said, glancing at Eva, 'One day when you come and work for me, you and the other workers can entertain us when we have our Friday end of week beers, hey my boy?'

'But surely Jay is going to uni?' Anna asked immediately.

'That's for you girls,' her father replied. 'Boys need to use their hands. Do an apprenticeship, not uni.'

'Funny,' Eva said, her hand moving involuntarily to her arm, 'my father had it the other way round. No university for girls. They needed to use their hands in the kitchen, bring up the children. I got punished one dinner time as a young girl for asking if I could go to university.' Peter said nothing.

'*Mutti* said I can go to uni, like Anna and Christa,' Jay said.

Peter glared at his wife.

'He can decide for himself,' she said.

Later that evening, Eva and Anna found themselves alone on the deck with their coffee. The others were inside watching TV.

'Talking about uni. How is it going with your studies?' Eva asked. 'It's your final year. Graduation soon, right?'

'Oh, I'm glad you said that. Reminds me I need to give you this invitation,' Anna said, scratching in her bag. 'It's still a way off, but they like to get these out early, they say.'

'It's been a struggle this semester I have to admit,' Anna continued, 'I have been so involved with the student union in the organisation of their latest festival. That's why I haven't been able to have Jay stay over. It's in Nimbin this time. I wonder if Dorothy still lives there. Remember she brought dad home once?'

'Oh God,' Eva exclaimed, 'I had forgotten about her. Yes, that's right; Dorothy. As much as we promised each other we would, we never did stay in contact. I have no idea if she is still there, Anna.'

Eva felt more and more uncomfortable as name after name was called out and she did not hear Anna's. She could not find her daughter's face amongst the students seated behind the invited guests either. The deans on the stage looked as bored as Peter next to her. He had complained in the car all the way about how little would be done on site with him not being there.

'My daughter hardly talks to me anymore. Why am I giving all this time to her? I have so much work,' he had grumbled as they parked the car a short distance from Sydney University's Great Hall.

The degree candidate marshal they sought out for explanation after the ceremony regarding Anna's absence, led them to his office where he pulled open a filing drawer. Inviting them to sit down, he flicked through several folders before finally taking one from the drawer. Without saying anything, he lowered himself into a chair opposite them and opened the file.

After a few minutes, he looked up with a puzzled expression.

'I'm sorry, there might have been a miscommunication between you and your daughter. Anna Baurst withdrew from all her courses months ago.'

CHAPTER 15

Aquarius

ANNA LOOKED BACK THROUGH the rear window of the old VW kombi, trying to catch a last glimpse of the Nimbin Rocks as their vehicle's complaining engine struggled with the final hill before Nimbin. The four students had pulled off the road earlier to enjoy the sight of the majestic rock formation that lay about two kilometres south of the town. A landmark of great cultural significance to the traditional owners, the Bundjalung people. Anna and her friend were hoping to meet the elders for guidance on accommodating Indigenous visitors travelling to the festival from far afield.

Standing with her chatting friends before the rock towers, that seemed to leap from the canopy of lush forest like stone age city skyscrapers, Anna initially tried to picture a volcano erupting 20 million years ago, creating these beautiful surroundings. But moving away to a quiet spot and gazing up at the rock faces, she began to sense the richness of the scene she was witnessing. She imagined she could see the spirits of the original settlers of maybe 50 thousand years ago, rising from the earth below the rocks, floating, dancing transparent figures. She thought she could hear the rhythmic clacking that accompanied the *shakealeg* dance they had seen Jay do for his year 8 project demonstration.

'Anna.' She jumped. 'Come on, we need to get set up before dark.'

They were just walking off to their Kombi when the sound of hoof beats behind made them stop and turn. A farmer on horseback trotted up to the nearby farm gate, his two dogs panting alongside his huge black stallion, salty lines of perspiration gathered on its glossy coat. The rider leant down in his saddle to raise the latch and, the moment he opened the gate, the kelpies slipped through, barking at the students gathered near their kombi.

'Bomber. Caster. To me. Down,' the farmer commanded. 'Sorry. They think there are no limits to their territory. Don't worry they're all bark and no bite,' he grinned.

'Sit,' he said sternly, with a downward hand gesture which seemed different somehow, to Anna.

'It's quite a view, isn't it?' he said gazing up at the rocks. 'More like small mountains than rocks, hey?'

As they were agreeing enthusiastically, another van pulled off the road, crunching across the gravel behind them. It was emblazoned with "ABC Radio" logos on either side and had barely stopped when a journalist, microphone in hand, followed by a sound man and his cable carrying assistant, clambered out. Ignoring Anna and her friends, they strode towards the horseman, coming to an abrupt halt when the dogs rose and growled menacingly.

'Brett Jarvis, ABC Radio sir, may we ask you a few questions?'

Anna noticed the rider did not reprimand the dogs. *Nor would I have, with that kind of direct approach,* she thought as she and the other students climbed back into their van, waving goodbye to the farmer. *Mr. Jarvis might have tried a 'good morning, sir' to start with.* She looked at the card the *assistant* had handed out to each of them as they left, like they were tourists who had just had their picture taken.

'*Send a cheque to this address to get your copy.*' 'Brett Jarvis, Journalist ABC Radio' the card said.

Waving away a waft of exhaust smoke from the departing kombi and keeping a wary eye on the dogs, the journalist went on, 'Sir, we're doing a report on what locals think about the upcoming festival and its impact on your town. You know, when it's invaded by thousands of, some might say, hippies seeking to celebrate an alternative lifestyle?'

As he dismounted from his horse and his two dogs came to him, tails wagging furiously, Tom, the farmer, reflected on how predictable journalists were, *shovel wielding Nimbin locals prepare to drive out dirty hippies.* He was the largest landowner in the area and one of the town's leaders who had thought the festival was a good idea, when the request to hold the festival in Nimbin had originally been tabled with them and the Bundjalung elders. Tom was one of the few in the area who still had a successful dairy farm, selling most of his milk to Norco in Lismore.

'Tom's the name,' he said, offering his left hand which had the journalist fumbling as he moved the mic from one hand to the other.

He responded to the question Brett had asked, by explaining how, generally, everyone around believed the festival would inject new life into a town which had experienced a sustained downturn resulting in the closure of many of Nimbin's shops.

'Aquarius - it's not referred to as "*the festival*" around here nowadays, we've kind of adopted it - has already had an impact,' Tom went on. 'Basil, for example, he owns the bakery, has taken on an additional baker in order to keep up with bread demands of the early arrivers and the general store has taken on more staff, ordered loads of additional supplies like shovels, plastic piping and so on. One or two other shops, long closed, are considering reopening too.'

'How do you feel about your kids being exposed to the hippie way of life, Tom?' Brett asked, moving a bit closer to the farmer now that the dogs had got used to him and calmed down.

Tom had given permission for a section of his land to be used by some of the young people for their camping set up. He had even allowed a few of them to fell trees for timber to build teepee frameworks.

'I don't have any family living with me nowadays, but if my son saw how these people live, he might appreciate the comforts of the home he had,' Tom smiled. 'Mind you, Steve is living in Newtown now. He plans to go to Sydney uni and I'm sure the area hasn't changed much since my time there. He will be seeing some unusual lifestyles and characters there too.'

Anna and her three student friends had been on the road since the early hours, departing Sydney along the nearly deserted Pacific Highway in pre-dawn darkness. Now, tired and thirsty, they were finally in Nimbin proper, keen to find a place to park the van and attach its side tent for the night. The sooner they got set up, the sooner they would be able to do something about their groaning stomachs. Get back some of the excitement that had faded over the last 10 hours of monotonous driving.

As the group's designated purchaser of provisions, Anna went in search of supplies while the others set up camp in a field of lush grass they had been directed to near Thorburn Street causeway, Nimbin's favourite swimming spot. Having walked all the way up Thorburn Street with its little cottages on either side, Anna made a right towards the town centre looking forward to getting her shopping done.

She was a little concerned to see, as she turned onto the path leading up to the general store entrance steps, that it was already occupied by two *locals* observing her approach. Stopped in her tracks, she saw there was no other way, she would have to walk past them to get to the steps. She knew that in any small town, new arrivals were often considered intruders; *always those two locals staring at you like these two, quick exchanges between them without taking their eyes off you, just a slight lean of one head towards the other.* They weren't normally aggressive, but these two Anna found very intimidating, the slow blink of a big brown eye observing her.

She took a step forward and the movement prompted one of them to turn from his side on position to face her, *oh God what now?* Suddenly a piece of a broken branch flew past Anna from behind, bouncing in front of her two oppressors.

'Go on scat you mangy bastards,' came a woman's voice over her shoulder. Anna knew immediately she had heard that voice before.

The Kiwi accent. The two roosters sprang in the air with loud furious squawks, combs bright red in the sunlight, before taking off half running, half flying, leaving a few feathers floating gently to the gravel path, marking where they had previously stood.

'They're feral roosters. People just dump them and they make the store their new home because of the park alongside: picnic scraps,' the woman said and turning to see her smiling face, Anna recognised her immediately. 'Nearly took a kid's eye out the other day when the toddler ran at one of them. Flew at him like a wild thing apparently. One very angry tourist yelling at poor Betty, the storeowner.'

Anna's rescuer did not seem to recognise *her* though. Anna was older with hair that was long now. In her last few years at university, she had cultivated, what she believed was, a 'new age' look.

'Dorothy, hello! You make a point of saving members of our family, don't you?' The woman's face was blank, a slight frown replacing her smile.

'It's Anna, Eva's daughter, you brought dad home that night. The Gap, remember?' Anna smiled.

'Oh my God. Anna?' Dorothy exclaimed.

Dorothy insisted she help Anna carry the various supplies she had bought to see her and her friends through their first night.

'I live in Thorburn Street, so it's on my way. My house is about halfway down the road to the creek where you're camping. You must have walked up past it to get here. So, you and your friends got here early. For Aquarius I mean. To get a good spot at the camp site?'

'You sound almost like you are looking forward to it, Dorothy? What about the disruption coming? Are the people not concerned?' Anna panted slightly, struggling with each arm around a large paper bag.

'No, on the contrary, we can do with a bit of disruption,' Dorothy said. 'Nimbin has gone backwards for so long, most in the town are happy about the event. We believe Aquarius might bring a new awakening. You know, tourism? New people? Shops reopening? Everybody has their own theory and wish list,' Dorothy laughed.

'Probably not quite what *visitors* are going to be looking for from Aquarius, though,' she added.

'Aquarius' always, not 'the festival', noted Anna.

'Goodness me, yours is not the only tent going up already,' Dorothy exclaimed as the camp site came into view.

The following morning, Anna had no trouble finding Dorothy's shop. There was only one main street, Cullen Street, and Dorothy was lounging in a recliner in the sun alongside a display stand of dresses and various other items made from hemp and cotton materials.

'If you're not buying, bugger off,' she laughed as Anna climbed the old wooden railway sleeper steps to reach her level.

'I suppose that's your thought each time a tourist arrives at your shop?' Anna smiled back.

'Not for the last few years, it hasn't. More likely, "please, please come closer so I can persuade you to buy something, rich tourist",' Dorothy said with an ironic smile. 'So, Anna, tell me what brings you and your friends here? All you said yesterday was something vague about a working holiday for you?'

Anna explained that she and her friends, regarded as the uni "forward party", were to handle certain festival logistics. There had been considerable effort to involve Indigenous people in the festival. Performing artists, people displaying crafts, as well as those just wanting to be there. Her group's job was to make sure, as far as possible, there would be support and appropriate facilities to accommodate their needs. Some will have travelled long journeys and getting organised first up would be intimidating in an unfamiliar place.

'Of course, the uni organising team has already requested permission from traditional owners to hold the festival on their land.'

'Yes, I read that somewhere. I think it might be a first,' Dorothy said.

'Yeah, it is and there will be another "first" because they have also asked the traditional owners if we can include a welcoming ceremony on the first day of the festival.'

'And how did *you* come to be selected to be involved in this?' Dorothy asked, shading her eyes with her hand, multiple shining bangles sliding down her thin wrist almost to her elbow. 'Come and sit down here with me or stop moving; I'm going bloody blind with that sun appearing from behind you every few seconds,' she added, patting a lounger next to her.

'I don't know. Maybe they thought because I have an Aboriginal foster brother, I might be considered knowledgeable about Indigenous culture,' Anna laughed, as she sat next to the older woman.

'Oh, now that *is* interesting. A foster brother. How did that come about?' Dorothy asked.

Dorothy could not get enough news about what had transpired

since they last met and Anna felt she had recounted her whole teenage life story.

'So where would I find someone who is abreast of all the "dos and don'ts" around here? Can give some tips on the best way to fit in with locals?' Anna asked.

'I can and will, but better still, go and see if Ben's working today. At the Hemp Factory, just down there. Other side of the road,' Dorothy replied with a gesture in the direction of Nimbin's main shopping area. 'He's lived here forever. Knows everybody and everything,' she laughed. 'He can introduce you to some of the elders as well. You will need their guidance with your Indigenous visitors.'

As Anna rose from her lounger, Dorothy added, 'Oh, and if you get the chance and you will, speak to Jack. He's our "top cop", the senior guy at the police station. He'll tell you about the "don'ts", especially his favourite, drugs. He says it's the first thing that will happen when, to use his words, "that hippie lot" arrive.'

Dorothy was right, Anna did inevitably meet up with Jack, at about the same time she met the man who would ensure Nimbin became her new home. These two were in conversation outside Travis' tent, or rather, Jack was speaking and Travis was listening intently as he was being lectured on the benefits of not been caught selling "dope", by Jack or any of his officers.

Anna was on her way back from the creek, that flowed past the camp site. She noticed the two of them as she came past the side of a tent and saw, what she decided instantly was, the best-looking man she had ever laid eyes on.

'Of course, he will have a girlfriend. Some gorgeous thing hiding inside the tent, no doubt,' she mumbled quietly, taking in the long, tousled hair and green eyes that smiled at her over Jack's shoulder.

This conclusion did not stop her staring anyway, as she passed unnecessarily close to the side of, what she assumed must be Travis' tent. Distracted, she tripped over one of his tent guy ropes and sprawled in front of them.

They both jerked into motion, hands outstretched to help her up. Anna, mortified, did not know what the best strategy might be to hide her embarrassment, as they hovered. Feign unconsciousness or laugh out loud like it was the funniest thing that had happened to her in ages, and she didn't feel uncomfortable at all? The latter thought brought back an image of her baby sister flying out of her pram into nettles; *the baby sister she had not seen for ages, missed so much*. Anna burst into tears.

Now, the men themselves were *mortified*, not sure what their best course of action was. Travis followed his instinct, dropping to his knees, helping Anna into a sitting position where he could hold her gently. Under the watchful gaze of Jack, he said softly, 'Are you okay? That was quite a fall.'

'I'm fine, I'm fine,' she sniffed into the back of her hand as he helped her to her feet.

'I'll get you some toilet paper. No tissues I'm afraid,' Travis said, disappearing into his tent.

'Thanks,' Anna said, and despite herself, edged a bit closer to the open tent flap to see who else might be in there, smiling at Jack at the same time.

'Sorry, I am so clumsy,' she said to him.

'You aren't the first person to trip over a guy rope,' Jack laughed.

Appearing back through the flap and handing her a wad of toilet paper, Travis said, 'Is there anything else you need?'

'No, I am fine now thanks,' she said blushing as she turned away. 'See you later.'

As Anna walked off, Jack recommenced the lecture he had previously been delivering to Travis, but the handsome man was not listening; he was enjoying the sight of Anna walking across the grass towards the student's kombi.

CHAPTER 16

Stepping Stones

STANDING BEHIND JAY, WAITING for the bus to arrive at their stop on Eastern Valley Way, Christa busied herself with the straps of his backpack.

'How many times has *Mutti* told you to remember to fasten these, Jay?' she said giving the back of his head a gentle shove. '*Clunk Click, Every Trip,* don't you watch TV?' she laughed.

'We should ask her if you and I can visit Anna while she's in Nimbin,' was his only response.

'Woo... your friends been telling you about hippie girls with bare boobs on show up there, hey?' Christa laughed.

'Of course, not,' he said gruffly.

'Blushing, are we?' Christa teased, stretching over his shoulder to look at his face.

'Don't be stupid Christa,' he said, pushing at her face but missing as she pulled her head back.

As the noise of another departing bus subsided, Jay half turned to her and said, 'It's just that with Anna being away so much, it's important we visit her, don't you think?'

She patted him on the shoulder.

'And how are we going to get to Nimbin? You going to borrow Mr Sharpe's Harley?'

Christa smiled at the earnestness in her stepbrother's face. Even though she and Jay had become close friends in the last few years, and supported each other in a stressful family environment, they both missed Anna not being at home.

Jay's heart was pounding as he clicked the bike into first gear with his foot and allowed the lever on the left handgrip of Mr Sharpe's Harley to slowly return to an open position. The throbbing bike below him seemed to be talking to him, made him think of a rodeo rider on a wild horse about to be released into an arena, *no Mr Sharpe to help you now, can you handle this?* he thought he heard.

After all the anxiety getting his learners license, the hours sitting on the stationary bike, practicing changing gears while Mr Sharpe helped, holding it upright. Riding behind his woodwork teacher while he described the technique behind the various handling manoeuvres being demonstrated...now it was down to this final moment.

Suddenly, he was moving across the empty tennis court parking lot near the school. He wished Christa and Anna were there to see him. He stayed in first gear for his maiden circuit around the lot, Mr Sharpe watching him, hands on hips, grinning.

'One step at a time, young fella,' Mr Sharpe had said earlier.

They were both hoping Jay would not freeze, would remember to reach for both the clutch lever and the brake lever simultaneously when he arrived back to where his teacher stood, who was ready to jump in and help him keep the bike upright once brought to a stop.

They Make Cheese in Nimbin, Don't They?

Standing next to Jay now as one bus after another passed, pausing long enough at the stop to pick up kids while those waiting for *their* bus were engulfed in diesel fumes, Christa wondered what he had thought about the post-graduation scene. They had heard Peter slam the car door and stamp up the steps to the front entrance, yelling insults back at Eva. He yanked open the door of the drinks cabinet, even though it was barely 3pm and called Jay to sit with him on the deck. *Come and talk to me my boy.* Christa had thought, *and hear about the inadequacies of women,* as she waited in the hall for her mother to come inside and explain what had happened at the ceremony.

By his third drink, Peter had moved on to why he needed Jay, a "man", to be in the family.

'Even Eva's father always said I needed a boy. A son who could piss on the lawn standing up,' he laughed coarsely, remembering his friends teasing him that first night on board their ship.

He poured a half a glass of beer for Jay, *drink with your Papi,* but it did not escape Eva's observation and she was out on the deck in a trice.

'Why do you take my son's drink?' he demanded as she removed the glass plonked heavily in front of Jay, before the surface of the amber liquid even had time to stop moving.

'Time for homework, Jay. Come now. Off you go,' she pointed at the open front door. A relieved Jay was up and on his way to his room before she had even finished her sentence. He heard Peter protesting loudly as he walked.

In their respective bedrooms, Jay and Christa sat distraught as another domestic war erupted downstairs. Christa was tempted to explain the situation to Jay, but she barely understood it that well herself. Why her father was like he was. Obviously, it had something to do with *the* war, that much had been relayed to her. Instead, she just sat and listened to the shouting below her.

Eventually on their bus, Christa was thinking, *Jay probably now thinks Papi is like he is because he had two daughters only and no "lawn peeing son"*. She laughed quietly to herself, sitting shoulder to shoulder with Jay, rocking together at the motion the driver was creating with his erratic lane changing. Jay turned in his seat and gave her an inquisitive look.

'What?' he said, but she just put her arm around his shoulders and gave him a hug.

'Will you miss me when I go to uni after the holidays, my little brother?' she asked.

'No,' he laughed. 'Get your creepy arm off me,' he said, leaning forward in his seat, but she clung on to him until he tickled her, making her scream, which to Jay's further embarrassment, had all the kids on the bus turning around to look at them.

Staring out of the window at the distant blue sea that popped into view from time to time between the blue gum covered hills, driving south towards Jervis Bay, Christa thought, *this is going to be a holiday of firsts*. It was the first holiday they were having without Anna. *She would be relieved,* Christa was sure and the first she would be having with a foster brother. Her mother had promised her that Peter and she would not have a fight on this holiday so that would be another "first" too, although an unlikely one. They had not been on any holiday for years, because they had always ended up in chaos, terminated prematurely by a parental row that left the whole family traumatised, driving home in silence.

Maybe another first will be when I meet a cute boy and lose my virginity during the holidays, she was thinking, when a finger poked her in the ribs, and she jumped.

'Money for your thoughts,' Jay laughed.

'Its "a penny" not "money" and mind your own business,' she said without turning from the window.

'Hey, why are you blushing?' he demanded, leaning forward to try and see more of her face. Eva turned around in her seat with a quizzical smile.

The house they had rented stood back from Hyams Beach, elevated on wooden stilts to cater for the steep slope it was built on, was surrounded by tall gum trees, part of a forest. Eva gasped, 'God, if there's a bush fire, we'll all be gone!'

'Nah, we'll just have to run like hell down to the water, *Mutti*,' Jay said, but Christa looked concerned and Eva regretted her words.

They were standing on the wooden deck that ran the full length of the house, a view of the sea in the distance below. Whilst the others talked over the shrieking of the lorikeets in the gum trees around them – where they stood, they were almost level with the canopy

- Peter beside them, was silent. He stared out at the ocean, lost in thought. Long after the rest of the family had moved in to change into swimmers and begun the process of *nesting* in their allocated rooms, Peter was still in the same position. He finally moved when they called to him to hurry up, so they could get down to the beach before it got too late.

'It's like standing at the rail of a ship,' he said to himself as he turned to join them. 'The endless ocean far away, below you.'

Christa was disappointed there were not many opportunities to meet other young people where they were, but she enjoyed each day, nonetheless. She and Jay took long beach walks, marvelling at the crystal-clear water all the way up to a naval academy at the far end of the beach. They dived into the surf from time to time to cool down, Jay claiming he had swum with one of the schools of silver whiting they saw flashing through the glassy sides of breaking waves as they strolled, the famous white sands squeaking with each foot fall.

One early evening on returning from the beach, as they reached the top of the road they had to climb to get to their rented holiday home, they found Eva standing halfway down the driveway looking anxious.

'Have you seen your *Papi*, Christa?' she called, looking over their heads towards the beach as they approached. 'He said he was going to fetch you in the car and take you into Huskisson for lunch?'

'He never said anything about lunch when we saw him buying flowers down at the shop. We came up from the beach to buy drinks,'

Christa said. 'He told us he was going to lay them at the monument for the destroyer that was sunk near Huskisson.'

'Yeah, one like he was on, he said. That sunk. In the war, *Mutti*,' Jay added.

'He told you that?' Eva asked, looking surprised. 'He normally says nothing about his time at sea. Anyway, you had better go and shower, dinner is nearly ready.'

Peter left his car in the parking lot of the Huskisson Hotel and walked across to the trees that bounded one side and from where he could look out over Shark Net Beach to Jervis Bay. In the distance he could see a helicopter heading for the naval academy.

He cast around for someone to ask about the location of the commemorative plaque. He had forgotten about the accident which happened a few years after they arrived in Australia, until he read about it again in one of the brochures Eva had got at the information kiosk they stopped at. One of the country's worst peacetime naval disasters, it occurred in 1964, when the aircraft carrier HMAS Melbourne sliced the Daring Class destroyer, HMAS Voyager, in two, 30 kilometres south-west of Jervis Bay. The ships had been involved in night flying operations and were "darkened" with only navigational lighting, when the Melbourne struck the much smaller Voyager, which had sailed across her bow, causing it to sink quickly, resulting in the death of 82 officers and men.

Walking across to the park as directed, Peter found where the plaque was mounted. After laying his flowers on the ledge, he read through the inscription carefully, mouthing quietly to himself the names of each of the seamen lost. He felt tears in his eyes as the image and sounds of that night on *his* sinking destroyer came into his mind.

'Sad, isn't it mate?' came a voice from behind him.

'A terrible loss, yes,' said Peter, turning to find a man of about his age standing near him. 'Some of them might have survived battles with *your* navy, only to die in peace time, hey?' he smiled, recognising Peter's accent. 'Or did I get that wrong? You look about my age. Were you in the war?'

'Yes,' Peter said, without a smile, looking back at the list of names. 'Yes, I was in the navy and was sunk like them.'

'Ah, no wonder you're paying your respects, mate. You must know the horror of a sinking ship. I can only imagine. It is good of you to take the time to honour them like you have.'

'Yes, I know the horror,' Peter said, looking past the man across to the waves and the sea beyond.

'You want to get a beer up at the bar, mate?' the man asked, pointing towards the hotel. 'I'm buying. For your show of respect here, mate. My name is Arthur.'

Later, when Peter mentioned where they were staying, Arthur was able to identify the house with a few questions regarding its appearance and position. Hyams Beach was small and Arthur, it turned out, had been doing electrical maintenance work for owners over there for years. It was nearly 9pm when he finally left Peter to go home. He had tried, unsuccessfully, to persuade Peter to head back to Hyams Beach since about 7pm, but Peter was in full flight and regaling all and sundry in the bar with anecdotes about the war, the building industry, the navy;

any subject that came up. Each new friend he made brought on another round of drinks and repeats of anecdotes already shared. Some in the bar were looking across at Peter and shaking their heads, telling each other that this was heading for trouble - but doing nothing about it.

In the middle of yet another anecdote, Peter suddenly stood up and swayed towards the bar entrance.

'I return soon,' he called without looking back, waving his arm in the air to no one in particular.

Walking unsteadily across the parking area, he headed for the lawn that led to the commemorative plaque. It was dark now, but he found his way to it easily in the moonlight. He could not read the words, but he put his hand on the cold metal plaque and mouthed the name, *Voyager*. Turning his back against the strong breeze that was whipping off the sea, he slipped his watch from his wrist and laid it in the stone alcove encasing the plaque. Then, after pulling his wallet from his back pocket and laying it alongside the watch, he turned and walked towards the concrete blocks protecting the embankment from the swirling water that gave passage to the Husky Ferry when it sailed through to dock.

Stepping unsteadily onto the first concrete block and then hastily onto the next, he made his way down to the water. He paused for a second, body rocking backwards and forwards, arms waving around for balance, but before he could take the next jump across the gap between the blocks, a combination of alcohol and a sudden gust of wind, had him toppling down onto the concrete. He gashed his arms and legs as he fell but somehow raised himself, although he was bleeding profusely. He stumbled off the blocks into the water and, after a step or two, sank into the deep dredged part of the channel used by the ferries and drifted away with the current.

A man, walking his dog, had spotted the dark figure collapsing into the shiny black flow. He ran to the spot where Peter had first stepped off the walkway onto the blocks and peered across them down into the water trying to see something, hoping to see a figure swimming back to the edge. Clambering out of the water, sopping wet, looking sheepish for *accidentally* falling in, but all he saw was a sinister boiling of the moonlit surface, no sound. Horrified, he was oblivious of his dog beside him, tugging on his lead, impatient to continue the run they had started. *You just don't know how fast they are until you see that fin cut through the water, as quick as a dry leaf whipped forward across a calm surface by a sudden gust of wind.*

CHAPTER 17

Change For the Best

Jay had woken her with a panicky voice, calling through her closed bedroom door, 'Gandyan! Gandyan outside, *Mutti!* Come quickly.'

Rousing herself from a deep sleep, she had been awake until after 2am waiting for Peter to arrive back home, before taking a sedative. She called out, 'What, Jay, what?' after his receding footsteps.

Hurrying down the hall, she saw the alternating red and blue reflection on the foliage in the front of the house before she even got to the deck where he was standing. The flashing lights came from a police car down on the road below. Eva thought, *déjà vu, well at least he's home.*

'Do you think there is any chance he is okay?' murmured Eva. So quietly, that the officer asked her to repeat her question. Christa and Jay sat stunned; the blood drained from their young faces.

Rescue boats had been out scanning the sea surface with their powerful beams for any signs of Peter, but the search had been called off until first light. Police and their dogs had also searched the beach in case he had been washed up or managed to swim ashore, but there had been no sightings so far.

'It's difficult to say. We are extremely concerned, given the witness statements we have taken, but I will call you as soon as we know anything further, once the search starts again at daybreak in a few hours, sorry,' he said zipping open a folder. Reaching inside, he handed Eva Peter's watch and wallet. 'These were found at the plaque,' he said. 'The fact that he deliberately left them there, where they eventually would be discovered, far from where he entered the water, is of concern, of course.'

Eva turned the watch over. It was inscribed on the back. A present from his mother when he turned 16. It was not an expensive watch, but he treasured it, she knew. As successful and as wealthy as he had become in Australia, he refused to wear anything on his wrist but the old watch. Eva sighed, he had even left it behind when he went off to sea during the war in case it got damaged or lost. *I have a cheap watch, maybe, but I drive a Mercedes for which I paid cash,* he would laugh when anyone teased him about his old watch with its tatty leather strap.

'The neighbours must be glad that flashing light has finally gone,' Eva said, after the police car had driven off. Christa sat quietly, staring at the wallet and watch that lay on the coffee table, *I should feel bad for not crying.* Jay watched their faces carefully, looking for a signal as to what he should do, how to react. His foster mother seemed to show no emotion. *Uncle Chook would say, 'sorry business coming'.* He wished Uncle Chook was here now.

Eva was in shock, yet acutely aware that her husband had suffered enormously for years with guilt from his memories and the nightmares it generated, *is he free of the pain now*? But she did wonder what the trigger had been, finally. Was it a perfect storm? *Close to the sea again, alcohol, a memorial to a sunken destroyer, drunken wartime anecdotes in a bar, away from his normal work distractions?*

Once again, the roosters she feared were hanging around on the path but after removing them by employing Dorothy's tactic, Anna climbed the steps and joined the others waiting to be served in the general store. She kept herself occupied by glancing down through the front-page headlines emblazoned across newspapers, neatly stacked on the shelves in front of the counter. One caught her eye and then another; she had a premonition that her day was about to change as she reread them.

Sydney Builder Drowned in Night Swim.

Holiday Disaster for German Family.

Reaching down past the person in front of her, she picked up the nearest copy and began to read.

'I am so sorry you had to find out that way *meine tochter*,' Eva said, when Anna phoned her. 'There was no answer from the number you gave us. We tried and tried.'

'I had to move from where I was living,' Anna said. 'The telephone bill has probably not been paid at the old address.'

'Today, I was going to phone the Nimbin police station and see if they could find you.'

'Don't be too concerned about me, *Mutti*, you know our relationship was not good. But you know, I feel sorrier for him than I do for any of us. It makes me sad that he suffered so much, knew how he also made his family suffer and did not ever want to find help. How often did you try and get him to see a psychiatrist and, when he did, would not cooperate with them. And then to drown himself?' Anna was suddenly silent. Eva wondered if her daughter was in tears. Then, 'Poor man, what torment. Poor *Papi*.'

'I am sorry for your loss, *Mutti*, especially as I know it could not have been an accident. Not after what happened at the Gap. He must have wanted to end the recurring memory.'

There was silence between them for several moments again.

'How is Christa taking it? And of course, Jay?'

'We're all trying to come to terms with this loss, we're shocked and sad but there has been so much ugliness in the past years. You know,' Eva said, surprising herself with her own sudden tears. In the newspaper reports, there was no mention of drinking or what the witness walking his dog thought he had seen. When Eva told Anna what the police had told her, she was silent for so long Eva thought the line was cut, but then she responded.

'No Dorothy to save *Papi* this time, hey? If only he had accepted help.' Eva was surprised again, this time at the sob in her daughter's voice.

The night after they had got back from their aborted holiday at Hyams Beach and Eva was in her own home with all the things she treasured around her, she had felt it sweeping over her. Like that night on board the ship, the realisation she had escaped the *gasthaus*, this time it was the escaping from under the dark cloud of Peter's mental illness.

On her way back home from Sydney, Anna had been driving north on the Pacific Highway for over five hours, the same images going around and around in her mind. She glanced down at the wallet and watch on the seat beside her. It had been several months since Peter's death, but any fading memories had become starkly real again following his memorial service and wake, held in the garden of the family home that weekend.

Uncle Chook had not been the only surprise attendee at Peter's memorial service. The barman from the *Big E,* invited by Uncle Chook because he needed a ride, and Mr Sharpe had joined Wolfgang and most of Peter's workers gathered in the shade of two large fig trees in the back garden. Looking at the neatly set out tables and their starched white tablecloths, it seemed to Anna to be more of a celebration of their boss' life than sombre reflection. Wolfgang and a few of Peter's German friends, chatted quietly together, preferring to stay in the background as the builders became more boisterous. Peter's foreman gave a short eulogy, mentioning his fairness to his workers and joked about his unwavering attention to detail. As the afternoon wore on and the drinks flowed, the conversations became increasingly animated, including anecdotes about Peter.

Anna wondered if their "nosy" neighbour had crept up to his fence to listen for some gossip.

The following morning, her siblings sat her down on the deck, determined to know everything about her time in Nimbin. The first questions related to the festival: *what unforgettable things had she seen or experienced? Why had she stayed on after Aquarius? Who did she meet that was famous? Was she coming back to Sydney one day? Could they come and visit?*

'Wow, slow down a bit, you two,' grinned Anna.

'But why didn't you come back? We miss you,' Jay said, wanting to get to the point. '*Mutti* never takes me to Redfern anymore. Not since you left. Yesterday was the first time I've seen Uncle Chook in ages.'

'Well, after the festival, like me, many had reasons to stay on. Some seeking out a new life. An *alternative lifestyle*. Tribes have formed, new communities settling on land offered to them by local landowners. You know, Nimbin made legal history for the first ever application of group title ownership of land in Australia,' Anna enthused. 'Many who came, did so because they had *always* wanted to find a different way to live, to get out of the rut they were in - *most* people are in. Aquarius was the opportunity to learn what their options were, to share thoughts and experiences about sustainable living. *Of course*, some *were* just hippies or plain old party people.'

Jay, bored, kept glancing at Christa, hoping she would get Anna to explain some of the things *they* had wondered about in the past months.

'Is that why *you* stayed?' Christa smiled, unconvinced.

'To escape city life with us?' Jay chimed in.

Anna was quiet for a few moments, watching their faces.

'No, I fell in love,' she smiled. 'After I first fell over a rope holding his tent up!'

Now her siblings were the quiet ones.

'Oh boy, you should see your faces,' Anna laughed. 'If you don't close your mouths, you're going to swallow one of these damn mosquitos,' she said looking down, slapping her ankle.

Anna was about to enlarge on how she met Travis when she was distracted by the intense aroma of Youth Dew wafting towards them, announcing their mother's arrival on the deck.

Sitting down alongside Anna, Eva asked with a smile, 'How would you like an all-expenses paid trip to Germany?'

Handing Anna Peter's wallet and silver watch, its strap dangling, she said, 'Your *Papi's* watch his mother gave him when he turned 16 and his wallet.'

Anna turned the watch over and read the inscription. Eva continued, 'I don't have any contact details for his mother and, of course, he never had his old home phone number written down anywhere. I had this idea that if you could visit them and give them these mementos, it would be a fitting way to break the sad news to her. You remember the way to the house after visiting them in East Germany with your father, don't you? What do you think?'

A few hours after arriving back home in Sydney for the memorial service, it had seemed to Anna her mother had undergone a change since she last visited. Besides the perfume, *probably better on a much younger woman* she thought, and the abundant blue eye shadow and eyeliner, there was something else new. There was a distinct difference in attitude. The last time Anna had seen her mother looking so animated was on board their ship to Australia, peering through a little round window in a serving door. Her mother and Rosa at the captain's table, glowing in the attention of the men around them. She was too young that night to have any idea what it all meant, but she had certainly recognised something new in her mother since boarding the ship, just as she did again now.

Anna had stayed on after the memorial for a few days, hoping to enjoy a catch up with the family she had not seen for some time and, although she had a good time with Jay and Christa, *delivered a surprise announcement*, she had seen little of her mother, who seemed to have many commitments. Christa had told her, as they were saying goodbye at her car, that their mother had started going out in the evenings quite often in the last few weeks.

Now, winding down her window to stop herself getting sleepy, Anna thought, *sounds like we have* Die Lustige Witwe *operetta on our hands*. She remembered the movie based on it, *The Merry Widow*.

Looking down at the watch and wallet next to her, thoughts began swirling randomly in her head; *he shouldn't have left it like he did between us. We could have at least spoken about it, even if he didn't apologise. Maybe he would have explained his reaction that night was born of his fear of losing his daughter. But why punish me? Am I being punished by* Mutti *now for disappearing to Nimbin without saying goodbye, not coming back until this happened? Well, at least I didn't disappear to another country forever, without saying goodbye to her.*

The thoughts took Anna back to the *gasthaus* in Germany all those years ago. The mortified look on the ashen face of her dying grandfather. She glanced down at Peter's watch and wallet again. She wondered if his mother was still alive. She remembered he called her from time to time, but her mother did not know how recently he had spoken to her.

Anna could picture the old terrace house in East Berlin she had visited with her father. It wasn't far from Checkpoint Charlie. She didn't know the address, but she could find it easily. *One day soon I'll take the watch and wallet to his mother.* Mutti's *right, she should know her son has gone, not die wondering why he stopped contacting her.*

Christa wondered how long the phone had been ringing as she noted the time on her bedside clock. Eleven ten. *Not again,* she thought. *Another sleepover Mutti?* Pulling on her dressing gown, she hurried down the hall, anxious at the insistent ringing. It was a man's voice that came through the speaker Christa had switched the phone to.

'Is that Eva's daughter or friend, by any chance?' he asked.

'Yes, it is,' Christa answered, feeling apprehension wash over her. 'Her daughter.' She felt Jay's hand on her arm as he appeared quietly alongside her.

The person on the phone was the manager of a hotel in Kings Cross. Eva had been in the bar there all night with a group of friends who had subsequently left. Eva was now alone with a man that the manager had some concerns about.

'I don't think your mother is in a fit state to catch a taxi and she certainly should not get a lift with the gentleman she is with. Can you fetch her?'

'Yes, we will, please keep her there,' Christa said without a clue as to how she could get there. She only had her learner's license.

'I'll try,' the manager said, putting the phone down. He slipped the piece of paper with Eva's number on it, one of her friends had given him before she left the bar, back into the drawer of his desk.

'I can ring Mr Sharpe. He'll help us,' Jay called as he ran to his bedroom to get his teacher's number.

Eva's gentleman friend and the manager were in a heated exchange when Mr Sharpe walked up to the bar.

'Come Eva, it's time to go home. Christa and Jay are worried,' he said gently.

Eva's friend swung around, but the expletive he was forming on his lips froze as he faced the large frame of Mr Sharpe holding Eva's coat.

CHAPTER 18

Escapes

WAY DOWN BELOW HER, surrounded by sparkling blue water, Rosa could see what she had only ever seen in pictures before, the stunning Sydney Opera House, its sails glistening in the sun. Taking in the beautiful image, she suddenly felt optimistic about her future, not concerned at all about being alone after living with Jorge for so long. Arriving in a country where she knew no one did worry her a little though, especially after losing Eva's details to an incensed and vengeful Jorge. She thought she might be able to track Eva down through the local telephone directory if she was listed, if she indeed still lived in Sydney.

After a lonely few months, Rosa decided the best way to make friends was to go back to studying, so after living in Bondi Beach for a while - she had heard about the suburb from friends in Stellenbosch - she moved to inner city Darlinghurst where she commenced studies in shiatsu massage and macrobiotics at the East West Centre. Sustainability and the environment also became her passions and she made friends with likeminded people. As the months went by, it was not long before she became known as a prominent activist, often referred to as a warrior for the environment.

Her white t-shirts, with her protest messages emblazoned across her large bosom, ensured Rosa had no problem attracting the attention of cameramen and journalists who were more than happy to accommodate her provocative attempts to broadcast her pleas to the government or logging companies. Editors thought images of her leading a march down George Street were great for their readership and viewership metrics. A part of her always hoped Eva, or little Anna, whom she missed so much, would see one of the newspaper or TV stories and find a way to make contact with her, as she had been unsuccessful from her side.

The Byron Bay hinterland became of special interest to Rosa, and she and her fellow environmentalists were involved in several rallies in the area. Later, in Sydney, she became increasingly active in movements seeking recompense for Indigenous people who had suffered as a result of colonialism. She rose to international notoriety for baring her breasts to the queen during such a protest at a royal event outside the opera house. While she and her friends laughed at the image broadcast on the ABC TV news, Rosa, slightly embarrassed once the heat of the moment had passed, thought, *at least Eva is likely to see this and make contact some way.* Unfortunately, it did not get noticed by either Eva or Anna, but it did by Jorge on SABC news as he sat sipping his coffee in his Stellenbosch lounge.

Jorge managed to persuade the editorial office at the ABC in Sydney that, as her husband, who had flown halfway around the world to visit her, he should at least be given Rosa's phone number if not her address.

He was desperate to make contact in the hope of a reconciliation after several years of being alone and lonely. His affairs with the women that worked in his house had inevitably led to a scandal when one of them reported him to the police for rape. No legal action was taken, but his reputation became so tarnished that he lost most of his friends. He was also keen to be reconciled with the money Rosa had withdrawn from their joint account in South Africa. Remembering the day he had opened his bank statement, shortly after Rosa had disappeared, still made him bristle with anger.

Jorge was in the midst of outlining his proposal for their new life together when Rosa replaced the telephone receiver gently. *I hear you calling for me, my beautiful Northern Rivers.*

Christa felt slightly sad about leaving Jay behind, but the chance to be away from her home environment was exciting. She understood why her mother, who after years of uncomfortable censored and anxious living with an alcoholic and undiagnosed, possibly bipolar, husband was determined to enjoy the years she had left. Nonetheless, feeling uncomfortable with some of Eva's pursuits, she enjoyed following in Anna's footsteps to Sydney University.

Jay was in his final year at school and, during this period, he lost a second mentor in as many years. It was announced that due to illness, Mr Sharpe would be on extended leave. Shortly before the end of the final term, at a special morning assembly, his passing was announced. It had been a rollercoaster few years for Jay, not made any easier by a recent succession of strangers staying in their house. What Eva insisted were *just boarders*, there to help pay the bills.

'So, why does Ernie, and the previous boarders, need to sleep in *Mutti's* room if we have a five-bedroom house?' Christa asked Jay when they next met at a café in Everleigh. Jay was visiting his friends around the corner in Redfern.

'To save costs, of course. Don't they teach you anything at uni, Christa?' Jay grinned with a wink.

'Yes, and we really need to save after all the money *Mutti* made when Wolfgang bought the business from her,' Christa laughed sarcastically. 'Anyway, what's this about "calling the fire brigade", you mentioned on the phone?'

Jay laughed.

'Oh that, it was to get Ernie down from the magnolia tree.'

'What the hell was *Mutti's* boarder doing stuck up a tree?'

Sitting in the huge magnolia tree in Eva's garden, the cockatoo cocked his head to one side for a better view of his would-be captor, now climbing onto an even closer branch. Seeing his earringed pursuer's blond, spiky hair and wide eyes drawing ever closer, the bird could have been forgiven for considering him some kind of giant predator intent on *no good*.

Eva had bought the cockatoo from a nursery one day when she was buying plants. The owners no longer wanted him and he looked so forlorn sitting on top of his tiny cage, she could not resist. He was obviously not a young bird, his plumage a bit scraggly and yellowish instead of white, but he could still get his crest up with a flourish when he got angry, which he was now, at the threat of impending capture.

The nursery owner said he never flew away; *knew he would not be accepted into a flock, too old, alone for too long.* Allowed out of his new, much larger cage by Eva to roam as he pleased during the day, he had, however, decided he wanted to be near the other parrots that occasionally landed in the magnolia tree. Now there was a *human* in his tree. He watched with concern as his stalker clutched a branch alongside him and leant forward into the space between them, extending an arm, seeds clenched in a closed fist. The hand opened slowly, cunningly, ready to grab an unsuspecting parrot around the neck when it went for a seed.

The cockatoo examined the open hand for a few seconds before reaching forward, exposing pink skin between thinning neck feathers, and clamped his nut cracking beak around one of the extended fingers, resulting in a loud yell of pain. He squawked and flapped his wings in alarm, as the human flayed both arms out like a giant bird before plunging downward, bouncing off several branches and landing upside down in a large azalea bush.

'No. No,' Jay grinned at Christa's exclamation. 'It was *Mutti's* new parrot in the tree. She named him after Ernie, the boarder, when he fell out of the tree trying to get him down. Poor guy broke his leg. Slipped when the parrot bit him as he tried to grab it. *Mutti* said he could not come back after he got out of hospital because he frightened the parrot; that's why it went up into the tree in the first place, she said.'

'Oh my God,' Christa managed through uncontrolled giggling. 'So, she blames the innocent boarder, throws him out and re-names her parrot after him. Why does she allow the bird out of his cage anyway? Did she at least pay for the hospital?'

'Yes, but she says he has to pay her back over 12 months. You know what she's like with money.'

'She says Ernie likes to go for a walk, *he needs freedom like she does*. She tries to trim his wings, but he just bites her or grabs the scissors with that big beak.'

Jay's final year at school did end on a high note. Eva received a letter from the executor of Mr Sharpe's estate to inform them that he had left his Harley to Jay. He had become a competent rider, having done a formal riding course through the RTA and been allowed to ride Mr Sharpe's Harley regularly over the years.

Eva drove him to the service station that had stored the bike for Mr Sharpe during his illness. Jay felt very emotional as he threw his leg over the saddle. He chose to ignore the expectant smirks of the motor mechanics appearing from under cars and engine compartments, amused at his small frame astride the big bike; he knew their expressions would change when they saw how professionally he rode the bike off the concrete apron to join the passing Willoughby Road traffic.

When he turned down the road their house was located on, he saw Eva in the distance, waiting on the curb at the bottom of their driveway. The moment he quieted the thumping engine next to her, she said, 'Thank heavens you're here. I was worried. Such a big bike?'

'You shouldn't worry, I was taught by the best. Now hop on, let me show you how stable and steady a Harley is.' Jay's voice came, slightly muffled, from behind his helmet.

'I need a scarf for my hair,' Eva squealed.

Under his helmet, Jay raised his eyebrows the way Christa did whenever Eva put on her *girlish* persona.

'No, you don't, your hair will be under this helmet,' he said, taking the spare helmet from the carrier behind him and handing it to her. 'Come on *Mutti*, put it on. You'll love this!'

Eva had a sudden image of her two brothers standing beside their bicycles outside the *gasthaus*, laughing and pointing at her little legs. She had begged them to teach her how to ride. She remembered her words like it was yesterday.

'Can't you make the saddle lower?' she repeated to Jay now with a laugh.

'What?' he asked.

'Nothing, just a memory from long, long ago,' she said as she waved at their neighbour who was having a sticky beak over his fence, having heard the motorbike pull up. He raised the hose in his hand above the fence with a self-conscious smile, as if it was his only reason for being there. Then shook his head in amazement as he watched Eva don her helmet and throw her leg over the rear seat.

With Christa gone, Eva was less inclined to go out and party, feeling guilty about leaving Jay on his own during the evening. Except when she had a *boarder* who did not enjoy going out to bars to watch Eva flirt with men half her age, under the pretext that she *loved to dance, that's all*. If her boarder wasn't her partner for the night, then she insisted they keep Jay company, which her foster son disliked even more than being left alone.

Eva's boarders were often strange, Jay found. Ernie had been the exception. They had got on quite well and he found himself asking Ernie questions – subjects he had heard alluded to at school during breaks - he would not have asked others, not even his Pa if he had still been alive. It was he who explained how sometimes single, unattached ladies found ways to *fill in the gaps*, as he said. Jay had blushed and changed the subject quickly.

Ernie liked to party, so he was seldom available to keep Jay company, preferring to go along with Eva, to keep the younger women at the bar company when they lost their escorts to her, approaching them with her hips swivelling, hands held out in invitation to dance. When Jay had mentioned to Christa over the phone one day, that he thought Ernie felt Eva was more a mother than a girlfriend, she merely laughed and said, 'Then why the fuck is he sleeping in his mother's bedroom?'

Jay took the phone from his ear and looked at it with a quizzical smile for a moment, *she's more upset about these damn boarders than she lets on.* Putting it back to his ear, he just laughed, 'Teach you nice language at that uni, hey sis?'

Jay loved it when there was no other man staying and things were almost normal again, he and his foster mother playing board games or watching TV together in the evenings. Nonetheless, he felt a little sorry for Ernie, seeing him summarily dispatched after the tree incident. But when Eva came bursting into his room a few nights later, yelling that Ernie was a thief who had stolen her jewellery bag, he was totally taken aback.

'He must have taken it, because I said he had to pay me back for his hospital bill. He must have seen where I hide it. I'll have to call the police,' she said angrily as she left his room.

Springing from his bed and following her down the hall, Jay called out, '*Mutti, Mutti*, hold on, are you sure you've looked everywhere?' Her kids knew she had a habit of hiding things in a *safe place* then forgetting that she had, but Eva was already dialling. He was relieved to hear her ask for Christa, not say she wanted to report a theft.

Jay straightened and looked behind him, hearing a man's voice say, 'Your dad's got you well trained, hey son. Hope he takes you for a ride after you finish cleaning it?'

'Actually, it's my bike,' Jay said and the young policewoman standing slightly behind her partner, smiled and gave him a wink. Over her shoulder, their car on the road blocked the driveway and Jay heard Uncle Chook in his thoughts, *gandyan can do that, Jay*. Eva came out onto the deck and both police officers exchanged glances when she said, 'Morning officers, I'm Eva, that's my son Jay. Come on in. Jay put the kettle on, darling.'

Eva had phoned and reported the theft, notwithstanding Christa's pleas to her mother to look through all her cupboards carefully, *this won't be the first time you have forgotten where you have hidden something*. Putting mugs and a pot of tea on a tray, Jay noticed through the kitchen window that Ernie was still missing from his cage. Gone since yesterday, they had scoured the trees in the garden but not spotted him. *Maybe he's decided it's now or never to join a flock*, Jay thought as he picked up the tray and made for the lounge room.

The previous day, returning from yet another search of the garden, climbing the steps onto the deck, Jay suddenly remembered that one of the parrot's favourite pastimes, when he was allowed out of his cage, was to amble down the deck until he found Eva's bedroom French doors and his reflection in their glass panes. He would spend ages, yellow crest raised high, nodding his head up and down or tapping the glass with his beak as he made strange chirping sounds. Ernie, the boarder, had always said he thought the bird was trying to persuade his friend in the glass to join him to form a flock. Turning the corner to the side section of the deck, Jay saw there could be no reflection today. Eva had both doors wide open and even the doors of the cupboards inside were open. She told him later she had decided, *no more boarders, getting rid of man smells from my room.*

Over tea, Eva explained her discovery the day before and her suspicions as to who might have been responsible for taking her jewellery, given his young age and the circumstances surrounding his departure. It was the first time Jay had been in such close proximity to police officers and he found it interesting to listen to their courteous, yet efficient, questioning. His only previous knowledge was based on anecdotes of police brutality. These two seemed okay, he thought but he felt awkward nonetheless when they started asking about Ernie, the boarder, not the parrot.

The lady cop, who seemed to Jay to be the senior of the two, a sergeant from the insignia she wore, asked if it would be possible to see the room from where the valuables had gone missing. *To the crime scene,* Jay thought as they all stood, Eva leading the way to her room. They surveyed it carefully, making notes, asking Eva how Ernie might have known what she kept in her bedroom.

Jay did not often go into Eva's room, so while they drew a sketch of the room's layout, he was having a good look around as well and that's when his eye caught a slight movement of the clothes cupboard door. There seemed to be a tap at the same time, but he thought he may have imagined it.

'You say the jewellery was kept in that cupboard?' the sergeant said, pointing at the one Jay was standing next to.

'If you have those doors wide open, anybody could have slipped in and taken from that cupboard, don't you think?' the sergeant asked, nodding at the French doors.

'Only like that for the last few days, for an hour or two, airing the room. Normally closed,' said Eva.

They stood before the cupboard as they spoke.

'Okay to open this?' the sergeant asked as she reached out and took a cupboard door handle in each hand.

She opened both doors simultaneously and, from the top shelf, with a loud screech born of anger at his night of captivity, wings outstretched, yellow crest raised - a cross between Pegasus and a mythical unicorn - sprang Ernie, claws extended menacingly.

The sergeant screamed as she stepped back, colliding with the other policeman and they both fell heavily onto Eva's bed, collapsing the legs on the far side. Eva's nighty, always neatly folded in front of her pillows, slid down the slope of the angled bed followed by her now exposed, *way to fill in the gaps*.

The thump, as it hit the floor, set the black plastic vibrator off at maximum and the rasping sound it made, moving itself around on the hard wooden surface, had the cockatoo, which had made an ungainly landing in the corner of the room, nodding his again raised crest vigorously. Jay having never seen a vibrator before, assumed it was some kind of police restraining device that one of the officers had dropped when they fell. He retrieved it quickly from where it danced before the concerned bird, wings akimbo, and handed it to the sergeant.

She involuntarily reached out to take it, before recoiling, shrinking back embarrassed. So Jay, recollections from his talks with Ernie seeping back into his mind, handed it to Eva. She was standing motionless, vibrator buzzing in hand, face crimson, when there was a voice in the bedroom doorway.

'Oh boy!' said Ernie, the boarder, looking ungainly and unpractised on crutches, taking in the scene. He held a toilet bag in his hand.

'Eva, the bag you put my clothes in, those you could not fit into my suitcase, had this lying at the bottom of it,' he said with a smile, handing the toilet bag to her. 'You are lucky neither piece of luggage was stolen from the bottom of the drive where you left it, is all I can say.'

Everyone in the room, except Ernie, the parrot, knew what was in the toilet bag Eva was busy opening, having finally quietened and dispatched the previous thing she had been handed, to everyone's intense relief.

CHAPTER 19

After Aquarius

Sunbathing on the edge of the small footbridge across Goolmangar creek, feet dangling below her, Anna watched Travis in the deep section of the water hole below the causeway, running under Thorburn Street. Nimbin's swimming spot was relatively quiet now that the festival was over and it was less likely to be used as a communal bath by those who had camped on the nearby field. Most had gone home, but some had formed communes during the festival weeks and moved to holdings they had been able to acquire from farmers around Nimbin after the event.

In the days leading up to Aquarius, against a backdrop of distant hills and the surrounding neighbourhood houses of Nimbin, a sea of tents and other makeshift dwellings had arisen near the stream. The tent town included everything from VW kombi camper vans to free standing teepees and conventional tents supported with guy ropes. One young festival goer had built himself a tree house, hauling planks many metres up into a gum tree's not always trustworthy branches, *widow makers*.

Anna moved her feet back and forth in the cool water, as Travis repeatedly allowed himself to slowly sink below the surface, then reappear above it, breaking the still glassy water gently like a hippo coming up for air. She loved the image, his hair slicked back, face dripping, eyes as green as the water he swam in. He had done the same thing ever since their first date here. Today on the grassy slope above them, two young girls sat sunbathing. Anna could see one was continuously looking towards Travis, over her friend's shoulder. Sighing with irritation, Anna pushed her fallen bikini strap back over her shoulder.

Since the morning they had first met, she and Travis had bumped into each other by accident from time to time. In between her other festival tasks with her group, Anna had roamed various events and shops on Cullen Street, trying to look inconspicuous as she attempted to make the *accidental* meetings happen. To her delight, one day after they met up, he finally made a move. As they parted, he said, 'Hey, come down to the water hole tomorrow. We can have a swim and a picnic. There's a barbeque place under the trees near the stream.'

Now, having sat on the hot wooden planks for some time, her wait for Travis to offer a little more than the wave she had got when she first arrived at the pool was over when he called out to her, 'Come on in, it's fantastic.'

She swung her dripping legs out of the water onto the surface of the little footbridge, readying herself to go round to the shallow area where she could walk in, but Travis called, 'Just let yourself slip in there. The water's not too deep. You'll be fine.'

Anna wasn't sure she would be able to execute such a water entry, without looking clumsy, so she just stayed where she was, feet making a wet outline on the wooden bridge, undecided. The two young girls watching her, suddenly broke into giggles and that made up her mind for her. Glaring at them, she thought, *stuff you*, and slid gently into the water, praying her top would stay in place.

Reaching back over her shoulder, Anna lifted the long, wet hair pasted to her back as she exited the water carefully over the pebbles that formed the shore. Adjusting her bikini strap yet again, she turned around to Travis, who was emerging from the water behind her. She was about to say something *amusing,* she thought, about the fact that men were lucky *they did not have swimming tops to worry about,* when she saw he did not have any apparel to worry about. The only thing *he* was wearing, was a big grin. Up on the bank, watching through fingers spread wide over their faces in false modesty, Anna heard the young girls giggle loudly once more.

The kombi spluttered into life and Anna gave her departing friends one last wave. Hearing the engine's hesitant, unsure start, made her think for a moment it was trying to tell her something. *Are you sure? Staying behind. With a boy you hardly know. In a place you hardly know.* She could feel her heart thumping, the tears welling up, but then she felt Travis' hand slip into hers, *be still my beating heart,* smiling at him.

Anna and her friends had stayed on for several days after the festival at the uni organising committee's request, to assist their Indigenous visitors where needed, before they started their long journeys home. Her friends had not seen much of Anna in the evenings and, realising she had embarked on a whirlwind romance, they were not surprised when she informed them she was staying on.

Anna watched Travis' eyes above the surgical mask he wore as the nurse handed him a pair of scissors. She expected to see anxiety or fear in them, at what he was about to do, but what she saw was joy. Tears slipped from his eyes and disappeared down his cheeks under the mask, as he lent forward to the umbilical cord held near him.

'Come on Dad, you're about to help your daughter start her independent life – earth side,' the midwife said quietly. Anna watched his trembling hand reach out and close the scissor blades on the cord, before turning his eyes to her triumphantly and saying, 'Oh darling, you're amazing. What a wonderful gift you have given us. You must be exhausted.'

Anna smiled, 'You will never know the half of it. Now can I have my baby girl?'

After she took Romy from the nurse and held her in her arms again, Anna looked up to smile at Travis. He was saying something, but all Anna could hear was her father, *this one is all yours now, but soon when you have a baby brother or sister, you will have to share gifts like this.*

Travis moved from the end of the hospital bed and laid his hand on Anna's arm.

'Anna, did you hear me? God what was in that epidural they gave you? I must get back. I need to irrigate the beds.'

'I know. I know. See you later,' Anna murmured with a faint smile as Travis bent over to kiss her and the baby's forehead; *left with half the chocolate.*

Travis said he needed a job so he could pay for their baby's needs. Pay rent he believed they owed to Dorothy, for the granny cottage at the bottom of her garden, although she insisted she did not want any, just enjoyed their company and, especially now, the baby.

He had been hired by farmer Tom, he told her when he arrived home one afternoon looking pleased with himself, to look after the vegetables he grew for his roadside stall, a common sight on the roads of the Byron Bay hinterland. Their colourful presentation had become a feature of the countryside.

Dorothy filled in a few gaps in Travis' job description when they spoke later.

'There is more to his job than he lets on, Anna. He is also growing "weed" amongst the farmer's vegetables and herbs and selling it in the area,' she smiled.

Dorothy provided meals to some of the needy around town, from time to time, and they were her well-informed source of local underground information.

'Jack and I have been friends since not long after my mother, bless her soul, and I arrived in Nimbin, so I have kind of watched your man grow up, Anna,' Dorothy had said. 'Travis breaks the rules, always has. He knows he can get away with it. It's the charm. His grin. Authority doesn't exist in his life, can't believe anybody in authority really means what they say.'

'But he better watch out,' she went on. 'If the farmer - everyone knows how sentimental Tom feels about that garden - or Jack find out, all hell will break loose.'

When Anna had discovered Jack was Travis' adoptive father, she understood his aversion to authority, or any aggression he was confronted with. Until he was old enough to leave, he had lived in a home where the topic of enforcement was always at the forefront. The festival meant Travis was suddenly surrounded by likeminded people avoiding hierarchy and the authority that went with it. Keen not to miss a moment in this new community, he even set up a tent with them during the festival.

But still, Travis was a loner. During and after Aquarius, when others were attracted to tribal living, he preferred to go it alone. When they started their relationship, Anna had to use all her skills to persuade him they should accept Dorothy's offer of the cottage and move from the room they had rented. He finally acquiesced when the baby was on the way, but never seemed totally at ease in their new environment, it seemed to Anna.

Although she loved his gentleness and his easy-going nature, his lack of responsibility concerned her, especially when it came to birth control. His whispered words in her ear, *we know this is a safe time anyway,* would be with her for months after she fell pregnant.

Being a de facto live-in "grandmother", Dorothy decided she had to build up her baby care skills. The visiting midwife from Lismore, who came to help Anna develop her nursing ability, was intrigued by Dorothy's diligent attention to everything she said, hovering at Anna's shoulder.

She laughed when she said one morning, 'Okay, have a go yourself, just remember the basics,' and *both* Anna and Dorothy had reached for a nappy off the nearby pile simultaneously. The midwife played along.

'Okay, Granny, let's see what you've learnt,' she smiled.

'Hell with your "granny",' Dorothy grinned, '*Au pair* maybe. Bloody gorgeous Kiwi au pair.'

They were reclining on the loungers, in the front of Dorothy's shop, beside her rack of home sown dresses she liked to strategically place in view of passing tourists. Anna pushed Romy's pram back and forth, absentmindedly. Without moving her eyes from the noisy, feasting rainbow lorikeets in the bottlebrush tree near them, Dorothy asked the question that had been on her mind.

'So, are you ever going to get around to telling Eva she has a granddaughter? Hey, it's no use hiding, girl,' she continued dryly, as one of the dresses, lifted by the breeze, enveloped Anna's head.

Pushing the clinging cotton aside with a laugh, Anna replied, 'I don't know what's stopping me. I know it's wrong, but I am so resentful.'

Dorothy turned to her, but said nothing as Anna went on, competing with the chirping birds.

'I think it was my dad's memorial, when she showed so little sorrow. She seemed absorbed in her new image the whole time I was there. It made me feel resentful. He *was* my father, even if we were estranged. I wanted her to be visibly sad, at least on that day.' Anna was silent for a moment and then sighed, 'Not telling her about Romy is getting back at her, I suppose.'

'Yes, but besides being a rather drastic response, it's also *getting back* at Romy, even if its unintentional. Eva is her grandmother, after all, Anna.'

They were quiet for a while before Dorothy added, 'Maybe that was just Eva's way of dealing with her sorrow. Focusing on herself intently.'

'I know, I know,' Anna said. 'Anyway, if I tell her, she will see it as just another disappointment. It will confirm ...'

'Hullo Dotty, hullo Dotty, hullo Auntie,' came a chorus of yelled greetings from a trio of young Aboriginal boys going by on their rusty BMXs. The startled lorikeets took off en masse, screeching loudly.

'I told you before, don't call me Dotty, you little buggers,' Dorothy yelled back, smiling though, and their laughter rang out as they raced down the incline towards the town centre.

'On those bikes, they remind me of Jay when he first came to live with us,' Anna said, as she popped the dummy back into the mouth of a momentarily wakened Romy.

'On those bikes, they remind me of my childhood friends in Wellington,' Dorothy said.

'No BMXs in those days. I was the only one without a girl's bike. Those Maori boys teased me unmercifully about it all the time, but we were tight. God help any boy outside our gang who made a funny remark about my bike.'

Dorothy turned from where she had been following the young backs disappearing down the road, 'Those are good kids, come to me to find a meal sometimes. Their parents seem to struggle, have their disappointments alright. Saying that, we were interrupted?'

'Well, I dropped out of university, I have an Aussie hippie for a partner, instead of the upstanding German boy my father always recommended, and I will be poor for the foreseeable future. I can't bring myself to face the look of disapproval on her face.'

Dorothy shook her head slowly.

'I think the only look you will see of her face, will be the one that tells you she is overwhelmed with joy to find she has a granddaughter, to be honest.'

Rosa was on her lounger too, on the deck of her new home, a small, converted church she had found in South Lismore. Not long after she had first moved from Sydney, having received Jorge's unexpected phone call and rented a tiny room in the town, her lawyer in Spain, the only one she kept up to date with her address, had written to her about an inheritance she had received from her uncle. As her parents were deceased, she was the next in line when the childless man passed.

Her attorney had enclosed a cheque for a considerable amount of money. It had prompted Rosa to tie up two things in her life she had been agonising over. She immediately wrote back to her lawyer, asking that she refund the money she had taken from Jorge, even though it was only half of their joint account, which she felt was fair at the time, and to initiate divorce proceedings.

Sipping her tea, Rosa gazed out over the oval with its white clad cricketers, amusing her with their excited antics occasionally, yelling 'Howwww.... zat?' In the distance was Leycester Creek and beyond it,

Nimbin Road and the cemetery with its headstones now glistening in the sun. Her mind roamed as she scanned the distant graves. *Wonder if any of those poor souls have been washed away in the floods? I love my little church, but the agent could have mentioned it had only been converted to a home after being badly flood damaged and sold cheaply by the church council to a developer. Will there be another?*

'Paranoia?' she asked herself out loud.

Rosa smiled at another image her gaze caught in the distance. A kombi, brightly painted with flowers, passing down Nimbin Road, alongside the creek before slowing to turn left towards the town centre.

'Heading into town for something not available in Nimbin,' she said quietly to herself, the edge of her cup poised just below her lip. 'Probably en-route to the maternity ward.'

Since the festival, there had been a considerable increase in the population around Nimbin, mainly babies born to the new arrivals. Living in Sydney, Rosa had not gone to the festival, but had met up with many people who had attended Aquarius events. What they told her about it and the intentions of those that stayed, she had found really interesting, *an attractive environment.*

Suddenly it came to her. *Why not?* She had been driving home a few weeks ago when she had to stop for a commotion going on at the roundabout near her home. Traffic controllers pulled her over, while a huge vehicle with an old Queenslander home on its trailer, negotiated the roundabout. Helpers wearing coloured vests, running to and fro, waving their arms and speaking into two-way radios. *Why not, indeed?* she laughed out loud as she got off the lounger to fetch the yellow pages.

'What's that?' Rosa inquired of the estate agent, pointing at a small, dilapidated brick building sitting on top of an incline at one end of the property.

'It's an old cheese factory,' he said as he led her up the hill, looking incongruous in his smart suit and tie, a sweat stain all the way down the middle of his back.

'What, or who, is Norco?' Rosa panted, taking in the faded sign painted on the weathered brick façade as they reached the top.

'It's what became the name of the old farmers' cooperative, formed in Byron Bay in the late 1900s,' the agent replied, as they reached the building entrance, and he slid the huge wooden door open. Norco, he informed her had used it as a creamery until about 1950 when they closed it down and someone else bought it for cheese making.

'Of course,' Rosa said, 'seen the name on milk bottles.'

'All went down the gurgler when the dairy industry and everything else was in recession in the early 60s, especially around here,' he said, looking back from the entrance, his arm sweeping in the direction of the surrounding hills.

What looked a bit like a raised, shallow square bath on legs, stood in the middle of the concrete floor and alongside it, an old drum sat on a rusty frame.

'This is what they call a *curd table,* the owner of the land tells me, and this over here is the vat they made the curds in,' he said, patting the surface of the drum which wobbled like the bath when Rosa leant on it.

Rosa imagined she could detect the smell of cheese wafting around the old room as she walked carefully between the remains of rusty steel legs that must have held several other tables, long since removed. A patch of sunlight on the leaf littered floor, made her look up. She followed the shaft of light up through the ceiling rafters to the glassless window opening in the roof high above her.

'Whatever,' she said, turning back to the immense barn door. 'I can always use it for storage or something I suppose,' she added, as they left the old building and started back down the slope. 'I like the view of the surrounding hills from that flat bit down there, just right for my little house. Okay, let's do the negotiation part where you agree to make sure the owner accepts what I offer him.'

'Sure thing,' the agent said with a grin.

'Shit, what the hell is this?' Jay said as Eva slowed for the first time since they had driven out of Lismore towards Nimbin.

'Your language has certainly deteriorated since you started working for Wolfgang. Is it a requirement of workers on the site to swear all the time?'

Ernie gave a squawk from his cage on the back seat and Jay laughed.

'No swearing Ernie, you heard *Mutti*.'

'Oh, my lily-white socks, it's a church on the back of a jolly big trailer,' Jay exclaimed in an affected voice. 'Goodness gracious, what's that all about?'

'Well, I've heard it's possible to move whole houses nowadays,' Eva said, ignoring his sarcasm, 'especially when they're made from timber like this little church. I wonder if "the flock" is following their church,' she laughed, bending forward to look up at the sky through the windscreen.

'Don't mention the word *flock* around Ernie, *Mutti*, you know it's a sore point,' Jay responded.

Suddenly serious, he said, 'They are going to need all the trades to set it up, I reckon. Maybe we should follow them. See if I can talk to them about a job.'

'Well, we can't pass them, so until we reach a detour of some kind, we are stuck here following them anyway,' Eva responded.

It had been a big decision for Eva, to leave Sydney. She had agonised for months over the situation she had got into with her jewellery; the scene she had caused. She convinced herself that between the embarrassed police sergeant and Ernie the victim of her wrongful accusation, the story of her assumed jewellery heist, and it's closing scene, was bound to become known. Her growing paranoia had her believing her neighbours, if not the whole of Chatswood, would be laughing behind her back.

With Christa at uni and Jay in his gap year, working for Wolfgang as an apprentice carpenter, the timing was right to escape for a while. And why not Nimbin? Anna was there - they were going to surprise her - Jay was always talking about the place; about being near Anna again and maybe Dorothy was still there. So, complete with Ernie the parrot and groceries for a year, by Jay's account, after having had to load them into the car, they headed up the Pacific Highway towards the hinterland of Byron Bay.

The rotating orange lights and the back of the trailer seemed to be slowing finally and they eased up behind it. The whole image became even more surreal as the horse and trailer made a careful turn off the main road. They could now see the church, with its little steeple, side on as it crept slowly past the fences that had been removed and laid to one side. It began its slow ascent to the top of a small hill, looking like a paddle steamer rising up on an ocean swell. Eva and Jay could make out a woman at the top of the slope. She seemed to be clapping her hands and dancing, hips swaying from side to side, arms waving above her head of long black hair.

CHAPTER 20

Lost and Found

UNLIKE ANNA'S EXPERIENCE ON the pathway to the general store, when Eva and Jay arrived in Nimbin for the first time, *their* introduction to the feral roosters was at a pedestrian crossing - the only one in the town and seldom used. Driving slowly down Cullen Street, Eva spotted them sitting on the crossing's iron "jaywalker" fence. Her attention caught by their large flaming red wattles, she was about to point them out to Jay when, suddenly, they opened their wings and dropped down onto the zebra crossing in front of their car.

As Eva came to a rapid stop, the larger of the two cocked his head in "one eyed" defiance directly at her, whilst the other bobbed his head a few times, before taking a stiff-legged step forward to peck at something on the tarmac. Jay laughed out loud, 'Only in Nimbin.'

At that moment, someone hooted behind them, and without looking back, he muttered, 'Fuck off,' under his breath.

'Jay!' Eva remonstrated as she pointed over her dash and downward in an exaggerated way, trying to show the driver behind her there was a hazard.

The situation was resolved anyway, when a woman with a stroller entered the crossing, forcing the roosters to take evasive action with loud squawks as she pushed towards them. The little girl sitting in the stroller, laughed gleefully, kicking her legs in front of her towards the birds.

'Saved by the granny,' Jay said, which prompted Eva to take in the woman's face a second time.

'Oh my God, I think I know her. That's Dorothy, I'm sure. She was the woman we told you about. The one who saved Peter that night.'

With the way now clear, Eva drove off but immediately pulled off the road into the first parking space she could find.

'Now what?' Jay asked.

Jumping out of the car with a "back in a minute" response, Eva took off back towards the crossing, past the quirky shopfronts of Nimbin, dodging between pedestrians, many of them tourists.

'He looks a bit scrawny, that bird,' a voice croaked immediately behind Jay, making him jump in his seat.

He had opened the window in the rear of the car so Ernie could get some air, while they were stationary, squeezed in as he was between suitcases and boxes of groceries on the back seat. The man straightened and moved his head from the window to stand alongside Jay who looked up at him as he spoke.

'His feathers are a bit yellowish, too. Does he smoke a lot?' the man sniggered. 'Nicotine smoke blowing around his feathers,' he said, waving his hands to indicate billowing smoke and began to laugh so loudly that passersby were turning to stare.

He continued enjoying his own joke until suddenly, the guffawing began to morph into a loud coughing fit. He bent over double, and

Jay thought he might collapse on the pavement right there in front of him.

The man was very thin, with long, unkempt hair just as discoloured as Ernie's old feathers. *That's definitely from smoking,* Jay thought. *And not just cigarette smoke, I bet.* Finally, he stopped coughing and between gasps for air, he asked Jay what his name was. Jay told him and he said nothing, just continued to gasp, bent over, his multiple-coloured braid necklaces and hair, dangling.

Straightening himself slowly he said, 'You couldn't give a man a few bucks Jay, could you son?' Ernie squawked his disapproval from the back seat and Jay imagined him bobbing his yellow crested head knowingly behind him.

Jay scrabbled in the glove compartment and found a few coins.

'All I got, sorry,' but before he could finish, the coins had disappeared from the palm of his hand and he got a wheezing thank you from over the thin shoulders as they moved away.

'Well at least we've met a local, hey Ernie.'

Eva had hurried down Cullen Street, poking her head into the doorway of each shop as she slipped between shoppers and browsers. Finally, she spotted the stroller parked on the veranda of a beautiful old building with an *Australia Post* sign attached to its aged weather boards. Below the sign were rows of post boxes buried in the old timber. Glancing up, Eva could see what she would come to learn was Blue Knob Mountain in the distance, behind the building. She decided to wait outside until the woman reemerged rather than try and talk to her in the line of people waiting to be served.

It gave her a chance to take in her surroundings for the first time since they drove into Nimbin, to take in the image of the town that would be her home for the next year or so. To try and sense the vibe of the place. It was certainly hippy-like alright, as she had been told by her Sydney friends when she informed them where they were moving to; *but it's nice*, she thought.

It has a happy feel about it, she thought as she took in the imposing, but joyful, image of the Hemp Factory shopfront a little further down the street.

At that moment, a woman carrying, what Eva estimated to be, a little girl just over a year old appeared at the post office entrance. The child wore a wide-brimmed sun hat pulled down over her face and was busy unwrapping a lolly. *The lady at the counter*, Eva guessed. As the woman bent to lift her back in her stroller out of the sun, Eva said, 'Oh my, should you be allowing your grandchild sweets without mum's permission?'

The woman looked up, about to tell her accuser to mind her own business, but seeing Eva, her expression switched from irritation to amazement.

'Eva! Well, I'll be damned. Here of all places.' They exchanged hugs.

'How nice to see you after all this time. Thought you had cut me off,' Dorothy laughed, leaning back over, to adjust the sun hat. 'Anna has kept me up to date with your news. Sorry to hear about Peter. Are you okay?'

'Oh yes, fine. You get on with it. And who is this?'

Staying bent, Dorothy played for time, undoing and redoing Romy's safety straps, her mind in turmoil. *What should I say, or not say, about Romy? Anna and Travis were only supposed to be away two weeks and it has already turned into four, without a word from them. Anna needs to talk to her mother.* She decided to stall some more, give herself time to work out how to handle this new situation.

'Look Eva, I have to rush, sorry,' Dorothy said as she straightened. 'This is Romy. I am babysitting and better get her home for her sleep. How long are you here? Can you come over for tea tomorrow?' Pointing down the main street she said, 'I live just down there, past the shops, in Thorburn, to your left. Number 28.'

Eva said, 'Sounds great. We are here for about a year, maybe more.' She laughed at Dorothy's surprised expression. 'Yeah, I know, but Jay and I want to catch up with Anna and I decided it would be nice to be away from Sydney for a while. From what you said earlier, it seems you've kept in touch with Anna, so do you know where she lives?'

'I believe she is away at the moment,' Dorothy replied, anxious to move off without being obvious.

'Oh no. That's disappointing. Mind you, give us time to get settled I suppose, while we wait for her to get back,' Eva said. 'Where has she gone?'

'It's only for a few weeks,' Dorothy replied, avoiding the question. 'Sorry, I must go but look forward to catching up tomorrow.' She pushed the stroller down the walkway. *I didn't really lie, did I?* she thought to herself as she hurried away.

'Bye Romy,' Eva called.

Travis was still going on about the hostility he felt in the presence of the East German border guards at Check Point Charlie, as they turned the corner to walk up the street that had been her father's home for most of his young life.

'They seemed really angry,' he said, 'like we had done them a disservice just asking for right of entry into their country.'

Unfriendly individuals, especially ones in authority, always warmed to Travis' charms, but not this time. Anna had seen that Travis, unlike her, was not unnerved by the size of the guards towering over him in their great-coats. To her they seemed like angry giants. He smiled at them warmly, but their faces were impassive as they studied Anna's German passport at length. Travis' Australian passport had attracted no more than a cursory inspection.

'I think for some, it's born of pure envy of those who enjoy the pleasures of the west. For others, maybe the opposite, I suppose you're unworthy of the DDR,' Anna said, looking around at her surroundings once more to make sure she had remembered the route correctly from her previous visit. *Now to find the house.* 'Depends how you have been indoctrinated I suppose,' she continued, turning back a second time to look at the street name plate, askew on its rusty pole. It seemed familiar.

Peter's will had bequeathed his portion of their estate to Eva, except for a token payment direct to Anna and Christa. Long before the lawyer's letter and cheque arrived, Anna had already planned to visit Peter's mother, knowing Eva said she would pay for it. So, with the extra money, she decided Travis and her could do the trip together. He had never been overseas.

It was important that Peter's mother knew of his passing and she felt it would be some kind of closure for her, given her deteriorating relationship with her father as she grew older, culminating in the terrible scene after her first date. Dorothy had been more than happy to have Romy all to herself for a few weeks. Well into her second year, Romy was already delighting them daily with her new words and antics. For her part, Anna couldn't wait to have Travis all to herself again, a second honeymoon; actually, maybe the first, *all the chocolate this time*.

Anna took a deep breath, smiled at Travis, and let the heavy cast iron doorknob drop against the flaking paint on the door. It was the third house they were trying and pretty sure they had the right one this time. There was a muffled voice calling to someone else inside before the door opened.

'*Guten Morgen, kann ich dir helfen?*'

Anna recognised the man who stood in the door frame greeting them, from her previous time. He was younger than Peter, but obviously his brother. She wished she could remember his name.

'*Guten Morgen, ich bin Anna, Peter's tochter. Und das ist Travis,*' Anna smiled. Travis offered his hand, assuming he was being introduced when he heard his name mentioned.

'*Oh ja, ich erinnere mich jetzt an deinen vorigen besuch mit Peter,*' he said, indicating he remembered her previous visit and shaking his hand, he introduced himself to Travis.

'*Ich bin Otto. Bitte kommt herein.*'

Thanking him, they followed Otto inside. He led them to a lounge room where, in front of a large hearth with a slightly smoky smelling log fire, sat Peter's mother in a wheelchair. She looked very old and frail, wrapped in a blanket despite the intense warmth from the burning logs. Otto had told them in the hall that she was unwell and had severe memory lapses.

'I don't know if she will remember you, or even Peter for that matter, if it is one of her bad days.'

Anna and Travis exchanged greetings with the old woman, and she seemed receptive, if not warm, to their presence after Otto explained who they were. Once they were all seated, Anna spoke of her sad tidings.

'*Es tut mir leid – ich habe schlechte Nachrichten.*'

She told them, as gently as she could, that Peter had drowned in a swimming accident. Both Otto and his mother seemed not to have heard her, but then Otto sighed heavily and stared into the fire.

Anna reached into her bag for Peter's watch and wallet and handed them to his mother. She took them but said nothing. Her face seemed impassive to Anna, as she stared at the two objects she held gently in her hands. But then she turned the watch over and, after putting on her glasses with trembling hands, read the inscription on the back. Anna saw a tear work its way down her pale, wrinkled cheek and leant forward holding out a few tissues she had pulled from her bag.

'*Dein Verlust tut mir leid,*' she whispered, putting her hand on the thin wrist of Peter's mother.

'*Mein Sohn ist schon lange weg,*' the old lady murmured, dabbing at her eyes.

Hearing his mother say his brother had gone a long time ago, Otto nodded slightly, not moving his gaze from the fire. They sat in silence, except for the odd crackle from the burning logs.

'Well, that was intense,' Travis said, as they walked back up the street an hour later. 'Do you feel it was worth the trip?'

Anna looked up at him, thinking he was being ironic, but the look of concern for her on his face told her otherwise. She slipped her hand into his and said, 'I don't want to talk about it right now. Later maybe.'

He gave her quick kiss on her cheek and said, 'Sure.' Then he said, 'Hey, I know, what about a quick detour to have a look at the Brandenburg Gate from this side? It's only about five minutes from here and then we can head back to the border crossing. Bit of a distraction, hey?'

A few minutes later, they turned onto *Unter den Linden* boulevard and in the distance, they could see the monument at the far end of the *Pariser Platz*. They were soon on the edge of the *platz* but held back by a barrier with an armed East German guard patrolling a short distance from it. They stood for a while, taking in the history of their surroundings, not oblivious to the menace of the guards nearby.

'This is silly, you can't get close enough to really see it properly. I wanted to see how they restored the war damage to the columns,' Travis complained.

Anna was surprised when he suddenly called out to the guard, who turned to glare at him, kalashnikov hanging from a strap over his shoulder. Travis tried to indicate to him that he wanted to get closer to the gate, but the guard ignored him and turned his back. With that Travis suddenly ducked under the barrier and Anna cried, 'Travis what are you doing? Are you mad?'

'Come on. They won't do anything. They know we are just tourists. No danger to them. Just being curious,' he laughed. 'Come on, quickly before they realise anything.'

Anna was mortified, watching Travis walk on, the only civilian on the spacious plaza. A guard, seeing him approach, called out to him, 'Can't you read? No further. Go back. This is the state border to East Germany.'

He was about the same age as Travis and today was his first time on duty since completing his training. He was totally taken aback at Travis' lack of concern and unsure how he should react, conscious of the senior guards watching the scene unfold.

'Don't worry, I'm not escaping. I just want to go to the Brandenburg Gate,' Travis laughed as he passed by, unperturbed and was warned again.

When Travis also ignored this warning, the guard shouted at him as he walked on. Alarmed by the yelling, two other border guards ran to the scene to block Travis from continuing any further. They stood in his path with their guns clearly in view.

Travis was suddenly surrounded by a triangle of guards. Anna called to him to return before shouting to the guards in German not to be concerned, that her man was just being silly, *would they let her come and get him, bring him back?* Travis finally seemed to realise he might be putting himself in danger and turned back to the first guard, who immediately shouted that he would make use of his weapon if he did not stop.

'You guys aren't shooting,' Travis answered, confident he would not be hindered forcefully, or shot at, while walking in this very visible public site.

He had covered about 50 metres before turning back and would have had another 250 to go before reaching the gate. The guard called out again, as Travis approached him, that he should stop and give himself up for arrest. Travis believed he could still defuse the situation and, as he neared the guard, he grinned and extended his hand in greeting, but the guard read the gesture as an attempt to take his weapon from him. The only other time the young man had seen a hand reaching towards the barrel of his weapon, was when his instructor was demonstrating what could happen if you got too close to your enemy - they could snatch your weapon from you.

Anna was sure the guard, who appeared extremely uneasy and anxious as Travis approached, had never had to deal with a situation like this before. He gripped the handle of his kalashnikov and pointed it, with one hand, at Travis. When the Australian, still grinning, did not stop, the guard aimed his gun at Travis and fired. Travis collapsed to the ground as the one burst of fire hit him in his stomach, chest and upper arm. Within seconds, he was surrounded by several guards and quickly manhandled from view, while Anna, screaming and sobbing, knelt alone on the cold damp paving of the *Pariser Platz*.

She had already been held by the *Stasi*, East Germany's secret police, for about a week when they gave her the news. A doctor had come to the room she was held in on the first day and administered drugs to calm her and help her sleep. They did little to numb the pain she felt. She was in a state of shock. She felt she was in an extended nightmare, wished it *was* a nightmare.

When they confirmed that Travis had been taken to the People's Police Hospital, where he had died, Anna was unable to respond – numb. She had known when the shots were fired, she had lost him. The only other information she got was, the guard involved had been awarded a medal for his bravery.

Her requests to be allowed to speak to the West German Mission in East Berlin had been denied from the start of the ordeal, because she refused to tell the *Stasi* which radical group she and Travis belonged to and what was behind their illegal activity at the Brandenburg Gate. Her repeated denials were met with contempt.

Jay's Harley Davidson had been delivered to the little house Eva rented on the outskirts of Nimbin the previous afternoon and he insisted they use it for their visit to Dorothy. Eva still felt a bit nervous on the Harley but as she had refused to allow him to ride it to Nimbin, it's *just too far and too dangerous for someone of your age, Jay,* she thought she should humour him and agreed with his suggestion.

Dorothy's BMX riding young Aboriginal friends were in awe when they saw Jay and Eva pass by. They hoped that what they were seeing was one of *their* mob, riding the big throbbing Harley down Cullen Street. They pedalled like mad things behind him, calling out and whooping as he and Eva rode loudly through the town centre, barely turning a head on the pedestrian walkway. Nimbin folk were used to unusual sights in their main street.

After entering Thorburn Street, the young boys still trying to catch up, Jay slowed as they counted off the house numbers, although most were missing or overgrown by flowering creepers.

'That's it, number 28,' Eva said loudly enough to make herself heard through Jay's helmet.

He brought the big bike to a stop in front of Dorothy's house. While they were removing their helmets the boys arrived, gathered around the bike, alternately whistling and repeating, 'Deadly man, deadly,'

'This is Dotty's house. You her *bunji*?' one of the boys asked.

'Nah, not my friend,' Jay said. 'She's my mother's friend.'

'Oh.'

'Our *bunji*, Travis, lives here too. He has good dope,' another added.

'Shut up,' the oldest of the trio whispered, giving the speaker a cuff across the back of his head.

'Who's your mob?' one asked Jay.

'Wiradjuri,' he answered. 'Dubbo area, way inland from Sydney.'

'We're Bundjalung around here.'

'We are all *bunji* then, if you know Dotty too,' the smallest of the boys concluded excitedly with a sweep of his arms.

'What have I told you lot about calling me Dotty?' came a yell from Dorothy's veranda and the boys all laughed as they scrambled onto their bikes and hurried off before she could get to the gate.

'So, you're the Jay I have heard so much about,' Dorothy said, as they followed her up the steps onto her deck where she had teacups set up on a small round table. 'But Anna didn't tell me you had such a big motorbike,' she said looking back at Jay with eyebrows raised dramatically.

'Oh, she didn't know, Auntie,' Jay smiled. 'It was given to me after Anna had left. And I didn't ever tell her about it, I wanted to surprise her one day when she visited us in Sydney. *Did* she know, *Mutti*?' Jay asked turning to Eva, who shrugged, resisting a comment about how little she and Anna spoke.

'I'll just put the kettle on,' Dorothy said as she walked towards the door of her cottage, then stopped. Looking back down to where Jay sat, she said with a smile, 'Oh and Jay, I appreciate the respect, but Dorothy is better, okay?'

'But not *Dotty*, right?' he laughed as she disappeared through the front door.

'Nope, only Romy is allowed to call me by that name,' they heard her say as she walked down the hall.

Listening to the muffled voices of Jay and Eva down the hall over the heating kettle, Dorothy gazed out her kitchen window towards the tiny cottage Travis and Anna stayed in. She marvelled at how fate had brought them all together. She recalled Eva's concerned expression as she opened her front door the first time they met. A much younger Anna behind her, alongside her little sister, both eyeing her torn blouse with its large safety pin holding it closed.

And years later, the serendipitous opportunity to have both Anna and Travis living so close by. To be, in some small way, involved in the birth of Romy; *darling Romy, how do we introduce you to your grandmother?* A woman, who soon after we met, was finding out from me why her husband had possibly tried to kill himself. Now I am about to inform her she has been a grandmother for over a year; *ah right on cue*, she could hear Romy calling as the noise from the boiling kettle subsided.

'That's Romy,' Dorothy called as she emerged from the kitchen. 'I'll just change her. Back in a few minutes. Want to make the tea, Jay? Kettle's boiled,'

They heard her say, as she went down the hall, 'Coming darling.'

'There you are, look who's come to visit. This is Jay and Eva, Romy. Remember Eva from yesterday? Say hullo, darling,' Dorothy said as she sat, putting Romy down in front of her.

Biscuit clutched in her little hand, Romy took in her visitors briefly, before turning away to bury her face in Dorothy's lap. Dorothy looked up at Eva to say something like, *don't worry, she'll thaw out in a minute*, but she saw the look on Eva's face.

'That's Anna's daughter, isn't it?' Eva said, and she didn't need Dorothy's expression to know she was correct. 'She's this old and I don't know I have a granddaughter?'

Eva had not been able to see Romy properly in town with the stroller hood down, in her sun hat but now she could see a *"baby Anna"* before her.

As Romy began sneaking quick looks at Eva and Jay, Dorothy said, 'All I can say, Eva, is Anna has been in a very confused place for the last couple of years and I can assure you, she has agonised over why she hasn't told you. I tried to get her to go to counselling.'

Eva seemed to not even hear Dorothy's words as she fell to her knees, tears in her eyes, arms open in front of the little girl saying, 'Come Romy, can Nanna have a hug, please?'

Romy was by now holding on to Jay's knee, insisting he take the biscuit she held out to him. As he observed her, flummoxed, she turned to Eva and leaving her biscuit on his knee, took a few steps before leaning forward into her new grandmother's arms.

CHAPTER 21

Revelations

CONCERNED THAT THE LAST time he had heard from Travis was nearly a month ago and knowing he was in East Berlin, an increasingly worried Jack decided he should make some enquiries about his son's whereabouts. Taking advantage of his connections in the police force, he was able to initiate the process of establishing Travis and Anna's whereabouts in Germany. Enquiries were relayed to the West German Police and the Australian Embassy in Germany.

The *Stasi* had finally relented and allowed Anna to make contact with the West German Commission in East Berlin and she was visited immediately by a case officer. They relayed her request to inform Travis' father of his son's death to the Australian Embassy in East Berlin, while the West German Government immediately secured Anna's release. The *Stasi* were less forthcoming about Travis, however.

Their response to the West German Commission's query on Travis was their standard response to border shootings, 'A border provocation of his own causing.'

It was known that the *Stasi* always tried to hide those shot in border crossings. The bodies were either cremated at *Baumschulenweg* or, if the person survived, they were taken to a *Stasi* run hospital. Should they recover they were sent to a *Stasi* prison after that.

The constable at the front desk of the Nimbin police station rang through to Jack to say the local area commander from Lismore was at the front desk to see him. With growing concern, Jack got up from where he sat at his desk. He could not remember any senior rank coming to Nimbin unannounced. The commander was a large man and Jack held his breath as grave-faced he lowered himself into the small standard issue office chair the constable had just positioned at Jack's desk. After the commander's first few words, Jack felt he had left his body. He was suddenly at the door to his office looking in, observing the commander from behind as he informed the officer, rigid behind his desk, that his son was dead. He felt sorry for the officer, relieved it was not he who had lost his son.

When Dorothy opened the front door of her cottage to find Jack standing there, she was taken aback at his expression. He looked stricken, lost, desperately trying to get his thoughts together.

'Jack, you look like you are about to arrest me, what's up?' she laughed but felt a prick of panic somewhere deep down inside her.

'Let's sit down,' he said, leading her down the hall to the lounge and a sofa where he was able to sit beside her. He took both her hands in his, her concern growing as she felt his hands trembling.

'Dorothy,' he said, stifling a sob. She was suddenly terrified. 'Our son has been tragically lost. He was killed in a shooting in Germany.'

Dorothy's whole body shook. She wanted to ask him a normal question, *by whom? who told you?* but all that came out was a strangled gasp and then a sob, before she lost control as he took her in his arms. Moving back from him after a while, in a daze, Dorothy forced herself to listen as he gave her the facts known to him thus far.

She decided, she was only going to survive the next few minutes if she started *doing stuff*. She made them tea. Went and checked on Romy having her morning sleep. Stuffed clothes into the washing machine – some not dirty. She stopped and returned to the lounge when Jack called out to her, 'You OK Dorothy? Where are you?' Rejoining him, she asked what Anna's situation was. Where was she? How had the authorities known where to contact him?

Without realising it, they had begun the process of acceptance when they started reminiscing about Travis. It had helped them to just talk, share memories. The decision she had to make, all those years ago, when Jack's wife, who had never been able to fall pregnant, suggested she and Jack adopt the baby that Dorothy had discovered was on the way.

Dorothy had felt she was nowhere near ready for motherhood, was already nursing a bed-ridden mother and trying to build up her business, so she could support them both. There were no jobs in Nimbin and Lismore was too far and would have meant the whole day away from her mother's bedside.

'At least the baby will be half mine by birth,' Jack's wife had said philosophically. Her initial anger after Jack had disclosed the affair, seemed to fade as she sensed an opportunity to fill a void in her life. Nonetheless, neither Jack, nor Dorothy, had ever stopped marvelling at her selflessness or forgiven themselves for their dalliance and lack of control.

Jack tried to persuade Dorothy to call a friend to come and stay for the night, but she said no. *Tonight I need to be alone, to grieve when Romy's asleep. Tonight's for weeping alone.*

'Should I ask Eva to come and fetch Romy for a few days?' he asked. Dorothy had told him about Eva.

'No!' she cried out, surprising herself with how emphatic she was. 'She is all I have left of my boy; my son who never knew I was his mother.' She wiped tears from her eyes. 'His little girl. My granddaughter.' Then more quietly, with a glimmer of a smile, 'She is what will get me through this.'

Jack sighed and looked at his lost son's mother. They had become close over the years. Since his wife died over five years ago, he had even thought they might get together again, but it would have been too awkward given Travis had no idea who his birth mother was, and they would have felt compelled to tell him. Jack's wife and he had decided they would not tell Travis that Dorothy was his mother, unless he specifically asked for the name of his birth mother.

He got up from his chair. 'I need to get back to the station Dorothy, find a way to bring Travis home. Call me if there is anything at all I can do for you.'

Anna felt a little better as the Boeing rose through the thick blanket of cloud hanging over Berlin into the bright sunshine above. She had not seen any sun for weeks. When she had finally emerged from the gloominess of the prison cell and was ushered into a diplomatic vehicle, waiting outside the heavy steel gates of the prison, it was grey and raining. The brightness, radiating through the little window alongside her now, made her think of being in Dorothy's backyard playing with Romy and she smiled despite herself. She mourned for Travis, trying to block the ghastly scene on the *Pariser Platz* that came to her over and over again. She could not wait to hold their baby girl in her arms, to be reunited with the sweet scent of her. To feel closer to Travis through her. To wash the scene of his death away.

Rosa was planting shrubs in front of her new deck when she heard the sound of a motorbike coming up the hill behind her. The deck was recently attached to her little church house which stood proudly halfway up her sloping property. It was on a flat piece of ground high enough up to give a 270-degree view over the surrounding green hills once adorned with red cedar, before being felled and devoured by sawmills.

She raised herself from her kneeling position and, removing her floppy cloth sun hat, wiped perspiration from her brow and face with it. The rider stopped his big bike a respectful distance from her and after quieting the engine began taking his helmet off.

'Gidday, mate,' Rosa called in a Spanish version of Australian dialect. 'You're my first visitor.'

'Gidday, Auntie,' said the rider, playing along. 'Like your house.'

'Thanks. I like it too. Still got things to do,' Rosa smiled.

'That's why I came. We saw your house being transported up the hill to you, few weeks ago. You looked happy to see it arrive, standing up here.'

Rosa giggled, 'My jig? The driver was impressed, laughed like a drain.'

'We were held up behind the big lorry carrying it for ages. Wondered if you might need things done. I've been working as an apprentice builder for about a year. Can do carpentry stuff. Quick learner and I need a job.'

'Who is "we"?' Rosa smiled.

'My mother and me, I'm Jay. We're renting a house just up the road. Between Nimbin Rocks and the town,' Jay responded, pointing in entirely the wrong direction, making Rosa smile.

'Oh, I see. And are you and your mother *Bundjalung*?'

'No, I'm *Wiradjuri*, she's German.'

'Oh,' said Rosa, trying hard not to look surprised. 'Okay Jay, that's enough questions. Let's go and have some tea and talk about what jobs you can do for me.' She led Jay up the steps onto the deck.

'Mind these,' she said pointing downwards, 'they're still slippery from the oil I just put on, and I'm Rosa by the way.'

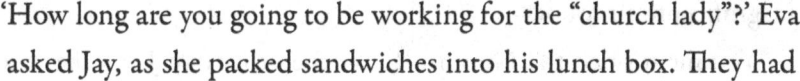

'How long are you going to be working for the "church lady"?' Eva asked Jay, as she packed sandwiches into his lunch box. They had bought it when he started working for Wolfgang. It had felt weird to Eva doing a lunch box again, something she had done for Peter for so many years.

'Auntie says once we have fixed all the things from the move, she needs help in the garden. I don't mind, its good money,' Jay replied.

'And what do you need all this money for?'

'Saving it.'

'What for?' Eva asked, snapping the lid on securely and handing the container to him.

'Just saving. You said it's good to "save up",' Jay answered, and Eva burst out laughing.

'Well, there's nothing wrong with that, my son,' she said giving him a hug, holding back an unexpected tear sneaking out of each eye.

'You tell your *auntie*, she's found a good one to have as a worker,' Eva said, tapping on the helmet he had just slipped over his long black curls.

As the days passed, Jay became more confident in his interaction with his new boss and asked her why she had moved to Nimbin. While they worked in the new garden, Rosa told him about her past activist work in Sydney and around Nimbin. Previously, she had travelled all the way from Sydney to be here for anti-logging protests but, needing to move from there anyway, she had decided to join the many who had stayed after Aquarius. Living here, she could continue the fight for the Terania Creek basin, one of the last remaining tracts of the once magnificent rainforest.

'You mentioned the Nimbin Rocks the other day, Jay. Like you and your mum probably did, tourists stop their cars when they see them, get out and admire them. I often wonder if they ever think of the protection the beauty they are enjoying requires. Being part of an ancient, eroded volcanic dyke, they are home to a number of threatened flora, as well as the glossy black cockatoo. And just as important, the millions of years of Aboriginal culture that needs to be secured.'

'You know, we didn't think of *any* of those things,' Jay said, shaking his head.

Panting slightly from her digging, Rosa sat down on an overturned wheelbarrow for a break. She took in Jay's concerned expression as she wiped her face.

'It's going to be down to you young ones to save this planet, *bunji* – sadly our generation hasn't done a very good job of it.'

One day, during his lunch break, Jay walked up to the top of the property to investigate the old building looking down on them day after day. Heaving the large door open, its rusty wheels creaking above him, he wandered around the room intrigued, kicking at the swirling leaves in the draft his entry had created.

'Old cheese factory,' he heard from the door as Rosa came in.

'Wonder if Little Miss Muffet worked here?' she added. Jay laughed but then became serious.

Hands on hips, he observed the old cheese tables with their rusty broken legs.

'They could be fixed up; I could make new wooden legs. No

problem with the top parts. They're fine, just need a clean. Only surface rust, must be galvanised.'

'Whatever for?' Rosa said from behind him, heading for the door. 'Come on let's get back to planting young man.'

It was a tearful reunion between the three. Romy's tears, sitting on her mother's lap, because she was seeing the two women she spent most of her time with, crying for the first time. They tried to explain she was seeing *together again tears* but the elephant in the room was what had transpired in Germany. Finally, Anna had to force herself to give the details of the incident to Dorothy.

'Travis and his authority thing again,' Dorothy smiled sadly.

Anna would only learn a little later in their conversation, why the words she delivered must have been so painful for Dorothy. Anna was relieved though when Dorothy said *she* would pass on the facts to Travis' father.

'I have some news for you too, Anna. Somewhat lighter though, I am pleased to say.' Dorothy told Anna about Eva and Jay's visit and her immediate recognition of Romy.

'She was upset at first, but seemed to understand your predicament, given the past. But you and her need to talk things though, my girl. And of course, our Romy here was the "oil on the water" during that conversation,' Dorothy smiled.

Anna sighed as she stroked Romy's cheek gently.

'We better make it up to Nanna, hey darling? It's time for all of us to come together, don't you think?'

'Nanna come?' asked Romy.

'Yes, on a big motorbike by all accounts,' Dorothy laughed. 'You should see them on it. The odd couple alright. Ah, and I can see plenty of grandparent competition coming, around here,' Dorothy smiled. She took a deep breath, 'On that subject I need to tell you I am *officially* a grandparent, not just a de facto, as you thought.'

'Sorry? I'm not with you,' Anna said puzzled.

Dorothy came across and sat next to her, taking her hand.

'I am hoping what I am about to say will help in some way. You see, I am actually Travis' real mum. His birth mother, one he never knew of. And while we are about it, Jack is his actual birth father. So, there it is.'

'Wow,' Anna said softly, and for a few moments the only sound was Romy fussing about, getting down from her lap to go outside. 'I think besides this *one*,' Anna gave a resisting Romy a hug, 'I just got a part of Travis back to love.' Romy squirmed and giggled, sandwiched by two soft warm bodies, she was immersed in a family hug.

Sitting back and smiling at Anna, Dorothy said, 'Now, on a more technical note – and happy note, stop frowning Anna, as "Nanna" has been taken; to avoid confusion, I'll stay "Dotty".' Picking the little girl up from her mother and kissing her cheek, she added, 'But that's *your* name for me, no one else, ok Romy?' Romy giggled as Dorothy swirled her around in her arms.

CHAPTER 22

Reunions

'**WHATEVER FOR?**' **IT WAS** the second time that day he had heard a woman's voice ask that question, he thought as he slid out and replaced each book. Watching Jay, standing poised precariously on top of a kitchen stool, Eva wished she had not asked him to stack her recipe books on the top shelf.

'Are you planning to start making cheese?' Eva laughed, flummoxed. 'You will never be able to read my handwriting.'

'No *Mutti*, I just want to see the picture you stuck on the cover, of the cheese making things. I remember seeing it when I put all your books up here. Check if the stuff at Auntie's place is the same.'

'What do you mean? Does she make cheese?'

Climbing down off the stool, book in one hand, pushing his hair back off his face with the other, Jay explained his discovery earlier in the day, of the small building up the hill above Rosa's "house of prayer", as he called it. That it had once been used for cheese making. And when he saw how easy it would be to restore the equipment, he had an idea that maybe there was an opportunity for them to become part of the Nimbin community.

'*Mutti*, I've heard you complain about the cheese you buy so many times. How it's not as good as you and *your Mutti* used to make when you were young, in Germany. Telling Anna and Christa about the different recipes you have. The different herbs you used. Let's start making some. Sell it in the town.'

Eva watched Jay's face as he spoke. Smiled inwardly at his youthful enthusiasm. His suggestion couldn't have been more unexpected. Cheese making, out of the blue, from a 19-year-old. Jay looked up from the cover of the book.

'I knew it. It's the same as in the old building, stuff just like this,' he said, waving the recipe book at her triumphantly.

Eva lay awake in her tiny bed that night, yearning for her wide, comfortable one they had put into storage, with the rest of their furniture somewhere in Paramatta. She questioned what on earth she was doing miles from Sydney, in a town writer Austin Pick had suggested was like *a smoky avenue of Amsterdam placed in the middle of the mountains...a strange place indeed.*

'Oh well. It's not forever and at least I can spend time with my new granddaughter. What a surprise that was. I wonder when Anna will be back,' she said to herself. She switched on the bed side light and reached for the recipe book Jay had got down earlier. She thought about what he had said, about making cheese. Eva tried to imagine herself and Jay cutting curds together, bent over his refurbished curd table.

God, that seems a long time ago, she thought, staring at the picture of the old *gasthaus* cellar. Her mind wondered back to her father. She wondered if he would have liked Nimbin.

'He would have been a hit with his *pfennige* trick in the Nimbin Hotel bar,' she smiled to herself. 'I wonder how he would have reacted if someone offered to sell him drugs in one of the lanes of Nimbin at night.' Christa had warned her about that. How does she know such things?

She started doing some calculations in her head relating to a cheese making business, but her eyelids refused to obey her and she slipped into a deep sleep, waking only briefly as her recipe book slipped from her hands and hit the floor with a soft clunk.

Bomber and Caster lay panting in the shade, under the dense foliage of purple basil and Thai chilli bushes. They kept a watchful eye on their farmer human, lest he should decide to do something less boring for a kelpie trained to move cattle around. Tom was clearing weeds from around the red onions growing in his large vegetable and herb garden.

It had been his wife's project, this garden. She sold the produce through the stall at the end of their driveway; an honour system, although recently they had put up a sign warning there was a security camera – which there wasn't. *Sign of the times,* she had sighed. He could still see her exasperated expression.

Towards the end, there were tears of frustration at not having the strength to work in her garden. To try and put her at ease, Tom would spend as much time as he could in it. Taking back anecdotes to her bedside, of any changes, progress her young plants were making, discovery of a new pest. She would listen intently, giving instructions for the following day. When she died, as busy as he was with his dairy farm, he had kept the garden going, in remembrance. Until he had gone off to Sydney, his son, Steve, had helped with it. Tom believed it had been a healing activity for both of them.

Glancing at his watch, Tom saw milking was about to start. Looking around the gardens one last time, he decided he had given Travis enough time to come back to work. He assumed the young man had lost interest or had found something else. He knew he had gone overseas, but that was supposed to be for just a few weeks. He had promised Tom he would get back to the garden as soon as he could.

'Better ask Jack what his boy is up to next time I see him,' he said to himself as he rose from his kneeling position, above the pungent scent of the long green onion leaves springing from their red bases, increasingly visible in the dark soil.

'Come. *To me*,' he called, and the dogs appeared in an instant from where they were hidden under the dense foliage, to execute simultaneous muscle stretching *downward dogs* before him.

Christa and Steve had been sharing an apartment in Newtown for over a year when she announced to him one day that her family was moving away from Sydney. Without a backup home, she wanted to arrange a long-term lease on their apartment, to give her more security. Their apartment was midway between the station and Sydney Uni in a road off King Street, so ideally located.

Steve was already living in the apartment when Christa had responded to his note pinned onto a pole in King Street, seeking a flat mate to share costs. With a slight smile, he said he was okay with a long-term thing, but he did not want to be too locked in.

'You never know your luck in the big city,' he laughed, 'I might find a partner one day.'

'No problem,' she said, 'I'll take it in my name, I'll talk to the agent.'

'If you're sure?' he said with a *you might regret it* inflection.

'Steve, come on,' Christa said, getting impatient. "So, who's our agent? I'll go and see them.' Steve had always handled that side of things, Christa just paying him *her* half of the rent.

'He's a dairy farmer in Nimbin, so it will be quite a trip for you,' he replied.

'Steve, stop fooling about,' Christa cried, slapping him on the arm gently, thinking he was being facetious, trying to remember when she had told him about Eva and Jay moving to Nimbin.

'Well, my dad owns this place. Nimbin's where our dairy farm is. So, your long-term tenancy is secure by default. Relax,' he laughed.

'Where are your family moving to?' he called later, from the kitchen, busy with their dinner preparations.

'I'll tell you over dinner. When we can enjoy it. I have to finish this assignment asap,' Christa called back.

'What?' he asked leaning backwards out of the kitchen door, so he could see her where she sat writing at their tiny dining table. 'Tell, me what? Enjoy what.'

'Later,' she said, without looking up.

Halfway through their meal, Christa asked out of the blue, 'They make cheese in Nimbin, don't they?'

Steve laughed and with a wink he said, 'Since Aquarius, there are plenty of interesting things being produced, Dad tells me. But seriously,' he continued, 'not dairy stuff anymore, all done in Lismore nowadays. That's where most of Dad's milk goes.'

'That's how my sister ended up in Nimbin. The festival I mean, not dairy stuff,' Christa said.

She went on to tell a now gaping flat mate about Anna and her new life in Nimbin and that it was the reason her mother and Jay were moving there.

Somewhat amused by her ever-increasing confidence on the back of the bike, Eva leant into each corner with Jay as they cruised past the Nimbin Rocks. Looking up at the immense cliff face she thought, *I hope this cheese factory business is an easier climb than that.* They were on their way to meet Rosa known as Auntie, Jay too embarrassed to ask her name after forgetting it, to discuss the possibility of using her old building as a mini cheese factory.

Coming round a curve, Jay braked the bike to give "Pothole Pete" a wide berth as he sprayed a large pink phosphorescent heart in the middle of the road.

'Hey, Pete,' Jay waved as they swept past. Jay had got to know him after driving this route every day to his job, stopping for a chat one day out of curiosity. He had told Eva, Pete had been saving people's wheels, possibly their lives, from potholes - a long-standing issue in the Byron Bay hinterland – spraying hearts around them.

'Sounds like he is likely to lose his *own* life if he's not careful,' Eva had snorted.

Now as they passed, he gave them a big grin and a double handed wave in return, spray can clasped in one.

The little church that had arrived to perch itself on a hill, overlooking the road to Nimbin, had become quite a talking point with locals since it had first been seen. No one drove past it without stopping at least once, to admire the new arrival in their countryside and, a few minutes later, as Jay and Eva came around a curve in the road, sure enough they saw a car parked on the road ahead. The occupants were looking up at the church, waving back to a woman on her deck.

Jay manoeuvered the Harley around their car and stopped in front of the gate at the end of the long driveway. He saw that a large gaudy hand painted banner attached to the fence had appeared over the weekend. It stated, 'No Logging in Terania Creek Basin.'

'What's that about?' Eva asked, as she got off to open the gate.

'Auntie and the environment, you will hear soon enough,' Jay replied.

Standing at the gate, Eva waved up at the woman and she thought she saw something familiar in the way the distant figure returned her greeting. Holding the latch with one hand, she gave Jay a theatrical bow, waving him forward, before closing it and climbing back on behind him. She had to hang on to him for dear life as they bounced over the ruts in the track up the hill.

Coming to a stop in front of the deck, Jay switched the engine off and waited for Eva to dismount so he could swing his leg over the saddle. But Eva was motionless peering up at the woman who had stopped dead in her tracks as she was about to come down off the top step.

'Eva?'

Rosa took a step down and stopped again.

'Is that you? Oh my God!'

Jay turned to look at Eva. She was still immobile, mouth wide open. 'Rosa?' he heard her murmur. Then much louder. 'Rosa!'

The bike lurched as Eva climbed hurriedly from her saddle to meet Rosa at the bottom of the steps. Jay felt glued to his seat as he watched what was unfolding before him. They clung to each other, both in tears. Then holding hands, yelling and jumping around in a circle.

Jay thought, *Some funny shakealeg, hey Jay?* Uncle Chook would say.

After a long tea on the new deck, Eva joined Rosa in the garden as Jay's replacement. Digging holes and smacking at incessant flies, they continued to swap endless anecdotes about their lives since they had last been in contact. Sometimes they laughed and once or twice felt a tear escaping. Once they simultaneously stopped their digging and, after exchanging looks, gazed out across the hills in silence, shaking their heads slowly. Reflecting on how they had come to be reunited in this least likely place.

Deciding he should give them time together, Jay had moved on to the other job he had started. He was up at the old shed, refurbishing the legs of the rusty curd table and vat, with large wooden posts he had had cut to size at the hardware store in Lismore. There were unused bolt holes in what was left of the old legs, so he simply bolted the new wooden legs to them. The rest was going to be hours of hard rubbing with steel wool to clean all the rust off the surfaces.

He would do the vat first so an electrician could begin rewiring and installing a new heating element. All the while, a glazier, Rosa said, had arrived just before he and Eva, stomped around on the roof above him repairing the skylights.

Eva was convinced that the key to their cheese making was finding a reliable supply of high-quality fresh, raw milk so she decided to visit Dorothy who knew everybody in the area and would be able to recommend a farmer to approach. Also, she had not seen Romy for days, so after getting Jay off to work and feeding Ernie, who showed how he felt about being enticed back inside his cage by trying to nip her fingers as she closed the latch, she drove off towards Nimbin.

Climbing out of her car and walking up to Dorothy's front gate, Eva discovered Romy sitting on the top step of the cottage deck with her dolls.

'Hullo darling,' she called as she walked down the path. A surprised, 'Nanna!' came straight back to her, accompanied by a big smile. As she bent down to pick her granddaughter up, she asked, 'And who's looking after my big girl out here?'

'*Mutti*,' the little girl said, pointing towards the front door.

'You mean Dotty, don't you darling? Dotty's looking after Romy,' Eva smiled.

'No, *Mutti*,' came the reply again as she held out one of her dolls towards Eva.

Hearing another quietly spoken '*Mutti*', this time from the doorway, Eva looked up from the little face to see Anna smiling at her.

'Anna!' Eva gasped.

As the two women embraced, Eva said, 'Oh, I am so sorry for your loss my darling.'

A little while later, Dorothy made them all something to drink. Anna and Eva had agreed it was time for the two of them to put things right. That at some stage, they would need to sit down and have a long conversation. Clear away the baggage that held them back as mother and daughter for so long.

When Dorothy rejoined them, Eva decided to tell them about the cheese making project she and Jay had embarked on. And then it came to her, Anna probably did not know about Rosa arriving in Nimbin.

'Anna you will not believe who Jay has started to work for here, through sheer chance. Someone who is also going to be our business partner. An old friend of yours,' Eva smiled.

'What? Up here? What old friend?' Anna asked, looking perplexed.

'She taught you to dance.'

'Dance? When? Come on *Mutti*, who?'

'Flamenco dancing? The ship?'

'Rosa? Rosa is here? How?' Anna exclaimed. 'I don't believe it.'

'Yes, she sure is and always the flambouyant one, she brought her own little church to live in.'

'Ah,' Dorothy said, 'so that's what the little church on the hill below the old Norco creamery shed is all about.'

'Yes, it is,' Eva smiled, 'and now let me tell you what that *old Norco creamery shed* is going to become.'

It was time for Romy's nap, so after Dorothy took her off to read her a story, Eva asked Anna what had caused the tragic *accident* that resulted in Travis' death. She was relieved to see that Anna seemed okay talking about it, although she kept her response to a high-level version, Eva could tell.

'Were you there because of my request after your father's memorial?' she asked.

'Yes, I didn't like the idea at first, but the only other way of informing them would have been through one of your brothers maybe, if we had had an address. Anyway, it was probably not appropriate, as I thought they deserved to see some sympathy and respect from us. I decided I would take *Papi's* watch and wallet back to his mother myself and inform them of his death. I knew you would reimburse me, and I was able to pay for Travis with the money Christa and I got from Dad's estate. It was his first time overseas.' Anna was suddenly in tears and Eva felt wretched for bringing the subject up.

'I am so glad we were able to let them know,' Eva said after Anna had composed herself.

Anna opened her mouth to say, *yes but at what cost to me*, but then stopped, *new beginnings*, she thought. Instead, she said, 'Well, they seemed appreciative that I had travelled so far to inform them. Peter's brother said to give you his and his mothers' regards.'

When Eva left, she carried with her the details on how to get to a farm owned by Tom, where she would be able to order and get the best milk in the district, Dorothy claimed.

As they said goodbye to Eva out on the deck, Dorothy said, 'You'll like Tom. He was the farmer Travis worked for. I've known him for years. Lovely guy. Sadly, lost his wife a few years ago. There is many a lady around here who regard him as very, very eligible,' Dorothy added with a smile.

'Maybe I should get into that line,' Eva said as she went down the steps.

'*Mutti. Mutti,*' Anna said shaking her head.

CHAPTER 23

'Nimbin New'

EVA DROVE ALONG THE windy rode up to Tom's farm very slowly. It was tarred but full of potholes.

'Where's Pothole Pete when you need him?' she said to herself, swinging the steering wheel violently from side to side. Finally, she saw the house, perched on top of a hill, *must give him a view all the way to the sea,* she thought.

Arriving at the start of the driveway, she turned off the tarred road and came to a stop in front of a gate with a long table protected by a corrugated iron roof, alongside it. Various vegetables were on display, below a sign that said, 'All proceeds to charity' and another that said, 'Security camera in use'.

Getting out to open the gate, she noticed the letterbox was hanging open and a few envelopes had fallen or blown out. She walked across to picked them up and stuff them back into the box, but as she did, for some reason she looked at the name on one. She nearly dropped it. *Why had she done that?* she would ask herself many times in the coming days. Disconcerted, she stuffed the envelopes into the box and closed the little door before turning and starting for her car. But she stopped and turned back to the post box, opened the door once more and slid one of the envelopes out. She scanned the name again.

'It can't be, surely? How can it be?' she said to herself as she moved shakily back to her car. Looking across the vehicle's roof as she reached for the door handle, in the distance she saw a lone horseback rider trotting up a grassy slope towards the house from the valley below.

Two dogs ran alongside the horse. She could hear their occasional barks, softened by the distance. Eva pulled the door open, banging her knee on the steering wheel in her haste to get behind it. She put the car into reverse and her wheels spun as she backed into the road before driving off erratically trying to avoid the potholes, which was difficult at the speed she was doing. After a tooth jarring thump through a large hole disguised by rainwater, she slowed and tried to calm down, as she headed for home.

'Just a coincidence,' she said to herself. 'Don't be foolish. It's not an uncommon name. Many with it in Australia probably.'

She drove on, vision blurred, tried to ignore the tears that ran down her cheeks.

'The hospital was gone. They were all gone,' she whispered.

'How did it go with the farmer?' Jay called, as he hung his helmet over one of the coat hooks in the entrance hallway.

'Think it would be better if you handled that, after all,' Eva said, hoping to avoid an actual lie. 'I did not like the look of the road up to the farm. Needs Pothole Pete badly.'

'Oh, okay, I'll ride over in the morning before work. Show me how to get there,' he said as he opened the map Eva left on the kitchen table. 'This poor map looks like it has been handled by someone who got frustrated trying to find the correct sequence of folding,' he laughed.

'Aren't they such a damn nuisance?' she said, picking up a teaspoon to point with.

Dismounting in front of Tom's large farmhouse, Jay enjoyed the magnificent 360-degree view before climbing the steps and knocking on the front door. There was no answer, so he strolled along the deck which seemed to wrap itself around the entire house. Approaching the rear of the house, he saw, not far from where he stood, what he assumed was a milking shed. In a paddock alongside, a herd of cattle were lined up, waiting for their turn at a trough of grain pellets while they were connected to the milking machine. At that moment, the farmer appeared from around the side of the shed and, seeing Jay, waved to him to go down and join him.

As he got closer, he heard the farmer call, 'Dogs, to me,' and two kelpies appeared from nowhere and, following a hand movement from the farmer, circled some of the cattle, moving them to where he held a large door to the milkshed open.

After Jay and Tom had introduced themselves, Jay told him how he and Eva had come to find the shed and their plans to make cheese. How they needed milk delivered to them. Just a small quantity to start with, but building up as they got their production going.

'Well Jay, who would have guessed the old Norco shed would ever be used again. Mind you, it was used by someone else after Norco, sold up in the 50s, until that land was acquired by a developer and divided up into smaller lots for sale.

'You know, I used to deliver milk to that place many years ago. Before you were even born, son. Before my own boy was even born. He's at uni in Sydney now. Okay, if you would like to wait around for a while, we'll finish the milking and then we can see what we can do,' Tom said turning back to the cows.

Jay watched, fascinated, as the dogs separated just a small group of animals from the rest of the herd and ushered them towards the entrance to the shed. *They understand every word he says to them*, Jay smiled to himself.

'Bomber, no!' Tom yelled as one of the dogs made to nip at a cow's leg. 'You don't do that. Even if it is just a bit of fun. Good dog.' Bomber wagged his tail and went and sat with the other dog, the two side by side waiting for further instructions. Or to be told they were off duty, Jay assumed.

Sipping his tea on the farmhouse deck, Jay told the farmer about his mother and him moving up to Nimbin and how they had met the woman who owned the little church.

'Her name's Rosa,' Jay said.

Tom smiled.

'So, it *is* Rosa who put the little church house there. I thought it might be when I drove past the other day and saw the banner on her fence. She's pretty famous around here. I'll tell you what, the logging companies don't like her,' he laughed. 'Good on her.'

'Yeah, she told me all about that,' Jay said. 'She's also our partner in the cheese making business.'

'Well, if she owns the shed, it makes sense, especially if you didn't want to pay rent. Now, getting back to milk, what is it you would like from me?' Tom inquired.

Jay scribbled in the notebook Eva had insisted he take with him, so he would not forget any of the information she wanted from the farmer. She had written a question at the top of each page. After getting a response to all Eva's questions, it looked like everything was going to work out well and, thanking Tom, Jay got up to leave.

'Before you go Jay, you said earlier that one of the things you had to do was create a herb garden for your cheese making. Well, here's an idea. I have a large, established herb and vegetable garden here. How about I offer you a job helping me maintain it and you can take what you like from it for yourselves and grow whatever else you require here as well. No need to find a suitable area on your hill, clear it and cart loads of topsoil to it,' Tom said, leaning back in his chair.

'Sounds interesting. Let me talk to *Mutti* and Rosa, but I think that would be great,' Jay grinned.

'Excellent,' Tom said. 'My previous worker went on holiday overseas and was supposed to be back working two weeks ago. I don't think my friend Travis is coming back, to be honest. Not to this job anyway, by the looks of it.'

As he spoke, Tom was perusing the clouds massing over the hills in the distance.

'More rain,' he murmured. Looking back to his young visitor, he was startled to see Jay's suddenly ashen face and open mouth.

'You haven't heard? Maybe it's a different person,' Jay stammered. 'My older sister lives here too. Very sad, her man died, was killed in Germany a few weeks ago. *His* name was Travis.'

With a deep sigh, Tom held the receiver above the phone and let it drop into its cradle with a clack before slumping back in his chair. He could still hear Jack trying to control his sobs as he had offered his condolences. The dogs at his feet watched him, concerned. They did not sense sadness in their human often. The girl, Caster, sat up and pushed her jaw across Tom's knee and he patted her head gently. She whimpered quietly as Tom murmured to himself.

'Poor Jack. He sounds really lost. Is that what prompted him, after all these years to tell me about he and Dorothy? How does a mother recover? I better not call her though; in case she doesn't know I am aware of their history.'

Bomber barked once, loudly, from where he now stood at the door having decided distraction was required. Wagging his tail. Impatient to get going.

'Yes, I know,' Tom responded, 'Time to get back to work.'

Glancing at his scribbled notes from time-to-time, Jay went through all the things he had discussed with Tom, Eva nodding in agreement as he spoke, occasionally interjecting to confirm certain things.

'Tom's milk is unpasteurised, right? I can only make cheese with *raw* milk,' she said, for what he thought must be the "umpteenth" time.

When he finished, she nodded her head slowly and said, 'I think it's a good thing you are working there, save us a lot of extra work not having to set up a garden.' Then she laughed out loud. 'And you'll have instant access to lots of cow manure for our herbs, they're greedy plants, need lots of feeding.'

'Great, can't wait for *that*,' he said, heading for his helmet hanging behind the door. 'Okay, I better get going again and help Rosa get the last of her planting done, if I want to be free to work at Tom's.'

Rising to walk with him Eva asked, 'So, what was our farmer, Tom, like anyway?'

'He's a nice guy. Seems kind, friendly. He was very interested in us, where we came from, why we came to Nimbin,' Jay said.

'You didn't tell him about what happened, did you?'

'Oh, *Mutti*, of course not,' Jay laughed, blushing as the scene came back to him. 'But I did tell him my mother was German and he was very interested. And, as I said earlier, about Anna and Travis...'

'Yes, it's going to be a bit awkward telling Anna you are now doing Travis' old job,' Eva interrupted with a frown, *very interested in my German heritage?* 'How do we handle that?'

'By being honest. Life goes on, *Mutti*,' he responded as he clattered down the steps off the deck.

'Yes, my 50-something teenage son,' she smiled, having followed him out the door. 'Why does he have a vegetable stall if he's a dairy farmer? Isn't that enough? Goodness.'

Jay turned back to Eva before he mounted the Harley.

'It's a kind of memorial to his wife, he says. She died a few years ago. And he likes to keep it going. He sells some stuff in Nimbin, but money from the stall is not important. In fact, he donates it to some charity.'

'Oh,' Eva said. She could not mention she had already seen the charity sign saying instead, 'He *does* sound like a nice guy.'

'He have a brother or anyone else staying there?' Eva asked as nonchalantly as she could, thinking of the name on the letter.

'Don't think so,' Jay responded. 'He said something about it being *just me and the dogs rattling around in this big house.* Why?' He didn't wait for her response, '*Mutti*, I must go.'

Eva had turned to go back inside when she heard Jay say from where he sat on the bike, boots planted firmly on the gravel either side, 'One thing though, when we shook hands, he used his left hand, never seen that before.'

She stopped in her tracks momentarily - flash back - before continuing down the hall without turning back.

༺ ༺ ༺

The first time she changed her sedated prisoner of war airman's dressing on his hand, it had been a shock. The *Oberin* had only mentioned the frostbite, so Eva assumed the bandage around Robert's hand was for frost bitten fingers as well, but as she removed the last of the dressing, she saw that his whole thumb had been severed. The surgeons had repaired the wound, stitching what remained, over the thumb joint.

'You will have to change the way you write,' she whispered to herself as she gently cleaned the wound. His eyes flickered at the sound of her voice, but he did not speak.

Romy raced gleefully across Dorothy's front lawn towards the gate when she saw Eva getting out of her car but stopped when she saw Rosa. Her shyness overtaking her excitement, kept her unmoving in the middle of the garden, a sudden garden gnome.

'Oh, I see what you mean, Eva. She is the image of Anna,' Rosa exclaimed as she followed her friend through the gate.

'Hullo my darling, come and meet Rosa, *my* lovely friend and your mother's as well,' Eva said, on her knees, arms open.

'Rosa?!' came Anna's voice through the opening screen door.

'Oh my God, Anna, what happened to the little girl I taught to dance?'

'She grew up and made another little Anna, everybody tells me, can't you see?' Anna laughed as she and Rosa hugged. 'And this is,' for a moment she was going to say, 'my *mother-in-law*' but switched, that was for Dorothy to announce, 'Romy's other granny, Dorothy, whom Romy, and only Romy, calls Dotty,' she smiled.

'Rosa, granny too?' Romy asked, looking earnestly up at her mother and they all laughed.

Sitting on Dorothy's deck enjoying a glass of wine, the four women marvelled at how life had brought them together in Nimbin, notwithstanding the tragedy that had overtaken Anna. Rosa said, while she was hoping she was not putting a damper on such a lovely, spontaneous gathering, she felt compelled to offer Anna her condolences.

'No, it's okay,' Anna said, patting Rosa on the arm. 'Dorothy and I have decided the only way to get over it, is to just get on with life.'

Giving Anna a wink, Dorothy said, 'The whole town will know about it soon Rosa, so if Eva hasn't shared it with you already, Travis was my boy.'

Rosa shocked both Anna and Eva when she said simply in reply, 'I am so sorry Dorothy. I know how you feel, I lost my son too.'

When Jay stopped his bike at the gate and dismounted to open it, Bomber and Caster came down the long driveway towards him at an electrifying pace, like they had just found a runaway; a cow which needed to be returned to the herd. They barked their greeting – or maybe a warning - all the way down the old track, before spraying pebbles as they skidded to a stop on the loose gravel. Notwithstanding their furiously wagging tails, Jay was glad he had not yet opened the gate. A distant whistle quietened them immediately and they trotted off, back up the driveway to Tom, on his deck waving a greeting.

Tom led Jay around the garden, about twice the size of a tennis court, pointing out the various beds of vegetables and herbs. He noticed there were little stakes alongside each bed with the plant's basic details written on the label attached to the stake. *Just what Mutti would have done*, thought Jay.

'This bed here, you have probably noticed, looks like what Nimbin is getting famous - or is it notorious? – for,' Tom winked. Jay had never seen actual hemp or marijuana but since he had been in Nimbin, it was hard to miss the drawings of weed everywhere, especially adorning the Hemp Factory.

'It's actually kenaf,' he went on. 'My wife, Anne, decided that with the increasing number of vegans around here growing, something that provided an alternative source of protein would be a good thing.'

Jay felt slightly awkward, knowing the farmer's wife had died a few years before, but he nodded enthusiastically, nonetheless.

'She wasn't wrong,' Tom went on, 'Just a bit early, because now it's in big demand. Since Aquarius and all the new arrivals with their desire for alternative living, we can't grow it fast enough. The Hemp Factory can't get enough of it. Fortunately, it does grow pretty fast as you will find,' he laughed.

'Tom says, you should go over to the farm with me one day to see the gardens and check out the milking process. He knows you are quite fussy about the milk you use. Go across for tea one afternoon. Arrive just before they start milking,' Jay said between bites of the sandwich Eva had made him for lunch.

She did not respond, gazing down from where they sat on a bench outside their soon to be cheese factory, towards the little church below and the hills beyond it.

She could see her father's three-wheeler Goliath parked alongside the gasthaus. She was helping him put the milk cans on the back seat so they could drive across to the milk shed and collect the milk for her Mutti's cheese making. Kurt would carry the heavy cans, full of milk, down the steps to Magda in the cellar with ease. Eva could see her face looking up to them as he started down. She looked so exhausted even then. Eva lifted her gaze to the hills above and beyond Rosa's church house. Where have all the trees gone? *Are my trees still there? The forest Papi drove me deep into? To find berries and the monster. I never even said goodbye.*

'Geez, *Mutti*. You don't *have* to go. Don't cry,' Jay teased.

Eva wiped her eyes and laughed. 'Just some old memories, Jay. Yes, I would like to meet Tom one day, but not right now, okay? Now, let me see the list of herbs he grows. See what we need to add to the garden.'

Jay sensed that his mother seemed distracted every time Tom came up in their conversation but said nothing as he walked away to get his notebook from where he had left it in the Harley's pannier.

Jay was dismayed when Eva told him that the last step in the cheese making process was a long one and did not require any work at all. Simply waiting for it to mature.

'Three to six months?' he cried. 'What do we do while its maturing?'

'We make more cheese,' she laughed. 'And the soft cheese, that we don't have to wait for.'

By the time their first day of cheese making arrived, he had been so absorbed in preparations, his impatience to have a final product had subsided. He was excited just to see the first cans of milk poured into the vat for heating. Forty minutes later, as he was leaning the vat over under the watchful eye of Eva, so the curds and whey could slip into the curd table, Rosa and Anna came up the deck steps with Romy.

'Did we make it in time to help with the first cheese made in Nimbin?' Anna called out as she arrived at the door, letting Romy slide gently from her arms to the floor so she could run across to Eva's open arms.

'Well, the first since Norco closed down in the 50s, according to the real estate agent. Or was that a creamery? Whatever. Congratulations,' Rosa said from behind them. 'You'll need a name, won't you?'

As Eva and Jay stirred the curds floating in the whey, Romy, standing on the stool Eva had found her, was leaning over, putting a finger down into the lumpy liquid. Straightening up she put it into her mouth before breaking into a smile, 'Yum.'

'Her latest word,' Anna laughed. 'I think your mixture just got a nod of approval,' she said patting her mother on the back. Eva, involuntarily seeing herself, a few years older than Romy, in the freezing cellar of the *gasthaus* hearing about 50 dead geese on the bloodied snow, forced a smile and said, 'We'll call it "Nimbin New" then, shall we? In case it's not the *first* cheese in town.'

CHAPTER 24

Part Closure

WATCHING JACK AND DOROTHY walking towards her down the "Arrivals" corridor at Lismore Airport, Anna sensed there was something that had changed between them. She had no idea how successful they had been in their quest to establish where Travis' body was, or whether they'd managed to have it returned to Australia, but *something* was different.

Driving back to Nimbin, Jack relayed that on arrival in Germany, their first visit was to the Australian Embassy in West Berlin, where visas for East Berlin were arranged immediately on compassionate grounds. Their next stop was the Australian Embassy in East Berlin and this is where the delays started. The West German Commission there seemed loath to meet with them, an official saying they would likely get nothing more from the *Stasi* than their unchanging response, 'a border provocation of his own causing,' to any border incident.

It was only when they insisted any additional information would be of great help to the victim's wife, *a German citizen,* that they agreed to speak to Jack and Dorothy. In addition, Jack found referring to Anna as "my son's wife" held more store than anything accurate – he had even taken to referring to Dorothy as "my wife".

It had been two days and they had still not heard from the commission regarding their meeting time. Dorothy had suggested some sightseeing to pass the time, but Jack was reluctant.

'What, a visit to the Brandenburg Gates? That would be nice, wouldn't it?' he said intending to be ironic, but it came out surly. 'Sorry,' he added, looking down at the traffic from the small window of his shabby hotel room.

'I know how you feel, Jack. It's okay. But I am going to go. I will be able to feel him, I know. And leave a bunch of flowers on the *platz*. Say goodbye.'

Dorothy heard what sounded like a slight gasp as he controlled a sob and she went to him at the window, putting a hand on his shoulder. Turning to her, under control now, he said, 'Yes, you're right, we should go and say goodbye.'

They stood together at the barricade, three East Berlin guards nearby. Dorothy's arms hung limply at her side, a bunch of flowers dangling from one hand, almost touched the paving. Peering across the *Pariser Platz,* the columns of the gates in the distance seemed ominous. A gate through which their son had been drawn, never to return. Tears were running down Dorothy's cheeks as one of the guards walked stiffly past them. Surprised the words were even coming out of her mouth, she heard herself say, 'Excuse me. Please.'

The guard stopped and looked back.

'*Ich spreche kein* English,' he said.

'I know, I know,' she said, guessing at his words. 'But people normally can understand a little?' Jack thought he saw a slight nod from the guard as Dorothy spoke again, 'My son died here a few months ago. Can I put these flowers a little further in? Maybe closer to where it happened?'

He came over to her, putting his hand out, reaching for the flowers she held. Jack tensed as he pulled the bouquet from Dorothy's grasp. The soldier walked away from them, further into the square, towards the gates before stopping abruptly and turning back to them.

They heard him say only one English word as he pointed down. 'Here,' then, '*Es ist hier passiert.*'

He lay the flowers on the spot and walked off diagonally away from them without another word.

Jack's police training ensured he saw the young man who approached them, as they turned away from the scene, was concealing something, probably a camera, inside his jacket. It was confirmed when he asked about what had just taken place and said he was a photojournalist. Jack did not hesitate to relay what had happened to his son. If a few more people knew about the atrocity, it could only help his task of trying to get justice.

The older, more senior of the two *Stasi* officials who sat alongside the West German Commission's diplomat laughed out loud, when

Jack asked if he could visit the *Stasi*-run hospital that Travis had been taken to.

'Impossible,' he said. He asked what could possibly be gained by such a visit and Jack said they would be comforted by talking to people who had nursed their son at the end. The man scoffed, 'There was no end really. Just confirmation.'

Jack felt Dorothy's hand slip into his and he breathed a little easier. The younger *Stasi* official was looking at Dorothy with what might have been taken for sympathy, *if you did not know what these bastards were about*, thought Jack.

'My son's wife says she is sure he was alive when they took him away,' Jack said.

'She is wrong. He was cremated at *Baumschulenweg* the same day. Border provocation of his own causing, that is all. Our guards are very brave,' the senior *Stasi* man said.

'Yes, his wife told us that the guard that shot our innocent son, received a medal,' Jack snarled.

The two *Stasi* officials got to their feet and stormed from the room, stopping only to deliver a short tirade in German to the commission's diplomat, quaking in his chair. At the door he looked back at Jack.

'No ashes,' he said, before turning his back on them.

Jack and Dorothy waited 10 minutes in silence before the elevator. Stepping through the finally opening doors, they prepared for a laborious return journey to the lobby of the West German Commission building. Seconds after Jack had pushed the lobby button the nearly closed doors suddenly clattered back open. There stood the younger *Stasi* official. He stepped forward with a slight smile and handed Dorothy an envelope. Stepping back, with one finger in front of his lips, he turned on his heel and walked off without a word as the elevator doors closed. Jack looked down at what Dorothy had taken from the envelope. It was Travis' wallet.

Anna could feel the tears running down her cheeks as Jack spoke, but she made no sound. She blinked once or twice to keep the road in focus, hands gripping the wheel tightly. She wished Dorothy hadn't left the bubble they had created for themselves. *Why did she have to go with Jack on this futile trip to get Travis returned in some way. Closure?*

Dorothy was silent as Jack spoke, but Anna could see out of the corner of her eye that she was leant forward, her hand on his shoulder, moving it only to hand Anna a new tissue or use one herself.

'Well, you two put yourselves through the wringer, alright. Do you think you have found closure now?' Anna asked.

'Not yet,' Dorothy finally spoke, 'but at least the plaster's been ripped off. The pain will go. At least we have been there. Felt it. Seen it. No more *imagining it,* every day.'

Anna glanced at Jack. He looked far away, *some place in the past, better times?* she thought.

'*Mutti,* can you go over and check the irrigation is okay at Tom's. I have to go to Rosa's. She just called and has some kind of emergency,' Jay said as he headed down the steps.

'What? How? I don't know what to...' she called, jumping up from where she had been kneeling, sweeping up Ernie's seed husks he sprayed all over the deck each day.

'Tom likes someone to be there while it's on, just in case, and he had to go into Lismore today. He's taken the dogs to the vet, so you don't need to worry about them. It's just for half an hour between 3 and 3.30, while it's running. Walk up the driveway to the house and you will see the gardens below you on the right.'

Eva's mind raced. She had thought a great deal about what she should do next about meeting Tom. Knowing once and for all. She heard the Harley roar into life as she thought, *no problem, Eva, he won't be there, you can put it off for a bit longer.*

At the top of the drive Eva turned onto the grass, into the shade of a giant Moreton Bay fig tree in front of the house. *This place must have been here a hundred years if this tree is anything to go by*, she thought.

She climbed from the car, but before moving off to follow Jay's directions to the garden, she stopped. The view was quiet stunning. She turned slowly, taking in the distant rolling hills, the valleys, one with a horizontal line of blue at its distant end, on the horizon, *the sea, she murmured.*

Closer, lush green fields ran away from the house, dotted with cows, heads down low, *turning grass into milk*. To the rear of the house, she could see paddocks and a large milking shed. In the front, a dam at the bottom of the slope and a large garden.

'Didn't really need directions, Jay,' she said to herself.

Unable to resist the temptation – *well no one is home* – instead of making for the garden Eva found herself climbing the steps onto the deck. The view from this higher vantage was even more interesting, revealing several smaller dams at the bottom of the slope, some with ducks on them and even a few, Eva guessed, wild black swans gliding effortlessly across the dark water.

She turned to sneak a look through the windows, but feeling self-conscious and guilty, she did not linger, seeing little, only that the rooms appeared very neat and tidy. *Well, that didn't tell me much,* she thought as she turned.

She caught her breath at the sight before her, *that "chk chk chk" sound I was hearing.* About 20 silver arcs of water were duelling across the garden and lawns around the house, slashing at each other like gleaming sabres, the collisions creating fragmented rainbows in the resulting spray.

'It's come on okay, Jay. So far so good.'

As Eva was arriving back from her walk to the dam, the sound of the irrigation system stopped abruptly and the arcs began to subside slowly, *ah now for those blackberries.* Standing almost inside the bush, its crown way above her head, munching on one berry after another, Eva was hardly aware of the faint barking coming to her on the cooling breeze. A few minutes later, seeing a movement through the dappled foliage, she moved to one side for a better view and there he was.

'Good afternoon, you must be Jay's mum?'

'Yes, I am. Hullo. He couldn't make it. Some emergency at Rosa's.' Eva barely got out, her stomach in knots realising it *was* him.

'My name is Tom. Nice to finally meet you. I apologise if I surprised you. The vet visit took a lot less time than I expected.' Eva could see he was studying her as he spoke, *it's coming to him*.

They were both quiet for what seemed like minutes but barely a few sharp breaths.

'Robert. Sorry I can't do "Tom" for the moment. I thought you were killed when the hospital got bombed. I can't believe it,' Eva said holding back the tears.

'Eva, *bist du es*?'

'*Ja, ich bin es*,' she said and now the tears could not be stopped. '*Ja, ich bin hier.* You still remember your German,' she said.

He made as if to reach for her. Then stopped, unsure, started explaining, 'They moved me that morning. I even asked them to delay my departure so I could say goodbye to you, but my escort was already there. They forced me to go. Saved a life they really did not want to save,' he smiled.

Eva, now a little more composed, said, 'Come on, we can't leave this without a hug. Come here, Robert, now known as "Tom."'

As they embraced, she could hear him saying in her ear, 'Somehow, I knew we would meet up again, me on a visit to Germany or something, but this? What a coincidence. Oh, and Tom is a nick name, from uni days, after the war.'

She laughed as they stood apart.

'Yes, making cheese in Nimbin and needing milk to do it, who would have believed it?'

Tom said, 'Let's have a drink and catch up on the last, what is it about 30 years? Bomber and Caster will be besides themselves with curiosity about what I am doing down here with a stranger, that's what all the barking is about. I locked them up in case they made you nervous, they can be boisterous to say the least.'

'Of course, it would be Bomber and Caster, what else?' Eva grinned. 'Robert really. Lancaster Bomber?'

Laughing he said, 'I know, sorry; hang on to me going up here.' He made to go round to her other side so he could hold her hand up the slope, slippery from the irrigation, but she said, 'No it's okay, I held that thumbless hand often for many months.'

Driving home she reflected on the last few hours, suddenly burst out laughing, *of course, Tom Thumb*.

Jay listened, astounded at the story of how Eva met Tom in the hospital in Hamburg, the most exciting part that he was a tail gunner in a bomber.

'What a coincidence. I can't wait to get some war stories out of him. Getting your thumb shot off. That's why he uses his other hand to shake,' he said nodding.

'I have the best bosses, nowadays, and one's my *Mutti* as well,' he laughed, giving Eva a hug.

'Yes, and your "*Mutti* boss" would like you to get that milk into the vat before it goes off,' she said pointing at Tom's dented milk cans in the corner, before walking across to what they now called their herb drying room to check on the hanging bunches Jay had been accumulating from the garden.

They had already made several wheels of cheddar, stored in the cellar under the drying room and she was keen to start experimenting with soft herb cheese tastes. She was waiting impatiently for the drying process to complete so Jay could start grinding with the large "pestle and mortar" they had bought.

Eva ran her hand across the dangling bunches, feeling how the leaves had already started drying. She paused at what Jay had tagged as kenaf, finding the foliage aromatic. She noticed that although almost all the stalks had pods filled with seeds, in addition, some had a strange looking flower containing seeds at their ends. She knew ground kenaf would give a very slight acidic flavour to the soft cheese she was planning but was intrigued to see what she could create once it was ground with fresh garlic.

Dorothy was finalising a receipt for a customer when she heard them start chattering amongst themselves on the edge of the road outside her little shop. Looking over her customer's shoulder, she saw the three of them astride their BMXs, feet on the ground gesticulating towards her shop as they argued. Returning to her writing, she smiled hearing, 'Dotty will know, Dotty will know.'

'Say "auntie", you dumb *boorie*, you know how cross she gets,' one of them said to the youngest.

Seeing Dorothy smile, her designer-dressed customer said, 'I don't know how you put up with *them* around here, especially the kids, so noisy.'

'"Them" are my friends, so if that is all? Thank you,' *Why don't you fuck off back to Sydney?* Dorothy added mentally.

The woman looked flustered, as if she had read the thought, then miffed before finally, at a loss for words, turned on her heel, walked down the steps and up the street under the watchful gaze of the three young boys whose cheerful greeting she ignored.

'What's up with you lot?' Dorothy called to the boys, 'Want a glass of juice?' had them scrambling to get their bikes leant against the fence.

Gulping their drinks down under the expectant eye of Dorothy, one of them said, 'Auntie, we want to know if we can do a little dance for *Kumanjayi*? He was our *bunji*.'

Dorothy was at a loss as to who they were talking about, but then remembering their culture precluded the mention of a deceased person's name *lest his spirit be interrupted in its journey*, realised they were referring to Travis.

'I don't see why not, but you will have to ask Captain Jack if he is okay with it - *and* get permission from your elders, I would think.'

'Oh no, Captain Jack will tell us off. He always shakes his finger at us when he passes in the hurry-up wagon,' the youngest piped up.

'Well, that's because you don't care about the road rules, like stopping at the traffic lights. We only have one in Cullen Street; you should be able to remember. And what about all the pot smoking in the park?' They looked sheepish, eyes cast downward to their empty glasses, *Dotty knows everything.*

'Captain Jack was his father, so you *have* to ask him.'

'Can't you ask him Auntie, please,' they begged. 'He likes you; we've seen. Waves when he goes past here.' They all started laughing, holding their hands up, blowing kisses.

Dorothy picked up a towel off the display counter and flicked it at them as they ducked for cover.

'Cheeky little buggers. Go on, get off with you, I'll ask him to give you a night in the lockup as well, while I am about it,' but she couldn't help laughing, hoping she had got them scattered far enough away before they could see her blushing.

Anna yawned into the window above the sink in the cottage she and Romy lived in. Her reflection was blunted by the mist on the glass from washing the evening's dishes. Wiping at it absentmindedly, she noted Dorothy's house was in darkness, not even a veranda light, which was always on during the night.

'Not home, must be staying at Jack's for dinner,' she murmured to herself. 'Probably making it for him,' she chuckled quietly.

As Anna had expected, being Travis' birth mother, Dorothy had taken it upon herself to help Jack as much as she could through the grieving process. It helped her as well, she had told Anna, to be supporting him rather than dwelling on her own loss continually. Much later, getting up in the early hours to settle Romy down after a bad dream, Anna let a little smile form in the corners of her mouth when she saw through the window that Dorothy's house was still in darkness.

CHAPTER 25

Breakaleg

THE INCONGRUOUS IMAGE OF a heavy-set East German guard holding a Kalashnikov rifle diagonally across his chest with one hand and a bouquet of flowers dangling from his other, striding across the *Pariser Platz* was syndicated worldwide. The Brandenburg Gate loomed large in the background of the photograph, taken by the rebel photographer they had met; he documented life behind the "wall". A sub editor at a Sydney paper captioned the story: *Guns and Roses: Remorse for Aussie boy's Death.*

Of course, that was not quite the truth but close enough for Travis' friends in Nimbin who were gathered around an expensively framed copy of the photograph sent to Jack by an anonymous well-wisher in condolence. Placed alongside a large one of Travis, the photographs formed the centre piece of the gathering in Nimbin Park for the people of the town to honour Travis and pay their respects to Jack and Dorothy. Since their trip together to Germany, it had become common knowledge that Dorothy was Travis' birth mother.

People were sitting under trees in the shade, many with young children almost impossible to control. Running around, playing catch, little girls screaming, boys yelling. *Travis would have liked it this way*, Anna thought. She wished Romy would join the other kids her age, but she refused to be taken anywhere near their activities.

'Loner, like your father,' Anna sighed.

Dorothy's three young friends, daubed in white paint, ready for their dance, were still gathered around the photographs, pointing and chattering, now and again glancing at Dorothy expecting at any moment she would "shoo" them away.

Anna watched Jack turn from his conversation with his area commander, resplendent in his uniform and medals and prepare to deliver the eulogy for his son, to the mostly long-haired, jeans and caftan-wearing throng. Smiling at the tie-dyed garments, splashing colour below the rows of solemn faces, she wondered if he was aware of the odd whiff of marijuana that floated on the breeze, rustling the gum trees around the park. *Could still be stuff bought from Travis before we went away*, she thought whimsically.

Looking down, when Romy tugged her dress and following the twiddling fingers she was using to point towards the edge of the park, Anna saw that her nemeses were edging their way into the area. There were three of them now. *Planning to take over. They look indignant, like we've invaded "their" park,* Anna thought. She looked in Dorothy's direction automatically, half expecting to see her readying herself to throw something at the roosters. She was standing very close to Jack, almost touching him as he began to speak, and Anna wondered if there might be another revelation before the day was over.

Jack opened his eulogy with a few comments regarding why they had the photograph on display. Conceding that whilst many might think it bizarre that they would have a picture of what could have been one of the guards that caused Travis to lose his life, it had significant other attributes as a token of remembrance. The newspaper headline they had all seen, implied the guard had shown remorse, but they were incorrect, Jack said.

'*I* know what that guard felt that day, it was not remorse. Travis would have been proud to see what transpired had he been there - or maybe he was,' Jack's voice wavered briefly and Dorothy put her hand on his back for comfort.

Gathering himself he went on, 'What the guard sensed was the searing pain in the heart of a mother. Unbearable sadness for not having said goodbye. As a "son" himself, he had no option but to honour the request of the mother before him, even though he was clearly disobeying orders.'

Jack put his arm around a now tearful Dorothy before continuing, 'So, I do not find this picture sad. It represents to me what the fearless love of a mother can do and Travis would have been, will be, comforted by it, as I am.'

When Jack finished his eulogy, Eva and Rosa moved closer to Anna, who was crying quietly as she held Romy, distraught at her mother's tears. Romy moved into Rosa's arms as Eva took *her* daughter in hers. Somewhere near the back of the gathering, fingers began strumming a guitar and the beautiful voice of a woman rose over the people. Her haunting words from *Bridge Over Troubled Water* had tears streaming from most eyes.

It was not a religious gathering, but when Romy called in Rosa's ear as the song came to an end, 'Look, look,' she thought one could be forgiven for thinking it was, seeing what suddenly appeared before the now silent mourners - especially when you knew they roosted in the old *parsonage* behind the police station. Nimbin's famous, splendid feral peacock, named Jesus, and his peahen partner, Mary, had wandered onto the scene, followed by their four newborn chicks. As everyone watched, Jesus stopped and fanned his magnificent tail feathers. Vibrating them, his train rattling was startling in the silence after the woman's singing. His signature tail eyespots appeared to float in the swirling sea of wispy feathers.

Eva stood back to admire the tables of refreshments she and Rosa had set up under a giant fig. Unpruned roots reached down from its lower branches 10 metres to the ground below, forming a curtain around the tree's trunk. She had used the post memorial refreshments to test her first ever batch of herb cheese, so glass jars, containing the soft white delicacies, were numerous on the tables. Each jar was surrounded by crackers and bread donated by Basil, whose bakery had flourished since the festival and the people it attracted, including some of the very people attending today. On each jar was a label with the name "Nimbin New" printed in large green letters and below, "Herb and Garlic Cheese". Anna had designed the label and couldn't resist the temptation to use a row of tiny hemp leaf images which ran along the bottom. On the back of the jar, above the mandatory technical small print was stated, "The Church Cheese Factory, Nimbin Road".

Eva's mind wandered back to her cheese-making in the *gasthaus* cellar, and she thought, *maybe I should have played it safe and stuck to my proven recipes, Quark and Kochkaese.* Moving her gaze from the table to the people nearby, beginning to rise from their sitting and lying positions on the grass, Eva said to Rosa, 'I wonder where that son of mine is. He's been dying to see one of our cheeses finally on offer and I haven't seen him since we unpacked the car?'

'He's around,' Rosa smiled equivocally and Eva gave her an enquiring look, but Rosa turned away as a rhythmic clacking sound started and the crowd parted to reveal three young dancers, stamping in time to the beat. Behind them Jay, body decorated in similar fashion to the boys with their white colouring, smacked two boomerangs together, creating the rhythm which he interspersed with his regular grunts.

Suddenly, one of the boys moved forward, his legs repeatedly whipped open as he took small jumps forward. Jay halted his movement forward with a 'One. Two. Three,' and without stopping his dancing to the beat, the boy retreated as the second moved forward with his shakealeg dance. The dancing continued for several minutes before Jay brought it to a close with a final, 'One. Two. Three.'

'That dance was to honour our *bunji, Kumanjayi,*' Jay said loudly and everyone applauded. Held in a tearful Anna's arms so she had a good view, Romy clapped her little hands together as well, delighted at the spectacle after such a boring few hours – except for the roosters and peacocks of course.

'This cheese of yours is delicious, Eva,' she heard from behind her. Turning with a pleased smile, she found Tom munching on the other half of the cracker he held in his hand, complete with a small fragment of cheese on his lip.

Before Eva could think of a way out of the awkward moment she faced, Rosa, standing with her, saved the day.

'You keeping that for later, Tom?' she laughed, reaching up with a tissue to remove the fragment. 'So, at last I meet our *milk man*,' she continued, not leaving anyone space for self-consciousness.

Eva breathed a mental sigh of relief, studiously screwing a lid back onto one of the jars before the circling flies could make a landing. Tom made to lift his hand to his lip, but checked himself, saying casually, 'And I get to meet the lady who can stop bull dozers in their tracks - saves what is left of our dwindling forests.'

'Well, me and quite a few other dedicated souls,' Rosa laughed.

As Eva turned back to join the conversation Tom said, 'Seriously Eva, what herbs are in this cheese? It's really different.'

'Thyme and kenaf, along with the garlic. The kenaf makes it a bit "lemony". I was looking for some acidity,' she answered.

Tom was grinning and shaking his head at her words, but before she could question his response, Ben from the Hemp Factory came rushing up.

'Eva, do you have any extra jars of that cheese? I'll take the lot off you and sell them in the shop. People love it. Let me set the price and I will give you 30 percent, okay?'

'Fifty percent and you can take the box of four dozen in the boot of Rosa's car over there,' Eva said.

'Done,' Ben said and rushed off to the car. Then stopped in his tracks. 'I nearly forgot; Jack says his commander would like to take a few jars. Theoretically, for his wife to try but he's been scoffing it straight out of the jar with a spoon since he discovered it.'

'Sure, give him a couple from that box in the boot. That's the last of them though and I still want my 50 percent off those. *Your* treat to Jack's boss,' Eva grinned. Ben just shook his head.

Rosa laughed, 'Hard assed businesswoman.'

'Nursing *and* business,' Tom offered. He looked at his watch and said, 'Eva, I have to get going back to the farm. Milking time. Would you like to come, there is something I would like to show you. I can run you back home afterwards.'

When Eva looked enquiringly at Rosa, she smiled, 'You kids go and have fun. I'll let Jay know and drop him off at home.'

Eva could hear the snapping of one of the dog's jaws behind her through the window of Tom's ute as they cruised down Nimbin Road towards his farm. As usual, the dogs were positioned on the back bed, either side of the cab, biting at the rushing wind.

They had not spoken since they drove off, Eva wondering if Tom might be composing his thoughts before he spoke - *I wonder when that night in the hospital will come up* - when he said, voice raised to counter the open windows, 'Has Jay ever smoked marijuana?'

'No. Not that I know of. I doubt it. That's a strange question?'

'Oh, I just wondered, that's all. More about whether he could spot any plant in the vegetable garden that was "weed". *The* "weed", I mean,' he laughed, over the wind noise.

Eva found the milking far more interesting than she expected. The last time she had seen a cow being milked, and tried doing it herself, was as a child in a cold, dark barn not far from the *gasthaus*. She had tramped across several misty meadows, frosty grass crackling under her little boots, towards the milking barn in the distance, nestling below a dark, forest covered hillside that hid the early morning sun. She held her father's hand as tightly as she could while she half ran, half walked, trying to keep up with him.

He had taken her with him that morning when he went to check on the workers. She remembered how badly her brothers had wanted to go, but he forbade them, saying they would make the cows restless, constantly pushing and shoving each other. Sitting on stools in the dim light, the workers, squinting at the smoke from cigarettes clamped in their lips, leaned under the stomachs of the munching cows. Pulling at the udders, long white streaks of milk squirting into dented buckets, white mist rising from the warm milk into the cold air of the barn.

Here, in Tom's humid milk shed, the udders were connected to a series of pipes which did the pulling, accompanied by the hum of sterile machinery. Everything seemed to have been painted white, seemed hygienic. The munching of the cows from buckets, containing pellets of food while they were being milked, was the same though.

Each carrying a mug of tea, Tom and Eva made their way down to the vegetable garden as the sun edged ever closer to its evening hiding place behind the surrounding hills. The dogs raced ahead when they spotted a white bobbing tail, only to return defeated by the rabbit's speed, a minute later.

'Jay mentioned that the vegetable garden is something of a memorial to your wife, Tom.' She had got used to the new name. 'Do you miss her a lot?'

'I do. Farming is a lonely life sometimes. It was just Helen and I and Steve for a long time. And he was away at boarding school most of the time. So, it was just the two of us, then suddenly she was gone,' Tom said, emotion in his voice.

Eva put her hand on his arm. 'I'm sorry. It will get better.'

He laughed suddenly. 'Didn't you spend a lot of time saying that to me many years ago?'

Eva grinned at him. 'And it did, didn't it? Look at you, the very eligible farmer now, I hear. You will find someone again.' He looked at her seriously but before he could say anything, Eva asked, 'Where *is* Steve nowadays.'

'University. Sydney Uni,' he replied turning away.

'Oh, so is Christa, my daughter. I wonder if they have ever met or...' but Tom had already moved away, beckoning her to follow him.

Tom was pushing his way through waist high green plants that Eva recognised as kenaf, similar to what Jay had brought home with the other herbs he harvested. By the time she caught up, he was holding the stalk of one of the plants.

'The leaves are more or less identical, but the flower is the giveaway. This is not kenaf, it's a marijuana plant. At the risk of speaking ill of Travis, on this of all days, I believe he was disguising his weed crop amongst my kenaf.'

Eva's mouth dropped open. *Of course, the flowers she had noticed, the aroma.* Tom laughed and patted her shoulder, 'I can see the look on your face, you saw a few of these flowers amongst your kenaf. THC takes much longer to take affect when it's ingested. I'll call you in the morning and let you know how I enjoy the evening. Pretty good I suspect.'

CHAPTER 26

The Morning After

JAY WAS JUST THINKING that it was the first time he could remember walking up the driveway from the roadside gate, where Rosa had dropped him, when he saw them. Two magpie adolescents were raising dust as they wrestled on the dry grass near the front deck of the house. A parent looked on, unconcerned, it's lightning-fast beak snatching now and then at insects in the grass around the commotion.

Jay had seen exuberant young magpies doing their mock fighting thing quite often, so he knew it would end without any dire consequences soon enough. As he watched, there was a flapping of wings above him and Ernie swooped off a branch of the gumtree nearby to land close to the magpies with a loud squawk, sending mother magpie off across the yard.

Jay burst out laughing.

'You tell 'em Ernie, no fighting on your block.'

Ernie was still bobbing his head and crest up and down as the young birds took off after their departing parent. A few flaps of his wings took Ernie up onto the deck railing where he stood head cocked at Jay, observing him expectantly.

'Alright, alright. I know we're late. I'll get your seed tray sorted.'

Jay recounted the antics of the birds while he helped Eva with the preparation of their evening meal. She laughed out loud at his description and demonstration of Ernie's bobbing head.

'Oh well, at least he had some fun. That's why I don't like him locked up in his cage permanently,' she said, using the pot's lid to empty boiling water into the sink. 'And *I* have some interesting news as well.' She handed him the pot of boiled potatoes to mash.

While she prepared their salad, Eva told him what Tom had discovered. Jay knocked the masher on the edge of the pot a few times laughing, 'Oh my God, I can't believe it! No wonder your cheese was such a big hit.'

'You've seemed very relaxed over the last week *Mutti*, I must say,' he said, pushing down on the steaming potatoes.

'Don't be silly. I've only been having tiny bits, tasting the mix. Couldn't possibly have any effect,' Eva said indignantly.

'Ah, I don't know,' he said in a sing song voice, and she swiped at him with a tea towel as he moved off to put Ernie in his cage for the night.

Jack's boss had been at the police annual party taking place at the Lismore Country Club for a few hours, by the time he found he was feeling increasingly good about life. As the evening wore on, he shared his description of the memorial he attended earlier, along with how beautiful the "shakealeg" tribute was, several times. Some, who failed to anticipate he was yet again heading in their direction, were eager to escape because they already knew every word of this anecdote by heart.

His officers exchanged glances with each other, knowing this magnanimous attitude was decidedly out of character for their commanding officer, as were the compliments he was handing out to their wives. He normally barely noticed anyone who was not an adult, white male, unless they were paying him a compliment. This included his own wife, who was looking somewhat non-plussed at her unusually gregarious, good- humoured husband.

Two of his senior officers were just sharing the fact that in the last hour they had both been promoted to the same position - as his second in command - when one, glancing behind the other, gasped at the scene taking place beyond the large patio sliding door, closed against the cold evening. There, in the bright lights surrounding the swimming pool, was their commanding officer on the paved edge, stripped down to his underpants. They watched in awe as he turned away from the water suddenly and made for the deep end where he began slowly pulling his heavy frame up the diving board ladder, one panting step at a time.

The officers were in two minds. Persuade him to not dive or simply enjoy the spectacle. It was at about that time his wife, a prominent politician, noticed what was about to unfold and yelled, 'Stop him. Stop him. In the name of God.'

It wasn't long before the boys got fed up with sitting in the car, regretting they had decided to come along for the ride. Parked outside the house, where one of their fathers was attending an after-funeral event in Lismore, it began to dawn on them that it was going to be a long wait. Finally, they left the car and crept up to the side of the house.

'*Sorry business* means lots of drinking and talking,' one observed.

'Maybe we should have stayed at home. Rode our bikes instead, hey,' another said, as they peered through the windows at people downing vast quantities of booze as they laughed and shared anecdotes about the deceased.

Watching the antics of adults soon became boring, so they decided to go and see what the bright lights they had noticed nearby were for. Maybe a footie game. It turned out, they were just bright overhead lights around a swimming pool.

'Let's have a swim, come on.'

'We got no swimmers.'

'So what, we can swim in our boxers.'

'It's too cold, man.'

'Come on.'

After sneaking through the fence, where it had broken away from its upright, they crept through the bushes towards the pool. About to emerge near the diving board, through the foliage they saw a large guy come lumbering towards them and start heaving himself up the diving board steps.

There were three young boys standing alongside the diving board by the time the officers got there, chorusing, 'Jump Jumbo jump. Jump Jumbo jump,' up at the commanding officer standing frozen at the end, staring down at the water and the wavy, white lane demarcations beneath its surface, knees visibly trembling, making the board shake.

'Scat you little shits,' the officers yelled as they arrived on the scene and the boys disappeared into the darkness, one yelling in a sing song voice as he ran, 'Jumbo's going to belly flop.'

They found themselves back under bright lights when they skidded around a corner of the clubhouse building into the parking area, almost colliding with a rack of the club's rental bicycles. Any thoughts that there might be *gunjies* right behind them were gone at the sight of the bikes.

'Deadly, man. Bikes,' one said.

They had been without their BMXs for hours, so the sight of the bikes brought joy to their hearts.

'Let's grab a bike and go for a ride,' the youngest whispered loudly.

'Hah, you're too small for those bikes.'

'Nah,' he replied, 'I can stand and pedal with my one leg under the cross bar. I'll show you.'

The non-paying bike renters had not gone far when the car coming up behind them flashed its red and blue lights before introducing a short blast from a siren. Small boys on oversized bikes and gaudy orange rental signage attached to the rear mud guards, was enough to make any policeman curious. It wasn't long before their joyride had become anything but, as they were bundled into the *van* and taken to the Lismore charge office.

Being high up on the diving board had been pure euphoria for the aspirant diver, until he looked down and realised how high he was. The acrophobia, he had forgotten he suffered from, flooded through his mind and body making him feel as though he had physically shrunk to half his size, imagined a giant hand crushing him. He was sure he was going to slip off the diving board and be killed. Terrified, he felt the same feeling of inevitability he always got when he experienced his height phobia washing over him; for an instant he thought, *just jump, get it over with, death is better than this*, but thankfully he couldn't move, frozen to the spot.

'Sir, turn around. Just walk back to the ladder. We will help you down,' called one of his officers as he began to climb up the metal steps.

'Get away. You'll make me fall, you fool,' his commander yelled back over his shoulder, but he did turn slowly, facing away from the water towards the top of the diving board steps.

He bent his knees slowly, trying not to look down, reaching for the sides of the diving board as he did so. He was aiming to get down on his stomach and slide his way back to the ladder like a snake – or maybe a seal. He felt his stomach touch the rough nonslip surface and, notwithstanding the grazing of his skin, he began to slip his knees out behind him in order to flatten himself onto the board's surface. Unfortunately, that meant they slid over the end of the diving board, changing his centre of gravity and before he knew it, his whole body slipped off the end scraping his ample stomach and chin as they too went over. He was left dangling, stopped from falling by his vice-like grip on either side of the board above his head.

The commander may have been overweight, but he had strong arms and for the moment he was safe, however, hanging the way he was meant his torso was somewhat stretched and his boxer shorts were looser than normal. Slowly but surely, before the transfixed audience drawn from the function room by the shouting outside, his boxer shorts began to edge downwards. He thrust his legs backwards and forwards in a scissor-like motion to try and stop them, but it was not to be. In fact, the motion exacerbated their looseness and the shorts slipped downwards even faster, prompting the women to recoil and move back inside.

Having a head start, the commander's shorts made it to the surface with enough time to float in triumph for a few seconds before his body crashed down on top of them - it wasn't a belly flop. Standing nearby with their "borrowed" bikes in the darkness the three boys struggled to contain their giggles.

The following morning, after his wife filled in any gaps from the previous evening over a very strong coffee, the commander was beside himself. His police training allowed him to analyse the events leading up to his incident with succinct clarity and by the end of his coffee, he came to the conclusion that the one thing that stood out when looking for a reason for his condition the previous night, was Eva's jars of herb cheese.

'Those hippy bastards with their damned drugs in everything,' he said to himself as he dialled the mayor of Lismore's direct line, the number written on a notepad before him. His wife, as the standing National MP for the seat of Lismore, had considerable influence, as the council was dominated by her party.

'It's for you, *Mutti*,' said Jay as he lay the receiver on the hall table and headed out the front door to his Harley for a hasty ride up to his vegetable garden *to remove the evidence*. Tom had called earlier and after he and Eva had had a good laugh, he had suggested Jay get over to the farm as soon as he could and get rid of the rogue look alike kenaf intruders *post haste*.

Picking up the phone as she heard Jay's bike going down the driveway, Eva had barely got the receiver to her ear and her greeting out when Ben interrupted, 'All gone. The whole lot. Some yesterday, but this morning there was a rush. Had to take the sign down advertising it before 10 this morning. Do you have more?'

Eva gasped. 'Four dozen in that time? Wow.'

'Yes. I had to limit it to one jar per buyer. But they were sending in their husbands, some of them. Someone even sent in their young son,' Ben laughed. 'I thought they were going to start trying to outbid each other. What did you put in that cheese?' he exclaimed.

That was when Eva started to giggle. She tried to cut it off, but it became uncontrollable. Tears ran down her cheeks.

'What? What?' Ben asked. 'What's so funny? Because I asked for more?'

Finally, Eva regained control and said, 'No. No I just thought of something funny, sorry. Seriously though, that batch is finished, but I will get onto another this morning. Give me a few days.'

'Okay, I will take everything you make, bye,' Ben said as he put the receiver down, shrugging and shaking his head at his curious workers listening in on his conversation.

'Who's this with Rosa?' Eva heard Jay say from their barn door as he shuffled in one of the cans of milk Tom had delivered earlier.

She joined him to see a man in a suit following Rosa up the hill. He looked unsteady as he traversed the steep slippery gravel track in his smart business shoes. When they reached the bottom of the steps, Rosa said, 'This is Mr Ableman from the Lismore City Council. I'm afraid he is not very happy with us.'

Mr Ableman stood slightly bent over, hands on hips, panting, unable to speak. Eva gave Rosa an inquiring look while they waited. Once he'd caught his breath, he put on his official voice and stood erect, trying to look dignified, after his scrambling climb, beads of perspiration running down into his white collar.

'Approval is required for certain activities, even for a home business like this and you must register with council, which you have not done.'

'Oh, we didn't know. Really, just for a little home business like this?' Eva said, putting on her most charming voice. 'Can we apply now?'

He ignored her and went on in the same voice, 'Should the operation involve food preparation, you are required to contact us prior to operation. Approval is required for certain activities and an inspection of the premises is essential before commencing operations.'

'Can we do all that now?' Rosa repeated.

'Not in this case. Because you have already begun production without approval and begun distribution, as we have been informed by the Lismore police, without approval, the council has to suspend the operation of the business for a period of 12 months,' Mr Ableman said. All three of the faces he spoke to looked back at him aghast.

'We are undertaking an investigation into the suppliers of your raw materials and, depending on the outcome, this may result in an extension of your suspension period and a fine for them. We are informed by the Hemp Factory owner that your raw materials come from a local farm. Is that correct?'

Mr Ableman's second uncomfortable experience of the morning came a few hours later when he was halfway up a pre-warned Tom's driveway, having left his car on the road and climbed over the locked gate. He knew he was in trouble halfway up the track when he heard a single whistle and two dogs came galloping down from the house towards him.

Bomber and Caster did what they did best when instructed to herd a moving object towards a gate of their owners' choice. In this case the entrance gate Mr. Ableman had climbed over a few minutes before. They were at their snarling, barking best as they guided him back down the driveway. With Tom nowhere nearby to keep an eye on him, Bomber couldn't resist a quick snap at one of the ankles trotting before him, which had Mr Ableman yelping and accelerating towards the gate.

Dorothy opened the door, expecting to see Jack standing there so she was startled to see the parents of her three young BMX riding friends instead. The grave faces made Dorothy fear the worst. *A riding*

accident, a speeding tourist, raced through her mind so she was almost relieved when the one father said, 'The boys got in trouble with the *gunjies* in Lismore. They put them in jail for taking bikes.'

'In jail at the police station or a youth detention centre?' Dorothy asked. She had no idea if there was one in Lismore, but the boys in their early teens, were very young for jail.

'In jail, like I said. I went there to ask for help when they didn't come back. They let me see them. They look very scared. They got thrown in the hurry-up wagon.'

'What happened exactly? What did they do?'

'I had to go to Lismore for sorry business. They wanted to come. Said they would wait in the car. But then I got drunk and took a long time.'

'They told me, I can't do anything until the boys go before the magistrate. He will decide,' the father continued. 'The *gunji* at the desk said probably youth detention where they will learn not to steal, he said. The boys told me they only borrowed the bikes for fun. Why would they steal them, they have their own BMX bikes here?'

Dorothy had made tea for the distraught parents and tried to reassure them that justice would prevail, but they were far from convinced.

'You the boys' friend, Dorothy. You know Captain Jack. Please talk to him. He can fix this,' one of the other fathers said as they all nodded.

CHAPTER 27

The Dancer's Return

'**Thanks for the ride,**' Dorothy said as she slipped into her seat and clipped in the belt.

Rosa patted her on the leg in response, 'Well, I was not going to let you *borrow* my car. Not the way you drive. Will they ever be able to get that wreck of yours back on the road?'

Dorothy laughed.

'Cheeky. It was only because Pothole Pete missed the biggest pothole in New South Wales, and I didn't.'

'Okay, so tell me what your plan is. How are you going to rescue your boys?'

'To be honest, I don't have any solution yet, but I do know I don't want to involve Jack, as the parents asked me to do last night. It's not fair on him. Too political in his state of mind,' Dorothy said shaking her head. She went on after a few seconds of silent reflection, 'I do think it might be worth going to the source of the problem. The Lismore Club. Talk to the manager, see what can be done, maybe?'

'Did *they* lay charges?'

'Don't know. Probably. Apparently, the boys just *borrowed* the bikes. Were going to return them.'

Rosa laughed, 'Okay then, as they say, the best place to start is at the beginning.'

Walking across the club parking area, Dorothy burst into laughter pointing at the rental bike rack in the corner against the clubhouse wall.

'Not exactly the ideal rides to steal, are they?'

Rosa agreed seeing the gaudy signage that proclaimed their "rental" status front, back and sides.

'Maybe they should have asked if they could rent them.'

'Yeah right. You can see some up himself manager letting *those* three take his bikes, can you?' Dorothy retorted.

'Nah, probably not, especially as the saddles would be chest height,' Rosa said.

Dorothy, with the most becoming smile she could muster, was about to greet the stern-faced manager striding importantly into reception – his assistant had informed him what their visit was about – when his eyes fell on Rosa behind her and a large grin split his face from ear to ear.

'Rosa! It's you! Where have you been all these months? It seems like years since you were last at dance classes.'

'Oh, Graeme, hullo. I know, I'm sorry. I moved to Nimbin and I have been so busy setting up my house I just haven't made it across to classes, yet,' Rosa smiled.

'You are looking so well; I have missed your beautiful dancing.'

'Well, thank you,' Rosa said, offering an alluring smile as she raised her arms above her head and did a classic flamenco pirouette.

Dorothy wasn't sure, but she thought she saw the manager gulp once before he clapped his hands together and said, 'Oh, I have missed your lessons so much. Come. Come to my office; Janet, can you get us some coffee please?'

'Come. Come,' he repeated, beckoning them to follow him from the club reception area, leaving an open-mouthed young assistant trying to take it all in.

As they walked down the hallway, Rosa whispered to Dorothy, 'Change of plan, the boys are my friends, not yours. You just came along, okay? Let me take the lead.'

Dorothy laughed, 'I think that's already happened. Your Graeme hasn't even noticed I'm here.'

As they sat down, Rosa said, 'This is my friend Dorothy. She kindly gave me a ride over as my car is being repaired.'

Graeme turned his head and smiled at Dorothy once briefly before saying, 'So tell me about your new house. And why did you move?'

Dorothy watched as the manager sat transfixed, while Rosa explained how she wanted to move away from Lismore because of the flood risk and then described her relocation of the little church house.

Occasionally the manager interjected with, 'Really?' 'That's amazing.' 'Only you could, Rosa.' But mostly he just sat silent, enraptured by the woman opposite him. Finally, Rosa said, 'You know what, why don't you come over one day for a drink and I can show you what we have done to it?'

Dorothy nearly burst out laughing at Graeme's reaction. He made a sudden involuntary jerky movement in his chair and, had she not known better, she would have believed he was doing a little jig under his desk; *it sounds like he is*, she thought. Suddenly he sprang up and Dorothy thought, 'Oh my God, he's going to do a little dance of joy,' but instead he said, 'Where's our coffee? Let me go check what Janet's up to,' and with that he bounced through the office door down the hallway like someone about to *miss their flight*.

Looking after him, Rosa said, 'What's that about?'

Dorothy giggled, 'Nervous energy. You have him eating out of your hand. Now what?'

'One more play and then we can go in for the kill,' Rosa smiled.

After Janet had left the room with her now empty tray, Rosa said, 'Before I forget Graeme, while I have been away from the dance studio, I've been thinking about how to handle my flamenco lessons better. You know I really need help with my teaching and as you've been doing so well, I was wondering if you would like to be my assistant? We could work on moves together before the main lesson. Just you and me.'

Dorothy watched as Graeme's face morphed from concentration as he listened to Rosa's words, to curiosity, to wonderment and finally outright ecstasy.

'Of course. Of course, I would. What a privilege, Rosa. Thank you.'

Rosa smiled and put her hand on the manager's arm, 'Thank *you*. When I was on my way here today, I would never have thought my grey day was going to turn out to be so happy with a chance meeting with you. I forgot you owned this club.'

'Well, not own it,' he smiled. 'But I am the senior manager, reporting to the board,' he added puffing out his chest; *like one of those damn Nimbin roosters,* Dorothy observed.

Putting on his assertive face, he asked Rosa how he could help her with the incident concerning the previous night's bike theft. It wasn't long before his expression softened as Rosa told him how the boys had been such good friends when everyone else had been slightly hostile to her as a stranger to Nimbin. Giving her support when she was down. Helping her set up her new home. Running errands for her, working in her new garden without payment and *on and on.*

It took all Dorothy's willpower to resist shaking her head in awe, the way Rosa told one "furphy" after another without batting an eyelid, looking like for all the world as if she was little orphan Annie. Rosa finally did bat an eyelid, Dorothy saw, as she let just one tear slip over her blue eyeliner and make its way down her cheek. It was Dorothy's turn to *enter left stage* and on cue, she pulled a tissue from her bag and handed it to Rosa with a flourish.

Graeme cleared his throat and said, 'I'll sort this out, don't worry, Rosa. Excuse me.' He reached for his phone. 'Janet, get the police station on the line please.'

'Yes Sergeant, all a misunderstanding I'm afraid. I forgot to tell my night shift manager that I had given authority for those boys to borrow the bikes for a few hours while they were waiting for their parents who were at a funeral. Yes, yes. It was a favour to a very good friend of mine from Spain.' He winked at Rosa across the desk, 'who is the boys' godmother. Don't ask me, Sergeant. I don't decide who is godmother to who." Another wink. "Thanks Sergeant, sorry for the trouble. She'll be over right away to pick them up.'

'Will you three turn the volume down already,' Dorothy said to the three chattering and relieved, boys in the back of Rosa's car.

'Sorry Auntie,' they chimed.

Turning back to the front, she said, 'What a performance. You deserve an Oscar.'

Rosa laughed, 'Well, as a matter of fact, I quite like Graeme. I could do worse hey? Not many single men around here with decent jobs,'

'Tell me about it,' exclaimed Dorothy.

'What do you mean? Jack's our top cop. That's a good job. You two are… aren't you? Especially after…you know…?' Rosa kept glancing into her rear-view mirror aware of three pairs of ears behind her.

To distract herself from her warming cheeks, Dorothy looked over her shoulder and said brusquely, 'So *what else* did you three get up to yesterday evening?'

Rosa and Dorothy tried to keep straight faces as the boys, at times talking over each other excitedly, relayed the events that took place at the pool. Having all been at the memorial service the previous day, it didn't take the story tellers and their audience long to deduce between them that the unfortunate person on the diving board must have been the Lismore Station Commander and that he had had too much to drink. Rosa knew better, having been informed about the cheese by Eva.

Dorothy said, 'How embarrassing for his wife. She's our MP, you know.'

All had been quiet in the car for a while when suddenly Rosa exclaimed, 'Of course. That's why we've been shut down.'
'What do you mean? What's been shut down?' Dorothy asked.
'The cheese factory. I'll tell you later.'
The three in the back of the car exchanged looks.
'We can ask Jay,' one whispered.

Eva and Rosa followed the rules outlined by the NSW Government regarding dissatisfaction with a council ruling. First appeal to the council, then the general manager of the council and then the mayor, in that order. They got a letter back from the council telling them what Mr Ableman had told them and confirmed in another letter after his visit. The general manager's office ignored their specific questions and suggestions and, instead, sent them an exact copy of the letter the council had sent them. The mayor's office ignored them.

A letter to the NSW Government small business department got them nothing more than another copy of the rules regarding "dissatisfaction with a council ruling".

'Well, fuck them!' was the *environmental warrior's* response. 'There is only one thing that gets the bureaucrats attention. When *the people* speak.'

CHAPTER 28

Priming the Musket

LEANING ON THE BALCONY rail, Steve watched Christa as she came down Alice Street, a sling bag full of textbooks over her shoulder, and turned into the small garden in front of their building. He was surprised when she did not stop to examine some flower or the other. He'd grown used to her stop start arrival routine whenever he happened to catch sight of her from their balcony. *Stops to smell the roses,* he always thought to himself as, bending over some plant, she would try to stabilise her dangling bag and hold her long blond hair back at the same time.

Puzzled, he watched the top of her head as she strode purposely towards the main entrance door without looking up to see if he was there and waving, as she normally did. He turned to respond to the buzzer he knew she was about to press – she always tried that first before searching for her key in case he was home.

When she opened the door, he was shocked to see her face was ashen. She dropped her bag on the floor and burst into tears. Something he had never seen before.

'Shit, shit, shit,' she cried, falling into his open arms. 'I got the time for my exam wrong. It was this morning, not this afternoon.'

Tom came over to their, now much less busy, cheese factory one morning to see how Eva was faring after her unceremonious shut down. Notwithstanding the council's order, she had decided to continue making so she could at least get some hard cheese into the lengthy maturing process. She was surprised at just how pleased she was to see him.

'I had a call from Rosa this morning asking me if I would support her protest against the closure,' he said as he dumped the can of milk he had brought on the concrete floor of the veranda.

'What are your thoughts? She said you were kind of *lukewarm* on fighting the council?'

'Being a politician is she, our Rosa?' Eva smiled.

'Just wants the best for you, I think.'

'Well, I don't think *me* and a bit of cheese are worth all the fuss, Tom.'

Unlike Jay and Rosa, since speaking to Christa, Eva had become ambivalent about the council's blow to their cheese making aspirations; after all, how long was she prepared to be away from Sydney? If she had been there, she would have made sure there were no exam timetable slip ups. *Maybe I should be back for next year? Get a place in Newtown near Christa. And anyway, Jay has to start thinking about what he does next, too. I just don't know what's best for us.*

'It's bigger than that Eva. The council has shut you down as a result of influence from one person?' Tom countered. 'I don't like it one bit. They need to be sent a very strong message. And Rosa can do that.'

'I suppose you're right,' Eva sighed. 'Ben did say that when he tells people he can't get supply from us because the council shut us down, he gets a lot of comments about how unjust it is when the Nimbin people are trying to live a sustainable lifestyle, growing stuff and making stuff. Looking after themselves and trying to rebuild the area.'

'Exactly,' Tom said.

'Maybe Jay and I should go into town tomorrow and talk to some people, get a feel for what they would like to do.'

'Now that's starting to sound more like the Eva I have heard so much about.'

'From whom?' she asked but he just bent and lifting the can, lugged it into the factory.

'Come on, show me how to make cheese, I've got the morning off. We can still make it for our own consumption, can't we? Do we have any of that *special* kenaf?' he winked.

Jay and Eva parked the Harley in a side road that led down to the swimming pool and park. As they were about to make their way back up to the Hemp Factory on Cullen to see Ben, they heard Anna's voice calling behind them, '*Mutti*, Jay, *kommt runter,*' and turning, they saw her waving them down to where she stood in the midst of 20 or so people gathered in the park. Halfway down, Romy appeared between the legs of those nearest and ran towards them, 'Nanna, Nanna.'

Anna came trotting up behind her to meet them and when she was still a way off, started talking excitedly. Eva lifted Romy up and hugged her.

'Look at them,' Anna said pointing back down to the park, 'I was taking a walk with Romy when a few of the people, who were at the service, came over to say hullo and told me how angry they were about the cheese factory shutdown. They called others over who were passing and suddenly we had a spontaneous rally for *Nimbin New.*'

'Ben's there,' she continued. 'He wants to ask Rosa to take the lead in a protest march to Lismore City Council offices.'

'Not all the way from here, I hope,' Jay interjected and she slapped him on the arm.

'Very funny.'

As Romy tugged at her hand, 'Let's go find the roosters Nanna,' Eva thought to herself, *wow they all have the "bit between the teeth" on this council thing, even Anna.* Heading off with her granddaughter, she said, 'By the way, I think Rosa is way ahead of everyone. She is already busy having t-shirts and banners done.'

'Really? What do they say?' Jay asked.

'Same message on both. Bright, "cheese" yellow letters, of course, *Council hands off our Nimbin cheese.*'

'No, Christa, you're not the *uni black sheep* in the family, that's me. You missed an exam this year, that's all, I dropped out altogether so stop worrying,' Anna said, holding the phone between her shoulder and cheek so she could open the crayon box Romy was holding up to her.

'Maybe, but you know they always said if we fail just once, that's it. We finish on our own. I don't have that sort of money,' Christa responded.

'Yeah, yeah, all talk, I reckon. Maybe when *Papi* was alive, but not nowadays. *Mutti* told me last night, after you called her, that she thinks it's her fault,' Anna said, 'because she was not there to keep an eye on you. I nearly reminded her that if she *had* been in Sydney, it would have been you and Jay having to keep an eye on *her*,' and the sisters laughed.

'By the way,' Christa said, 'we tracked down your Mr Jarvis. He did leave ABC Radio, their switchboard was correct, but Steve's got a friend there and he's just gone back, but to TV this time. They obviously haven't updated their lists yet.'

'Okay, I will look up the TV number.'

'This is about the protest, isn't it? You're really getting into it, Anna, aren't you?'

'Well, I need the distraction. Keeps my mind off other things. Romy, no darling, not on the wall! Christa I'd better go.'

'Okay, just quickly, something else to keep your mind off things. I am coming for a visit. Steve's visiting his dad who lives near Nimbin, so I am tagging along. Don't tell *Mutti*, I want to surprise her. I'll let you know when.'

'Brett Jarvis, speaking.'

'Ah good morning, Mr Jarvis, it's Anna Baurst here.'

'Hi Anna, 'fraid "Mr Jarvis" is my dad, I am just Brett, his wayward son. What can I do for you?'

Anna laughed, 'Okay. Sorry Brett, you won't remember me, we did not actually meet, but we nearly did a few years ago near Nimbin when you stopped to speak to a local farmer.'

'Actually, I remember it well. Your group, sightseeing. There was a beautiful blond lady about to climb into your old kombi as we pulled in.'

Anna said nothing, smiling to herself.

'And those dogs of his. Tom, I think his name was, I thought they were going to go for us. Yeah, it comes back,' Brett said, his voice trailing off absorbed in the scene he had recalled.

'Well, I don't know if you would be interested in a follow up story, but I thought I would ask you anyway.'

Anna gave him a snapshot of Nimbin's last year or so and the latest developments around the cheese factory saga.

'So, everyone's up in arms and planning a march in Lismore sometime during the next few weeks,' she finished.

'Hmmm interesting,' Brett said. 'There's a state election soon and Lismore is a seat on the edge, currently held by the Nationals. The last thing they want is something unexpected that could show the National dominated council in a bad light. *Unfair treatment handed out to a small business trying to do good for a struggling little town and it's not very affluent people*. Leave it with me, I'll do some digging around and get back to you Anna, thanks for the heads up.'

CHAPTER 29

Getting a Lift

Tom glanced from face to face of the passengers, as they walked towards gathered friends and relatives there to meet them at Lismore Airport *Arrivals*. They looked relaxed, ready for their long-awaited holiday, he supposed – or just relieved they had got there safely. As always, when he came to meet someone at the airport, he couldn't resist wondering how arriving passengers might have enjoyed their flight if they had been sitting with their knees bent – like a high diver doing a somersault - in a glass bubble attached below the fuselage of their aircraft. *A slight tingling where his thumb used to be.*

It wasn't the flight he was waiting for and so he sat back and let his mind wander. After `the revelations of the last few weeks, his thoughts had tended to dwell on the past. Memories of his time in hospital during the war slipped into his mind again. Being cared for by Eva, as his frost bite wounds slowly healed and the anxiety attacks reduced. Trembling between sterile, starched sheets at night, wondering if the droning bombers he could hear in the dark sky above the hospital were manned by his very own squadron. He imagined their faces, momentarily lit up by the raking German search lights; flak lighting up the sky, like an out-of-control fireworks evening.

Deafened in their metal tubes as they counted down the seconds to releasing their lethal load, obliterating him and everyone else in the wards around him.

These were the nights, if she was on duty instead of going to the hospital air raid shelter, Eva would come to his bedside and take his hand. Speak to him softly, mostly in German so he could not understand much, but comforted by her reassuring tone. Returning slowly to the present, he thought, *well Eva, do either of us want to start over again after losing life partners? Re-learn routines, smells, sounds, movements, compromises?*

He was jerked from his thoughts by a disturbance behind him. Turning, he saw a group of squealing teenage girls surrounding a young man not much older than them, surly looking security guards either side of him. Tom had seen the trio passing earlier and assumed he was some boisterous teenager who had created a disturbance, being escorted from the airport building. *Looks more like a high school kid than a celebrity* he chuckled to himself. One of the girls was holding up a marker pen to her idol, insisting he autograph the front of her t-shirt, but the security guard eased her gently away from him, this time with a smile.

Looking back, his eyes alighted upon a new group of arrivals, including a very attractive young woman with long blond hair. Getting closer to where he was sitting, her blue eyes seemed to catch his and he felt momentarily embarrassed, but she turned her face and whispered into the ear of the young man whose arm she was holding. This was the moment he recognised her friend, previously head down searching in his bag for something, was Steve. Tom waved – *of course I had seen you Steve, that's why I was staring* - and the girl and his son waved back.

After father and son had exchanged hugs, Tom joking about not expecting to see him arriving arm in arm with anyone, Steve said with a smile, 'Yes, sorry Dad, I should have mentioned that Christa and I decided to travel together as she wanted to visit her mother, who by sheer coincidence, also lives in Nimbin and I know, I have been promising you a visit for ages.'

'Funny, I don't remember seeing a Nimbin address on the rental contract we did last year. Must be old age, hey?' Tom smiled.

'No. No,' Christa laughed, 'we lived in Sydney. I moved out when I started uni. She only just moved up here.'

'I see. Anyway Christa, thank you for getting my son to finally visit his dad.'

Squeezed between Steve and Tom in his ute, Christa could not help but see the hand on the steering wheel. Picking where Christa's eyes were directed, Tom said, 'War wound. Lost it to a Messerschmitt pilot one night.'

'Wow, really?' Christa said.

'Don't get him started please, it will turn into a long trip.'

'But I'm interested. My *Papi* was in the war. The navy apparently. I don't think he ever left it behind or rather, it just refused to let *him* go.'

'Our navy boys did a great job,' Tom said. 'What did....?'

'Her father was in the German Navy, Dad,' Steve cut in. 'Now can we change the subject please?'

'Oh. Sure. So where am I taking you Christa?' Tom asked after a slight pause.

'Ironbark Drive.'

A sudden epiphany hearing Christa's response. Of course, what other German woman had only recently moved here? She had told him she had a daughter at the same uni as Steve.

'What number?' Tom asked her, but was thinking *serendipity?*

'I can't remember. Hang on,' Christa said, reaching for her bag between her feet on the floor.

'This might take a while,' Steve laughed.

Smacking Steve on the leg without looking up, Christa fished around in her sling bag before handing Tom a piece of paper with Eva's address on. Tom said he knew the road but was not familiar with the numbers, *in the country we just remember houses.*

'Once we get there, we'll just drive until we find the number, hey?' he said, but he was pretty sure which house they were going to end up at.

Eva heard Tom's ute coming up the gravel road towards their drive before she saw it and, after confirming it *was* his through the window, quickly headed for her bedroom to change her old clothes and sort out her hair. She was just studying the results of her frantic mini makeover in the mirror when the doorbell rang. She hurried up the hall to the front door and, with a last passing glance in the hallway mirror, she pulled open the door saying, 'Well hullo stranger where ....?' but instead of Tom, she saw Christa, wearing a big grin.

'Surprise!' she called out and Tom and Steve appeared from where they had been hiding to one side. Tom, laughing along with everyone, was still wondering at the coincidence Christa's arrival had revealed.

Eva, after her initial squeal of delight at seeing Christa, looked from her to Tom to Steve and back to her daughter, her mouth gaping.

'How on earth!?'

Christa explained that she had discovered Steve's dad lived in Nimbin and they had decided to come up together, which was very convenient given that she needed transport from the airport. Anna, who was in on the surprise visit, would have had to borrow Dorothy's car, only it was being repaired.

'Tom squeezed me into his ute,' Christa concluded.

'You and Steve know each other from uni, of course?' Eva responded.

'*Mutti*, I've told you before we live together. That is, we share an apartment,' she added as her mother tried to hide her anxiety. Busy running himself a glass of water at the sink, Tom smiled at the conversation behind him.

Christa found herself slightly irritated at the attitude her mother was displaying, and she wondered how long it would be before she'd ask whether her and Steve were in a relationship or not.

After Tom and Steve had left, Eva and Christa began catching up with each other's lives during the last few months, including Christa's debacle over her final exam. Eva put her daughter's mind at rest when she said she would support her until she could complete the course. When Eva told Christa about her chance reunion with Tom, how she had nursed him during the war and then thought he had been killed when her hospital was bombed, Christa was incredulous.

'What are the chances of that happening and on top of that, me sharing an apartment with his son!? Amazing. Tom seems to be such a nice man. Kind. Caring. Steve's lucky he wasn't left with a father struggling to cope with life after the loss of his wife.'

Eva was silent for several moments, playing scenarios in her mind and then she said, 'So, you and Steve, do you have your own rooms?'

Christa was about to respond angrily when they heard the sound of the Harley coming up the driveway.

'There he is. I would know that sound anywhere,' said Christa distracted, jumping up and making for the front deck. Stopping briefly to give Ernie a scratch on his chest, which elicited a loud squawk and the raising of his yellow crest, she ran down the steps to meet an already waving rider.

'I could stay with Steve and Tom if you have no space here, *Mutti*. I can see you only have two bedrooms and they have already said I could stay at the farmhouse if I needed to. I'll call Steve quickly and...' Christa was saying.

'No,' Eva cut in, a little louder than she intended. 'No, stay with Anna. It will be better,' she added and both Jay and Christa looked at her curiously and then at each other. 'Don't you want to get to know her little girl, Romy? Anna would want you to stay there,' Eva added.

'Why don't we go over and see her then?' Jay said. 'She's at Rosa's place, I've just come from there, they're planning the protest. You can see the cheese factory at the same time.'

'What protest?' Christa asked.

'Ah, that's the part I was just getting to when Jay arrived,' Eva said.

Christa smiled down at Romy sitting behind them on the floor with her crayons, as the sisters hugged each other.

'So, this is the niece I have heard all about. And what are you drawing Romy? That looks beautiful.'

'Say hullo, Romy. This is your *Tante* Christa,' Anna laughed.

'Oh God, no. Not auntie, please,' Christa said as she dropped down on her knees next to Romy who promptly began furiously drawing random zig zag lines across her page to hide her shyness.

'So, what do you think?' said Rosa as she appeared up the hall from her bedroom, arms outstretched. 'Oh sorry, I thought it was just Jay and Eva I heard arriving,' she said, seeing Christa on the floor with Romy.

Anna said, 'This is baby sister, Christa. Remember?'

'Wow,' Jay said.

'Jay?!' Anna said, swiping at her brother's shoulder as he looked away awkwardly from the tight t-shirt Rosa was wearing. It said, '*COUNCIL HANDS OFF NIMBIN CHEESE*' emblazoned on the front. *The words "HANDS OFF" strategically placed*, Jay thought.

'Not our jerky little dancer from the ship?' Rosa exclaimed. 'Oh yes, I remember those beautiful dimples now.'

CHAPTER 30

Reacquainting

The sudden splutter from various points in Tom's expansive vegetable garden had Romy looking up from her digging in surprise and Jay and Christa quickly heading out of the garden with their hoes. They sat down together on some discarded sandstone blocks, watching Romy resume her digging, the handle of the little spade they had given her, clutched in both hands.

Rotating jets of water from the irrigation system slowly reached their full trajectory, glistening in the morning sun as they arched above the plants.

'I wonder if she's far enough from the bed to miss the drops?' Christa whispered.

'No way,' Jay said with a quiet chuckle.

'I can understand you and *Mutti* being upset, but how come the whole place is up in arms?' Christa said.

'Rain, rain!' an excited Romy cried, jumping up hands above her head, fingers wiggling.

'Rain gone,' she said after a few moments, looking disappointed. She wiped at the drops running down her face.

'It'll come back in a minute, sweetie,' Christa said.

Jay said, 'Well, I think our little factory has meant different things to different people. Anna has benefitted from the distraction; anyone can see that. *Mutti* would have got bored with small town life, remember we didn't know she had a granddaughter living here and, for me, it's been my chance to spot an opportunity and run with it. It has probably been an indication to *everyone* that there *are* opportunities here, you just have to look for them.' Christa smiled inwardly at how much her little brother had changed.

'So, everyone is saying no way, you can't just switch us off like we don't matter. We're going to push back. And anyway, Rosa is always up for it, our "warrior" loves a good protest. It won't be the first time she and her friends have taken on people in authority around here and in Sydney.'

Jay turned to Christa with a large grin.

'Her fight for the rights of Indigenous peoples when she lived there had her lifting her t-shirt to the queen at the opera house – a lot of people read the message on that t-shirt.'

'What?' gasped Christa.

'Yup. International news apparently.

'Rain. Rain,' yelled Romy as the stream of water reached her again.

'Nimbin has started to recover so the council's arbitrary shutdown of the cheese factory is a threat to all. In their eyes, it's bureaucracy at its worst. Well, that's what they kept yelling at the meeting in the park the other day, *this is what we came here to get away from*. And then there's the *old* locals. As far as they are concerned, it's the Lismore City Council being a bully. Ask Dorothy, she's got plenty to say on that subject,' Jay grinned.

'Oh God, we promised we would go back to say hullo to her, we should go soon?' Christa said.

'Sure,' Jay said as he got up to help Romy, who had slipped and was trying to push herself up from the now wet soil.

'Hullo slaves. Downed tools or what?' they heard a voice from behind.

'Oh no, it's Farmer Steve. Come down from his posh house to whip us poor workers,' Christa said in her best "southern American" drawl, hands on her cheeks in mock dismay. Romy joined in, muddy hands smearing her face.

'She looks half drowned, what have you two been doing to the poor kid?' Steve asked. Without waiting for an answer, he waved in the direction of the house. 'Come up for something to eat and drink. Dad's got some kenaf cheese he made at Eva's factory the other day,' he said laughing at Christa's perplexed expression. 'Tell her the story, Jay,' he called out as he walked off back up the track.

'It's some guy named Brett Jarvis from the ABC for you, on the phone,' Dorothy called from the deck to Anna who was hanging up her washing.

'Oh good, at last. On my way.'

'Romy has gone with Christa and Jay to Tom's farm,' Anna said, as she arrived at the steps to the deck. 'You were in the shower and they were in a hurry, so they will say hullo when they bring her back.'

Reaching for the phone she wondered what prompted her to check herself in the mirror above it.

'Hullo, Anna here.'

'Hi, Anna. It's Brett Jarvis. I have some news for you.'

Anna was excited to hear the ABC TV had decided to send a team up to Lismore to cover the rally they had planned that would take place in front of the council chambers. As a journalist, Brett's editor had covered several protest events Rosa had led in the past.

'It was Rosa that had him convinced. Well done for mentioning her as your co-organiser. He told me about how she made international news once.'

'What for?' Anna asked.

'You had better ask her about that,' Brett laughed.

'By the way, one of my contacts tells me that some politicians here have got wind of something contentious between the council and Nimbin and they are getting very anxious about it. Remember I told you about the upcoming election, the Lismore seat?'

'Oh, yeah. I'll mention that to Rosa. Maybe another banner?' Anna said.

'You didn't hear that from me.'

'You know, I can remember clearly doing the same thing with him when I was about that age,' Steve said as the three of them watched Tom and Romy come up the track from the milking sheds. He was walking very slowly, holding Romy's hand as Bomber and Caster bounced around them barking occasionally.

Tom bent down and picked up a stick for the dogs, sending them galloping off, racing each other for the prize. Romy laughed delightedly as Caster, having claimed the stick, returned and dropped it at their feet. Telling the dogs to *sit*, Tom retrieved it and handed it to her.

Christa got a lump in her throat as she took in the scene, *he must miss his wife; with Steve gone as well, it must be very lonely.*

'He's loving having her,' she murmured, more to herself than the others.

'I think it's been a while since there were kids running around here alright,' Steve said.

Romy tried to throw the stick, but it ended up at her feet and the dogs pounced, nearly knocking her over. Tom grabbed her and swung her out of their path, to loud giggles.

Seeing Steve's stern expression, Christa teased, 'You jealous?' placing her empty coffee mug on the deck table.

'Nah, it just triggered some memories - my mum, that's all. Bit of nostalgia.'

Feeling awkward with all the emotion from the other two, Jay said, 'Christa we better get back, Anna is going to want to put Romy down for her nap and *Mutti* might need the car back. I'm sure Dorothy can't wait to see you as well.'

Rosa tied the last of the banner's corner strings to her fence and walked across to the other side of the road to see what it looked like.

'Probably should have put an exclamation mark after *COUNCIL*,' she said to herself.

Before she could cross back, a car came towards her gate and seeing the sign, they hooted and gave her a thumbs up. She waved back and thought, *well it's in motion I believe.*

Starting up the gravel track back to her little house, she paused to collect the mail from her post box. Rosa saw from the post mark on one of the envelopes that there was a letter from her lawyer, so putting the bills and junk mail under her arm, she tore it open in the hope it was confirmation of her divorce from Jorge.

Unfortunately, it was not the news she wanted. According to her lawyer, she had received a rambling, irrational letter from Jorge in which he refused to sign any papers sent to him and demanded Rosa return to him forthwith, *or else*. Her lawyer said she had no idea what "*or else*" implied, but she felt the tone of the letter was concerning and threatening. Further, she said they could confirm that Jorge was served with the divorce application by filing an affidavit and the fact they had been apart for many years, indeed in different countries, meant the court would grant the divorce anyway.

In conclusion, she remarked that she felt reassured knowing Jorge did not know where Rosa lived in Australia. Rosa sighed. *Well, there is some progress, good; and if little Jorge thinks I'm scared of him, he can think again. He knows, even if he did find me, if he was to start something, it would end badly for him, little womanising weasel.*

※ ※ ※

'Whenever I watch her go through those final slow blinks before she falls asleep, it reminds me of you,' Anna said to Christa as she came up the path from putting Romy down for her nap.

'You mean when I nod off in front of TV?' Dorothy said.

'No, I mean Christa, when *she* was a baby,' Anna laughed. '*Mutti* made me take care of her every day. There was so much to do in the *gasthaus* and our grandfather was a tyrant. One of my jobs was to take her out in the pram, to get her to sleep. I would push and push, watching until her eyelids closed and I could go and play.'

Turning to Christa, Anna continued, 'Sometimes, just as I wheeled you back through the *gasthaus* door to *Mutti*, you would start fussing and I would have to start all over again. It drove me crazy,' Anna grimaced.

'Hence, you letting my pram take off with me in it from the top of a hill?'

'That's sounds scary,' Dorothy said.

'Scary is not the half of it,' Christa said. 'I feel itchy just remembering the version I have been told. Go on "wicked sister",' Christa laughed. 'Tell Dorothy what happened.'

Anna's account the day she pushed Christa's pram down the hill was punctuated with uncontrolled giggling that the other two found infectious and soon, all three were rocking in their chairs, tears streaming down their faces, the story line interspersed with loud laughter.

Bringing herself under control finally, Anna took a breath and said, slightly nostalgically, 'Actually, all my childhood resentment of you when you were a baby came about because of a slab of chocolate, would you believe?'

'Well, that's a new one. You've never told me that before,' Christa said.

'I only just heard about it recently. Mutti told me about the incident the day she called me to tell me about *Papi* drowning.'

Both Christa and Dorothy were taken aback by Anna's account. Dorothy was first to respond, 'Almost sounds like Peter intended for you to *take up arms* against your baby sister, Anna. Very strange.'

'Oh well, we ended up all good by the time we got to Aus, hey sis?' Christa said giving Anna an affectionate slap on the knee.

CHAPTER 31

The Rally

HEARING THE LATCH ON her front gate, Dorothy looked up from her newspaper to see Jack striding down her path resplendent in a t-shirt with *Council Hands Off Nimbin Cheese* emblazoned across the front.

'What the...?' she gasped. 'What do you think you're up to? You're the town cop. Not a damned activist.'

'Right after Rosa informed the Lismore station you were holding a march and a rally, the commanding officer called me, to tell me he wanted me *undercover* on the march. Telling him I was probably on first name terms with everybody on the march did not dissuade him. So here I am, undercover, my dear. When do we leave?'

'I was just waiting for Eva to pick me up and we will be on our way. Yes, you better come with us if you're undercover,' grinned Dorothy. 'By the way, where did you get the t-shirt?'

'Rosa has been everywhere handing them around. One of the constables grabbed one and brought it back to the station as a joke. Little did he know!'

The Premier of New South Wales leaned back comfortably in the rear seat of his car, his aide in the front editing the speech he was to give in the House that morning.

'James,' he said to his driver, 'let's go via the harbour bridge this morning rather than the Anzac. I feel like seeing the opera house and the view towards the Heads on such a beautiful morning.'

'Sure, sir,' came the reply.

The premier sighed contentedly. Yes, things were going well. Provided none of their marginal seats went "belly up" they had the election in a month's time, *sewn up*. Picking up the Sydney Morning Herald his driver had bought earlier, he scanned the headlines – nothing of importance to the election – and then turned to the second page. A headline halfway down caught his interest – *Rosa Garcia leads protest in Lismore* - he thought he remembered that name, so he began reading the story.

Suddenly he sat bolt upright.

'Oh, for fuck's sake,' he said loudly. 'How could she be so stupid? How did she let this happen?' Looking up at his startled aide he said, 'Call the member for Lismore and the mayor. I want a conference call with them in an hour.'

'For fuck's sake,' he shouted loudly again, hurling the newspaper down beside him. The report in the newspaper said there was to be a rally, a protest against the harsh penalty given by the Lismore City Council to a startup home business in Nimbin. The rally leader was none other than the infamous activist Rosa Garcia. *The incident at the Opera House* - the very landmark the premier was currently glaring at from his car as it crossed the harbour bridge slowly in heavy morning traffic.

The article went on to report that it had become a matter of principle for the *whole* of Nimbin, as the community claimed the ruling handed out arbitrarily by the Lismore City Council had the potential to impact on all their endeavours to build the village into a prosperous community. The article had a photograph of the Labor member for Lismore and quote saying his party fully supported the protest.

'Are you telling me that your husband, no, that *you*, allowed your husband to phone the mayor and bully him into this?' the premier asked through gritted teeth, his eyes on the speaker phone before him.

'Yes,' the member for Lismore said meekly, praying the premier did not ask how her husband got the mayor's direct number.

'Mayor?' the Premier asked.

'Well, I don't know if bully is quite correct....' the mayor started.

'So, here is where we are with this,' the Premier cut in. 'We are very close to winning re-election provided we don't have any unexpected swings. Right? And you Mr Mayor, with the help of the honourable member here,' he made a point of not using her name, 'are using your council, which is well known to be National dominated, to push nearly two and a half thousand voters towards Labor. It has to stop. This *earth soldier*, or whatever she calls herself, is going to put our whole fucking campaign at risk. Do you understand the situation?'

'Yes.'

'Yes, Premier.'

'So, fucking fix it!' the premier yelled as he slammed his fist down on the conference phone button.

The glistening surfaces of the Leycester Creek and Wilson River behind Rosa, as she addressed the gathered *Nimbin New* supporters, brought to Tom's mind the past floods that had resulted in so much hardship for the Lismore population. *Why had they ever built the town right on two riverbanks?* he wondered, but then remembered the river junction he was looking at was the very reason the town had been founded.

It was perfectly located for the shipping industry that had started in the 1800s and had still been going in the 1970s, before finally succumbing to rail and road networks in the region. As he listened to Rosa's voice outlining their route through the town centre before stopping in front of the council chambers, Tom was imagining a large paddle steamer gliding behind her, pushed below its load line by the heavy logs it was taking to some sawmill upstream. Logs of red cedar, that in the mid-1800s had created a "gold rush" movement of people hoping to make money logging in the hinterland. Bananas and cattle would have been carried by this same steamer by the end of the century when the denuded forests were turned over to dairy farms.

A loud rallying "whoop" from Rosa brought him back to the present. She seemed larger than life in this environment, a natural born leader of those protesting against injustice. The camera crew from ABC TV panned across the people gathered before Rosa, but inevitably kept returning to their star attraction.

Brett, mic in hand, was in deep conversation with Tom, and Anna assumed it would be a *live interview* that was addressing how things had changed since the last time the two had spoken. Suddenly, they both looked towards her and Tom pointed in her direction. Before she knew it, Brett was beside her.

'So, it was you Anna, you were the person I saw climbing

into the car that day. Why didn't you say so when we spoke on the phone?'

Anna bought herself some time by having to respond to one of Dorothy's three BMX riders who had interrupted to ask if he could push Romy's stroller.

'And who will ride your bike?' Anna smiled.

'You can, Auntie,' he said nonchalantly. She laughed out loud and so did Brett.

'I will,' said Jay, taking the bike from the young boy, doing a circuit around all of them, to the delight of the boys and Romy.

Anna turned back to respond to Brett's previous question, but he had spotted some kind of commotion taking place between Rosa and Eva and an official looking man who was waving his finger at them.

Mr Ableman from the Lismore City Council pushed his way through the sea of white t-shirts, trying to catch up with Rosa and Eva who were leading the procession. He looked totally out of place in his suit and people assumed he was an official there to disrupt, or maybe the Labor MP who had said in the newspaper he supported them.

Finally, he made it to the leaders and standing before them panting, tie askew, he said, 'I have good news. You can stop the march. The council has withdrawn its ruling, your business can proceed provided you do the paperwork.'

'Goodness, Mr Ableman, every time we meet, you're bent over and panting,' Eva smiled.

'And sweaty,' Rosa laughed.

'Okay, okay, can you call off the protest? Send everyone home,' he said.

'No way,' Rosa said. 'We have nothing in writing. Why should we believe you? You don't have any credibility with us after what you pulled.'

'It is official. I am official. You have to stop,' Mr Ableman yelled getting desperate, Brett held the mic near his flushed face before moving it to Rosa's for her response.

'Not going to happen, sorry. Please go away Mr Ableman,' Rosa said, and he turned and ran off to his car - Brett and his camera man struggling to keep up - yelling back to them, 'I'll get a letter from the mayor.'

Eva said, 'Maybe we should call it off Rosa. I'm sure it's true, what he's said.'

'So what, we've got the perfect launch for *Nimbin New* going here. Anna has got us ABC TV and all the local rags are here. Everyone will know about *Nimbin New* by this evening. It's going to be a winner,' she yelled, hugging Eva briefly.

They were moving again now and as word spread of the council's early capitulation, the mood of the march became more and more celebratory. Walking with Tom, a few metres behind Rosa, Eva watched as Christa gave Steve a series of playful jabs in his side, tickling him, laughing as he squirmed. When he tried to move away from her, she pulled him back to her by the arm. Watching Eva's anxious face, Tom said, 'Relax Eva, they're just young people enjoying themselves. Showing affection. What is worrying you?'

Eva made a sudden decision and, moving up close to him, she put her arm through his and began speaking. With happy people all around them it was quite noisy, so she had to put her mouth near his ear as she spoke. A minute later, Tom stopped dead in his tracks, people behind them had to squeeze past. Eva watched his face, her concern growing as she saw tears in his eyes. Then she saw the smile begin to appear on his lips.

Jack was walking next to Rosa - *where else would an undercover cop walk?* Something was worrying him. He didn't know what, but his instinct said he should be wary. When Dorothy noticed his anxiety and asked what was wrong, he grinned, 'Oh nothing, I'm sure. Too much "policeman" DNA, I suppose.'

The words were barely out of his mouth when in his peripheral vision, he saw Rosa's shoulders jolt like she had been hit with a defibrillator, before spinning and crashing face first to the roadway. Jack was over beside her in a second, turning her gently to find her whole front red with blood. Yelling, 'Call emergency, she's been shot,' he ripped off his t-shirt and bunching it, pushed down over the wound.

Eva moved her leg to take a step towards the fallen Rosa, but it felt as though it had gone to sleep, like an arm that had been slept on. It simply collapsed under her, and she too found herself lying on the road, Tom kneeling over her. Seeing her go down, Jack assumed, correctly, she had taken a bullet as well, possibly one that had gone through Rosa or a second that had missed Rosa and got her. He went for the former and estimating the trajectory, whilst keeping the pressure on Rosa's wound, looked for a possible site the shooter may have aimed from.

By now, most people around them had scattered in the chaos, screaming and hiding behind cars parked on the side of the road or face down themselves. Staring in the direction he decided the bullet had come from, Jack was able to see between two buildings. There was a hill behind the buildings, open space with a few trees. A car was just moving off rapidly. Jack was pretty sure he recognised the "No Birds" logo of a car rental company.

CHAPTER 32

The Dimples

THE IMMIGRATION OFFICER AT Sydney Airport examined Jorge Garcia's documentation, glancing up alternately at Jorge and his computer screen. Passing the passport back to him, he said with a smile, 'I see you're a wine maker Mr. Garcia.'

'Yes.'

'Been up in the Hunter Valley to steal our wine making secrets?' he asked laughing.

Jorge's face was impassive.

'No. I was on holiday in Byron Bay,' he said glancing around behind him, wishing the official would get on with it.

'So, you were not doing any business in Australia?' the official asked.

'No. No, as I said already,' Jorge said hastily, and the official glanced up at him from his note taking.

He looked back down and was silent for several minutes while he stared at his screen, tapping the keyboard occasionally. Then, rising from his chair he said, 'Sir, if you don't mind waiting a few minutes, I just need to reboot the server in the office over there. My screen has frozen.'

Jorge stared back blankly and said nothing.

'Computers? You can't live without them, hey?' the official smiled. 'Back in a mo.'

Jorge glanced around again. Some way off were two policemen. They were not looking at him, but certainly were scanning the departures hall. They seemed to be just sauntering, but nevertheless, were getting closer. Suddenly, one put his hand to his ear and, after a few seconds, spoke into the mic attached to his shirt before looking in Jorge's direction.

Putting a mug of coffee on the deck table in front of Tom, Steve said, 'Dad, I need to talk to you about something.'

'Look at those two. They never give up with those rabbits. Sorry son, yes what is my boy?'

Steve sighed, trying to remember what Christa had told him to say. They had rehearsed it on the plane, but had burst into a fit of giggles, attracting a glare from the old guy reading his book across the aisle.

Finally, he just said, 'Dad I should have told you before; I'm gay.'

Tom smiled. 'I know son, Mum told me when you were 13. She said I should have a conversation with you if I wanted to, but I didn't.'

'Why not?'

'Well, as I said to Mum, why would I?' Tom was silent for a few seconds, watching the dogs in the distance. 'I have never had a conversation with you about how you walk, or laugh, or talk, or breathe, Steve. Those things are yours; they don't affect me unless any of them are threatened. For the same reason, why would I talk to you about your sexuality?'

They were both quiet for a few moments, gazing towards the surrounding hills.

'The only things that concern me are your happiness and that you love your old Dad.'

'Whoa,' Tom laughed. His mug went rattling off the table, following the spilt coffee to the floor as Steve jumped up and bent over to hug him.

As she awoke from her anaesthetic induced sleep, Eva listened with eyes still closed to the sounds around her. Sounds she had last heard as a nurse in the hospital in Hamburg. The repetitive knocking of small wheels as a trolley rolled by, a metallic clack as it went over a joint in the concrete floor; *someone on the way to surgery? Someone on the way to a recovery room Or, if they didn't make it, on the way to the morgue?* She shuddered, *Rosa, had she made it?*

The thought opened her eyes, *amazing, 30 odd years since I was in one, they still look - and smell - exactly the same.*

'Ah, you're awake Eva,' the doctor at the end of her bed holding a chart, said quietly. 'You had a lucky escape, didn't you?'

'Not sure if being shot is a lucky escape,' Eva murmured hoarsely. Her leg was raised slightly under the bed cover, held in some kind of contraption.

'Well, having passed through the other lady on its way to you,' *he didn't say, 'and killing her',* 'meant the bullet had slowed down enough to lodge in your leg rather than smash through a thigh bone. You'll be up and about in a few weeks no doubt,' he said, hanging the chart up at the end of her bed, 'provided you have total rest and stay off that leg for at least two weeks.'

Eva was too petrified to ask about Rosa, expecting the worst. *Why doesn't he say something, 'the other lady' you know 'the other lady', come on,* she thought.

'I am afraid your friend, Rosa Garcia, is still in surgery. I am sorry I have no other information, but they will let you know when they can, I'm sure,' the doctor said as he left the room to see his next patient.

Eva let her eyes close and as she drifted off, her thoughts returned to the hospital she nursed in all those years ago. She thought about Tom – Robert then – and how she had helped *him* recover in hospital. She had made him feel loved to draw him, slowly but surely, back from the dark place in his mind.

Eva was standing in front of the hospital ruins in Hamburg. Trying to move away from the heat of the burning rubble, she was weeping and repeating over and over, *they're gone, Rosa and Tom, both gone.* She tried to lift her hand to shield her eyes from the swirling ash, but it wouldn't move.

Opening her eyes, she found Christa holding it tightly.

'*Mutti* it's okay, you were dreaming. Tom's here, Rosa will be back soon. All of us are here. Anna's outside phoning to check on Romy, she'll be back in a minute.'

'I had to send Steve off to organise the milking. Cows don't wait for anyone, I'm afraid,' said Tom.

Eva looked down at Christa's vice-like grip on her hand. She laughed, 'Darling you are holding me so tightly, are you afraid I'll run off somewhere on one leg?' and they all laughed. One by one they all kissed her on the cheek and stood beside her bed.

The blood drained from the premier's face when his aide informed him what had transpired during the march earlier.

'Oh my God, don't tell me they hired someone to shoot her?' The aide suppressed a smile as she said, 'Hardly, Premier. I think an unfortunate coincidence for us, sir.'

'Of course, but who knows what conspiracy theories are going to arise. Especially with the press all over it. Heaven help us. I've never liked that Brett Jarvis. How did he get wind of this so early, anyway?'

The premier turned in his chair and stared out his office window for several minutes then he said, 'The loggers. They hate her. Can't we put it on one of the logging companies? Could we leak something? Move the attention across to them? They have a motive after what she and her cronies have done to them up there in the past.'

'I'll look into it, Sir,' the aide said as she left his office in a hurry.

Eva looked from one face to the next before she said, 'There is something I have to clear up finally, and everyone I need for that, is here around my bed, so I am going to tell you what has been on my mind for some time. Experiencing what I did today, how quickly life can change, has made me realise I'd better take advantage of my lucky escape and tell you what I have kept to myself for so long.'

Christa surmised that Eva was about to bring up the subject of her and Steve and she said, '*Mutti*, if this is about your dilemma over Steve and I then its academic. And anyway, in front of everybody?'

'Steve wanted us to come up together so I could give him some support after he decided to tell his dad he was gay,' Christa continued, 'which it turns out, Tom has known for years anyway, and never cared about,' Christa concluded, smiling at Tom.

Eva said, 'Well that *would* have been the solution to my dilemma, but it is not what I wanted to talk to you all about and when I do in a minute, you will see why it was a *dilemma*. Let me just say first, that the only reason I have not told you this before, what I have known for so long, was because I thought he, all those years ago, had been killed by the bomb that destroyed the hospital I nursed him in.'

Eva was silent for several seconds whilst she looked from one perplexed face to the other. She took a sip of water from the glass next to her, then she said quietly with a quiver in her voice, a sparkle in her blue eyes.

'Christa, Tom is your birth father.' Looking away from her gaping daughters, she turned her head on the pillow to a smiling Tom. 'He only found out when I told him during the procession today.'

A nurse came through the door, hesitated at the expressions on their faces, but finally said, 'Doctor Riceland asked me to give you a message. Rosa is out of surgery but still critical. She has a good chance of a full recovery if she gets through the next 24 hours.' She turned on her heel and departed, her shoes tapping as she walked rapidly down the passageway to ICU.

Jay and Anna looked at Christa, trying to guess what thoughts she was having, how she felt. Anna's mind was in overdrive. *So many things over the years made sense now.*

Christa said nothing, her mind racing, trying to assimilate. Tom watched her intently, heart pounding. After a few moments, she smiled at him and said, 'Ah, so I got my dimples from you?'

www.ingramcontent.com/pod-product-compliance
Lightning Source LLC
Chambersburg PA
CBHW011549070526
44585CB00023B/2514